VENGEANCE
FEMINISM

Also by Kali Nicole Gross:

A Black Women's History of the United States
(with Daina Ramey Berry)

*Hannah Mary Tabbs and the Disembodied Torso:
A Tale of Race, Sex, and Violence in America*

*Colored Amazons: Crime, Violence, and Black
Women in the City of Brotherly Love, 1880–1910*

KALI NICOLE GROSS

VENGEANCE FEMINISM

THE POWER OF
BLACK WOMEN'S FURY
IN LAWLESS TIMES

SEAL PRESS

New York

Seal Press
Hachette Book Group
1290 Avenue of the Americas, New York, NY 10104
www.sealpress.com
@sealpress

Printed in the United States of America

First Edition: September 2024

Published by Seal Press, an imprint of Hachette Book Group, Inc. The Seal Press name and logo is a registered trademark of the Hachette Book Group.

The Hachette Speakers Bureau provides a wide range of authors for speaking events. To find out more, go to hachettespeakersbureau.com or email HachetteSpeakers@hbgusa.com.

Seal books may be purchased in bulk for business, educational, or promotional use. For more information, please contact your local bookseller or the Hachette Book Group Special Markets Department at special.markets@hbgusa.com.

The publisher is not responsible for websites (or their content) that are not owned by the publisher.

Print book interior design by Amy Quinn.

Library of Congress Cataloging-in-Publication Data

Names: Gross, Kali N., 1972– author.
Title: Vengeance feminism : the power of Black women's fury in lawless times / Kali Nicole Gross.
Description: First edition. | New York : Seal Press, 2024. | Includes bibliographical references and index.
Identifiers: LCCN 2024003473 | ISBN 9781541603462 (hardcover) | ISBN 9781541603479 (ebook)
Subjects: LCSH: African American women—Violence against. | African American women—Crimes against. | Women, Black—Violence against—United States. | African American women—Crimes against—United States. | Lex talionis—United States. | Justification (Ethics) | Retribution.
Classification: LCC HQ1410 .G76 2024 | DDC 305.48/896073—dc23/eng/20240404
LC record available at https://lccn.loc.gov/2024003473

ISBNs: 9781541603462 (hardcover), 9781541603479 (ebook)

LSC-C

Printing 1, 2024

For Ma.
We Love You Always.

CONTENTS

Preface   1

Introduction   3

ONE   Their Honor:
           Black Womanhood on Offense   23

TWO   Their History:
           Lawlessness and Black Womanhood   49

THREE Their Weapons:
           Danger and Survival, on Multiple Fronts   75

FOUR   Their Games:
           Black Badgers, Better Days, and the Limits of Fury   109

FIVE   Their Dead:
           The Three Marias and the Babies in the Privy   133

           Conclusion   159

           Afterword   167

           Acknowledgments   *169*
           Notes   *173*
           Index   *229*

PREFACE

THIS IS A BOOK ABOUT BLACK WOMEN *NOT* BEING KILLED by batterers.

This is a book about Black women *not* being railroaded by police or the legal system.

This is a book about Black women *not* being forced to bear or raise children they did not want.

This is a book about Black women who did *not* tolerate dishonor.

This book is about Black women lashing back, often violently and not always righteously. It's about the extremities Black women used to escape total victimization.

They were not always wholly successful. Still, they were exceptional by most metrics. Their efforts sometimes produced surprising outcomes in criminal cases. This was especially unique because many in this small group were wanton, lascivious, intemperate, and generally not the folks most likely to receive the benefit of the doubt. Yet even those who had educations and jobs and held to traditional social mores and middle-class aspirations realized that doing things in respectable ways might not spare them from the state's attacks, surveillance, or degradation.

After all, this book *isn't* about women who fought their battles in the *right* ways.

This book focuses on Black women in lawless times. It's about women who seized upon unanswered wrongs in ways that exercised and exorcised fury—a fury at the violence directed at Black womanhood in America, fury at their own powerlessness, fury at having no protection.

These women reacted in ways that reflected their lived experiences. Theirs was not a clinical or dispassionate practice, however. Their embodied eruptions seemed to function as a salvo and its own kind of salvation; like a cooling balm for skin ripped and rubbed raw from deeply cut rope burns on newly loosed hands and feet. Many of their methods might demand reproach and condemnation, yet I can't help but find some comfort in them. Their existence proves that Black women were not always long-suffering hostages, buffeted around helplessly by the savagery of the systems.[1] In their stories, I see not just the spirited need for revenge but also the unexpected space, dialogue, and outcomes created when Black women act on fury in the name of vengeance.

INTRODUCTION

ON A LATE OCTOBER DAY IN 1886, MARY JOHNSON headed toward the home of Edward Sydnor, the father of her child. Under a sky that portended rain, she probably passed Philadelphia's Walnut Street Theatre on the way, only four blocks from Edward's residence at 1204 Clover Street. Perhaps she strode past the famed opera house or the Chestnut Street Theatre, both of which were even closer. He lived in the heart of the city's theater district, a vibrant if sometimes-seedy locale that could have served as the backdrop for Mary and Edward's courtship. That Edward remained a married man might have been the primary reason the embers died out. Perhaps the realities of child support tempered a once-steamy affair. Whatever passion led to the birth of their child now ran cold.[1]

Anxiety and trepidation might have haunted her steps as she moved through the city's streets, casting a gray pall like the darkening clouds high overhead. Maybe anger animated her steps too.

When she arrived at Edward's, tensions flared. She asked Edward if he had paid the five dollars owed to their child's nurse. He said no. Mary asked if he would give her the money, as the nurse needed to be paid somehow. He ignored the question and went out. She followed. He entered a nearby carpenter's shop, close to a saloon that Edward owned and operated, and announced to the shopkeeper that Mary was following him. The situation was escalating.[2]

Mary placed her hand on her hatchet. Her possession of the weapon might have reflected her trade, as most Black women labored as servants. Hatchets would have been used around the house for firewood and the like, so it is unsurprising that she owned one. Still, meeting with Edward essentially armed could suggest she anticipated some kind of conflict. Maybe she was threatening him; perhaps she sensed that she would have to defend herself. Whatever the reason, that instinct proved correct, as Edward rained down multiple blows on her head. Striking him back, she sank her teeth into his hands. She would be accused of pummeling him with the hatchet as well.[3]

Officers brought Mary in for "attempting to kill Edward." It was a serious charge, one she contested at the arraignment. Edward started the row. All she did was finish it.[4] She testified that while she had placed her hand on her hatchet, she hadn't raised it. Mary told Magistrate Smith, "Sydnor then hit me two or three times on the head. Then I hit him." Though Black women were usually the ones doing time regardless of claims of self-defense, Mary nonetheless made her case. What's even more extraordinary is that it worked. The magistrate discharged Mary after hearing her testimony and that of Edward. Magistrate Smith went further, once he learned that Edward had fathered Mary's child out of wedlock. Edward took Mary's place in custody. Newspapers reported that he did so to the tune of $1,100 bail—$500 for assault and $600 for unlawful cohabitation, the total amounting to roughly five times a domestic servant's yearly earnings. According to the trial docket, however, though he stood accused of "Adultery in having carnal knowledge of the deponent he being a married man," and also with "Assault & Battery on deponent," Edward was discharged the same day.[5]

Mary disappears from available records after this, so her ultimate fate is unknown; presumably, she went on as she had before, struggling to make ends meet. Still, what we do know is illuminating. We learn about her financial struggles and what mattered to her, like the care of her child. We know that Mary walked with a weapon, suggesting fears navigating the city as well as her personal life. The hatchet also tells a story about her resolve to protect and avenge herself. On some level, she knew she was in jeopardy, and she had a plan for how she might strike out against it.

Mainstream presses were quick to unilaterally assign guilt and criminality to her. Perhaps the best example in this instance being the *Philadelphia Evening Bulletin*'s piece, simply titled in block capitals, "MARY JOHNSON VIOLENT." The account made no mention of Edward's attack on her, or his infidelity, itself a violation at the time, concentrating instead only on her retaliation. That she ended up in police custody offers a glimpse of how the authorities treated women like her.[6]

Her method of combat is also revealing.

She did not meekly accept abuse or ill treatment. When Edward struck her, something combusted. And he was arguably worse for the wear, as her teeth tore at his flesh, never mind the specter of the hatchet. That violence seemed to comprise and express a fury at the circumstances, such as having to chase this man down for child support, almost as much as it was a response to the physical conflict itself.

Throughout my research into the lives of Black women, I have routinely come across cases like Mary's. Messy clashes featuring Black women fighting, sometimes even fighting dirty, if necessary, against elements of sexism and racism, including the basic forms of disrespect resulting from them. The numbers are small, but I believe these instances are significant nonetheless, as the ways they lashed back point toward a pattern and ideology not simply of self-defense but also revenge.

In an era when many Black women opted to embrace tactics such as dissemblance and respectability, the actions of these women offer us another form of resistance to consider. Most of these women were not walling off their sexuality or laboring arduously to adhere to white middle-class notions of femininity. The women seemed eager to live in bold, uncompromising ways. They did not necessarily seek out conflict, but they did not appear to be deterred by it either. More often, they seemed to seize upon opportunities to enact vengeance when wronged or otherwise affronted. Because police, prosecutors, justices, and juries routinely failed them, vengeance allowed these Black women to punish wrongs that might otherwise go unaddressed by the state. That these women found ways to protect themselves and enact some measure of retribution might seem unsurprising, but the virulence in how they struck back warrants our consideration.[7]

Over the course of 2019 and 2020, as I participated in dialogues with other scholars about Black women and feminism, I realized that I hadn't spent a great deal of time considering the Black women I studied, women embroiled in the criminal justice system, as political actors in a de jure sense, let alone as political theorists. It's an odd oversight in retrospect, because so much of my work has been about challenging the idea that only certain kinds of figures are worthy of historical study and deep intellectual engagement. I started to ask different kinds of questions: Did the women have their own kind of feminist politics? If so, what was it? What did it look like in practice?[8] The answers to those questions startled me, but they also birthed fundamental observations about the uses of Black women's violence in service of vengeance as a viable, feminist practice—as alarming as that may sound.

I use *feminism* in ways that are largely aligned with how Beverly Guy-Sheftall defined it in her pioneering anthology on Black feminist writing, *Words of Fire*—namely, "the emancipatory vision and acts of resistance among a diverse group of African American women" whose work mapped the complexities of Black womanhood as well as "the interlocking nature of the oppression" imperiling it. Much of that writing shows that feminism's origins in America do not solely lie in white women's rights activism, particularly those following abolition; rather, they are glimpsed in the earliest forms of struggle when Black women fought against enslavers and would-be rapists and abusers. We see early models in the legacies of freedom fighters such as Harriet Tubman and Sojourner Truth as well as in the political lectures and writings of forerunners such as Maria Stewart in the 1830s. For our purposes, however, the emphasis is on exploring Black women's vengeful *acts* against racist oppressors as well as other misogynistic foes.[9]

More broadly, Black feminism is typically understood as an ideology that seeks to dislodge misogyny, which is the hatred of women, and it aims to dismantle misogynoir, the specific hatred of Black women; it also seeks to embolden women and afford them equitable access. Firmly rooted in the long collective struggle for justice for Black people, Black feminism challenges racism and patriarchy. And at its most expansive and intersectional, especially in more recent decades, Black feminism contests heteropatriarchy as well as mass incarceration, homophobia and transphobia, and poverty. Black feminism has tended to eschew violence as among the "master's tools," which in theory will never lead to true liberation for oppressed peoples. Black feminism has also been deeply concerned with structural inequalities and has often mobilized the legal system as a means of redress (though there are groups of Black feminists who did not and do not adhere to the latter, particularly abolitionist feminists). Still, generally defined, Black feminism aims to uphold everything and everyone; often in the noblest of ways—through nonviolent social protest and other forms of civil disobedience, grassroots organizing, petitions, lawsuits, and through art, literature, the uses of the erotic, and scholarship. Under this umbrella, Black feminism is often charged with restoration and repair.[10]

When I started this project, I envisioned a book that would map a form of feminism undertaken by a band of Black women who took matters into their own hands, because the same legal system that so often moved swiftly to punish them offered little in the way of protection or justice against racist and gendered wrongs. But in encountering Mary's case and those of other Black women of the era, women who sliced and diced their way out of tight corners, women who lied, robbed, and cheated in the process of enacting a particular kind of revenge, I realized that this book is as much a meditation on Black women's *fury* as it is about Black feminism. I use *fury* more often than *rage*, partly because of its origins in ancient mythologies, tales of fierce female deities that violently administered justice—goddesses of vengeance. But also because fury and Black feminism have always been inexorably linked, as they represent an anger that is deeply concerned with justice, the lack thereof, and also efforts to find new ways to administer it. Yet it wasn't until more recently that I came to understand the women I study as some of its key architects and proponents.[11]

Although predicated upon many of the same core beliefs as traditional Black feminism, particularly the veneration of

Black womanhood and bodily sanctity, this type of feminism rotated on baser axioms. There was an immediacy to it, as it helped women act quickly to address everyday wrongs on the ground while at the same time, as much as possible, avoid punishment and other adverse repercussions from a corrupt legal system. It was not concerned with community uplift or institutional reform—that's not where these women lived. These were everyday Black women confronting crises—those that burst forth spontaneously and yet still somehow also touched upon a chronic, collective kind of pain.

Many of these Black women's crimes in late-nineteenth-century Philadelphia bore distinct feminist logics, but it's complicated. How they affirmed their womanhood far exceeded anything that I had ever learned about or considered within traditional definitions of white or Black feminist activism.[12] Black women have been so castigated and caricatured for being angry that many of us have been trained not to express it, let alone act upon it, even when it is warranted. Scholarship documenting and decrying the angry Black woman trope is wide and deep at this point, so I won't belabor it here, except to say that it was refreshing and instructive to explore histories of Black women who not only refused to swallow their anger but rather drew decisively upon it.[13]

The women employed a kind of Black feminist violence or vigilantism, sometimes for self-defense but also to avenge outrages that uniquely affected or offended them as Black women.[14] We have a growing body of literature that attests to Black women's extraordinary abilities to collectively organize and wring out effective strategies to push back against myriad injustices. After enslavement, we know they hustled hard, working multiple jobs and toting pans to provide extra food for their families. They formed one of the first civil rights organizations and raised funds to help protest racial and sexual violence. They founded newspapers, schools, and clubs and pressed for democracy in the face of the nation's lawlessness. *Lawlessness*, in this work, references misogynoir erected and sustained by biased laws and their antiblack enforcement through unequal policing, adjudication, and confinement.[15]

But some Black women resisted in a different way. With razors, pistols, hatchets, blackjacks, and balled-up fists. With loud hollering and trembling tears, playacting for courts and crowds and racist marks. They resisted and took revenge. The tactics fall across individual actors and their respective calamities, yet when taken together, a method in the melees comes to the fore.

While much of their violence revolved around their attempts to attain a kind of justice, it also seemed to exorcise their rage at misogynoir. Yet rather than running from racist or misogynistic stereotypes, some managed to weaponize and repurpose the attributes—they leveraged these disadvantages for their own benefit. Others appeared to have largely let go of mainstream notions of respectability and morality, too, particularly regarding premarital sex and reproduction. They could be brazen, cold, and often brutal. The patterns were shocking but also seemed to give more than just a rare sounding to the anger and frustration that Black women felt and likely continue to feel as a politically, economically, and socially marginalized group; one especially vulnerable and yet far removed from equitable access to formal protection and justice. Their stories serve as potent examples of Black women who acted on fury and offer some extraordinary outcomes when they did.

I have taken to calling their actions and the underlying principles structuring them *vengeance feminism*. In the pages that follow, I map its characteristics and contemplate the importance and urgency of its legacy.[16]

I must caution readers: vengeance feminism was often violent and extralegal. And yet, it's imperative that we engage with these women where they were. Let me also say for the record that my aim in pondering vengeance feminism is not to glorify wholesale acts of violence against misogynists, nor is it to suggest that every criminal act a Black woman committed in the past can or should be interpreted as feminist activism. Rather, first and foremost, it's to recognize this as a type of Black feminism, and to stress that it largely served its proponents' needs during a period when they were subjected to gross racist and gendered double standards. It is also about exploring the advantages of female fury, as it allowed the women guided by it to create spaces for themselves where they weren't constantly powerless victims; where they were not always the only ones forced to cope with unanswered violations.[17]

Vengeance feminism is most closely aligned with those strands of Black feminist theory that engage anger and the need for retribution. From both a historical and ideological standpoint, Nikki M. Taylor's *Brooding Over Bloody Revenge* serves as an important examination of enslaved women's deliberate killing of enslavers and their kin, which she posits as a Black feminist practice of justice. In many ways, her discussion of their violence situates these enslaved women as potential forerunners for key aspects of what I observe in the post-Reconstruction period and beyond. Works that explore rage and anger from a more contemporary context would be *Black Macho and the Myth of the Superwoman*, for example. Michele Wallace's 1978 critical intervention powerfully voiced Black women's frustration with sexism and patriarchy in society certainly but also within the Black Power movement and the Black community. Audre Lorde's rousing 1981 essay, "The Uses of Anger," excoriated the silencing of Black feminist rage and that of women of color; it championed the productivity that comes from anger as a response to racism and the limitations of white feminism. bell hooks's work, too, channels Black feminist rage and fashions it as a potent weapon against racism, sexism, homophobia, and racial capitalism. More recent scholarship has emerged revisiting Black feminist rage. An evocative collection of essays appeared in a 2019 special issue of *Signs*. In it, the authors "theorize rage, harness rage as a resource, and use academic work to help foment the productive rage that forces change."[18]

Plus, a bevy of newer works has been published that recognize the need for alternative forms of Black feminism; works that map Black women's activism around food insecurity and the ongoing struggle for better housing and quality education for their children. Books like Brittney Cooper's *Eloquent Rage: A Black Feminist Discovers Her Superpower*, which is a love letter to the complex range of Black women's emotional and sociopolitical responses to injustice; mapping conflicting tensions, she tackles poverty, middle-class status, and Black women's difficulties finding partners while still somehow managing to find joy and to thrive. Still, other new works call for holistic, principled ways forward as we continue battling for civil rights, use feminism as a catalyst for prison abolition, explore queer feminism, and work to continue *Making All Black Lives Matter*. All this scholarship, past texts, and more recent works are phenomenal and have created a rich and vital archive of Black feminist history, theory, scholarship, and activism. These works are incredibly valuable for advancing Black women's equality, and this book is not intended to detract from them.[19]

But here is precisely where vengeance feminism diverges.

This feminism was about hitting back—not always figuratively, and not necessarily nobly either. Vengeance feminism is not healing or productive in the conventional sense. Typically, when we refer to those kinds of outcomes, it is with the expectation that Black women are undertaking reparative work in a manner that benefits the Black community if not the whole of American society itself. This isn't that. Vengeance feminism is defined by Black women defending themselves against dishonor, violence, and lawlessness, and taking control of their own bodies with respect to reproduction by whatever means necessary. With volatile blends of anger, fear, desperation, and acrimony powering their approaches to achieve those ends, they mobilized physical violence but also, intellectually, they leveraged their deficits, manipulated misogynistic stereotypes, and used chicanery and anything else at their disposal to avoid formal punishment. Vengeance feminists grasped those tools that were available to extract payback when wronged and to privilege their own safety and sanctity; sometimes they worked collectively to achieve those aims, but more often than not, women struck out on their own. Normally, as a historian, I would not deign to call the women something that they did not choose or identify for themselves. However, since the phrase is derived from their specific histories of revenge against racist and gendered wrongs, I think we can respectfully do so here.[20]

And we need to be clear: theirs was not an eye for an eye—Black women's relative low status did not permit such a thing. Theirs was a finger for an eye. Such a metric allowed them to counterpunch and take vengeance in a way that was painful for the objects of their ire, even as the women themselves did not have the status or resources or physicality to respond exactly in kind.

It was not justice, because that didn't exist for Black women. It was retributive, anarchic. Navigating the vicissitudes of American justice demanded nothing less.[21]

On that end, the narrative of this book is at times unwieldy and uneven, as vengeance feminism resists clean lines and linear thinking. The latter is likely worsened by my own wayward penchant for periodically dropping in and out of the writing. Some of this is down to my own by-now-obvious adoration for all manner of unruly Black women, women who knew the deck was stacked against them (from floor to ceiling, quite frankly) but managed to strike out in ways that built new spaces and avenues to inhabit. The other part is a disorderly by-product of the fact that I continue to wrestle with the full import of vengeance feminism.

I know the expectation is that scholars should have all the answers, but for me, there is a richness in wrangling with ideas, stories, and all manner of Black women's mysteries. Even as Black women's history, and studies on Black women more broadly, continue to grow, there is still so much that we don't yet know. Given this, this project also endeavors to center and weave Black women's stories together in a way that animates their lives, as much as it punctuates the tenets of vengeance feminism and the historical context in which it is studied, primarily Philadelphia in the late nineteenth and early twentieth centuries.

Throughout the book, I introduce new historical cases and revisit some of my favorite old ones. I must confess now that in instances where the sources permit, I have been rather indulgent in recounting the gory details. I do my best to make sense of conflicting evidence, and where documentation is wanting, I strive to provide as accurate a retelling as possible. I use speculative and descriptive prose to give readers a better sense of the context. So, for example, when I discussed the weather on the day Mary was arrested, I did so based off a weather report printed in the paper that day. I had information about where both Mary and Edward lived and, using maps for the period, speculated on what her journey may well have looked like as she made her way to his home. Also, given that the stories and details about them are extracted from nineteenth-century papers, periodicals riddled with racist caricatures and inaccuracies, I scrutinize accounts, corroborate as many details and aspects as possible, and often read against the grain.

Most of the book—and my scholarship, for that matter—is grounded in Philadelphia's history. As a native New Yorker, I have long been accused of committing a kind of unforgivable treason because of my affinity for the city. But its importance to this study and the themes explored is unmatched. It was central to the nation's founding, and as such, it reflects all the highs and lows therein. It suborned slavery while it professed deeply Christian and democratic ideals. It was also among the earliest to end enslavement after it hosted the Constitutional Convention, which would give rise to one of the largest populations of free Blacks in the country prior to the Civil War, and it was among the earliest to witness the launch of equal rights for women. Philadelphia is central to the modernization of justice and punishment and the turn to incarceration.[22]

One could argue that Philadelphia initiated the long, horrific legacy of the violent overrepresentation of Black people in the criminal justice system, beginning with the establishment of the Walnut Street Prison's "Penitentiary House" in 1790, the first such penal institution of its kind. More recent history also finds the city without rival when it comes to homicidal antiblack policing. We need only revisit the events on May 13, 1985, when authorities using a Pennsylvania State Police helicopter dropped "military-grade" plastic explosives on the headquarters of MOVE, a Black liberation group in West Philadelphia. The flames that engulfed the house on Osage Avenue also rendered the lives of six adults and five children, as well as sixty-one nearby homes, to ash. The city would be ground zero for the mythology surrounding "crack babies" and the feared lost generation during the late 1980s and early 1990s. Indeed, it figured prominently in the rhetoric that placed Black mothers at the center of renewed caricatures of urban decay—itself an extension of a longer historical pattern of the racist lampooning of Black women, such as those images featured in the cartoons of Edward Clay in the city in the 1820s.[23]

Yet Philadelphia was also the birthplace of pivotal Black organizations and religious orders, some still operating. The African Methodist Episcopal Church owes its founding to a core group of deeply religious free Black men who refused to be segregated in St. George's Methodist Episcopal Church in the 1780s. After fundraising and buying land in 1791, their labors eventually resulted in the establishment of Mother Bethel

Church, which would go on to serve as a crucial anchor for the city's Black community. Mother Bethel exists as an early example of the long history of the Black church answering both the spiritual and civic needs of its congregation, as its founders and parishioners were also ensconced in working toward Black freedom and citizenship. The *Philadelphia Tribune*, founded in 1884, is the oldest consistently running Black newspaper in the country, and W. E. B. Du Bois pioneered ethnographic research with the publication of his 1899 study, *The Philadelphia Negro*, when he was employed by the University of Pennsylvania. All this to say: Philadelphia history is American history. And Black women's experiences are central to it.[24]

At various points in the book, the city itself and its more notorious districts function almost as characters unto themselves as details about cases and their circumstances unfold. Beginning with the wild and chaotic flavor of life on Lisbon Street, the first chapter explores the ways some Black women used feminist violence when they took revenge for physical abuse as well as umbrage at insults about their womanhood. It explores how they navigated their own notions of honor and how the women defended those boundaries when breeched.

The second chapter contextualizes the embers fueling vengeance feminists' fury by taking stock of key statutes sanctioning enslavement and Black women's sexual exploitation. It also charts the resulting, loathsome cultural dictums about Black femininity that spread like the fetid pustules of some deadly plague. It shows how that history and those ideas endured and adversely impacted Black women at various points when they encountered the legal system.

From there, Chapter 3 turns to the countermeasures that these Black women deployed, examining their own configurations of survival. It takes stock of the multiple sites of jeopardy as they battled attackers, accusers, and the justice system alike. Specifically, it focuses on two cases where Black women faced death sentences, one for murdering a Black man and one for murdering a white woman, to consider how they mobilized a variety of methods to navigate perilous terrain.

The fourth chapter examines how the women weaponized racist and misogynistic stereotypes through the wily cunning of a distinct group of female thieves. It charts how these women often robbed white men and largely evaded punishment. At the same time, it explores the women's actions against the wider context of the daily vitriol lobbed at Black women traversing city streets. This chapter also considers cases that are similar to but not completely within the milieu of vengeance feminism, as it fans out to discuss the limits of the ideology.

Chapter 5 considers what might be vengeance feminism's furthest reaches as it studies instances of abortion and infanticide. Although there were probably myriad reasons why some women chose to end pregnancies as well as why they killed newborns, and many of those motives are largely unknowable, this chapter ponders whether Black women's actions were also enactments of their own fury at the inequitable stigma assigned to unwed and unwanted pregnancies.

The conclusion shows that while this study of vengeance feminism is situated in the past, in many respects, the concepts and practices are historically porous; there are glimpses further back in Black women's history, and examples of it exist in our own time. I also contemplate the enduring lessons undergirding it and question whether it holds value for women today.

Vengeance feminism was hewed out of an aggrieved cry for a just reckoning. It was routinely extralegal, volatile, and at times nihilistic. That constellation of words might normally be used in a pejorative sense, but there was power in nihilistic action and volatility was sometimes the only weapon the women had. Their actions outside the bounds of the law were not necessarily unjust. The uncomfortable truth is that it was practically impossible for most Black women to adhere to or trust in the law because it was never universally applied. Vengeance feminism, with all its odious, malevolent, and awesome contours, was a poignant response to the conditions they were under.

It is for this reason that I turn our attention to this sanguine swath of Black women's history.

ONE

THEIR HONOR

Black Womanhood on Offense

I think I would be almost glad . . . if more of our women so treated would do the same thing.

—EMMA RHOADS, 1885

I think she is a hero in a true sense of the word and has rid the world of a villain.

—ROBERT PURVIS, 1885

THINGS HAD GOTTEN OUT OF HAND, BUT SUCH WAS USUally the case on Lisbon Street. The "malodorous thoroughfare," dubbed Murderer's Row, routinely found its denizens at the center of its many bloody calamities. Loud and belligerent arguments were a regular feature, as dice games became deadly, as pugnacious deeds resolved disputes rather than words.[1]

Anyone brave enough to visit the place after hours would have witnessed such scenes firsthand. They might have run into men such as John Blackston, a notorious figure on Lisbon Street. In 1893, Blackston, who also ran an illicit resort on Lisbon, was already under indictment for keeping a disorderly house after a police raid in August, when he was again arrested three weeks later. This time Blackston attacked a long-standing rival, William Brown, also a resident of Lisbon Street, while the man ate oysters at a nearby saloon. Blackston made good on past threats by submerging a steel blade into Brown's side. Of Blackston, the *Times Philadelphia* reported, "No one is better known to the police than this man."[2]

And yet on Lisbon Street, John Blackston was but one among many: Young men like twenty-year-old Frank Love, of Hurst and Lisbon, who viciously stabbed another Lisbon street resident, fifty-two-year-old Josiah Elliott; Edward Palmer decided to settle his beef with Frank Howard with a revolver on Lisbon Street late Saturday night, October 14, 1893. He struck his adversary in the neck and thigh; James Elliott of 517 Lisbon, was "accidentally shot in the left hand" while trying to disarm William Turner of 530 Lisbon Street.[3]

City dwellers wandering down the corridor could expect to be propositioned by bold women, such as Tenie Hogan, also known as Tennie Cornish, of 521 Lisbon Street. Tenie, an enterprising, if notorious, Black woman, ran her own disorderly house that doubled as a fairly active crime scene. In 1890, a man had been stabbed in a drunken fracas in the parlor, and a few days later, an Italian man would be robbed of $200 there. Details vary, but the most consistent telling is that as Domenico Fabrizio walked down the street, Mamie White accosted him for beer money. When he refused, she snatched his hat and ran into Tenie's spot. He followed and reportedly offered her ten cents for the hat's safe return. As Fabrizio fished for the coin, he inadvertently revealed a *roll of notes he happened to have on his person.* Mamie snatched the bills and disappeared. Fabrizio left to summon the police, giving Mamie enough time to divide the plunder with Tenie and two others in the house before hightailing it to New Jersey, where she was later apprehended.[4] In all likelihood, Mamie was soliciting under false pretenses—pretending to sell sex so that she could rip off wannabe johns. The city's slums were rife with such scams, and Lisbon Street was no exception.

But another kind of melee took place at Blackson's spot on Saturday night, September 16, 1893—one about honor. It involved another Lisbon Street regular named Ida Payton. Even as she and her peers rejected the more restrictive attributes of respectability, such as chastity, temperance, and submissiveness, they seemed to insist upon a basic standard of civility and respect for their womanhood just the same. When breeched, they mobilized characteristics typically associated with male honor, particularly the nerve and gumption to violently defend their pride when injured or when their character had been otherwise besmirched.

Through Ida's story and those of other Black women like her, such as Annie Cutler, who was tried for murder in 1885, we can begin to understand how otherwise rare and extreme individual acts could nonetheless compel the public to grapple with the larger implications of the sanctity of Black womanhood and the utility of Black feminist violence. This is important because African American women had long been branded as immoral and thusly placed outside patriarchal notions of protection. Yet whether they lived and labored on streets like Lisbon or attended every Sunday service and stayed virgins until marriage, they did not surrender to those damning, exclusionary notions. Many Black women defined honor for themselves, but vengeance feminists defended their own honor.[5]

INDEED, HONOR WAS SOMETHING THAT BLACK WOMEN on Lisbon Street took seriously. Perhaps it's because they knew how the outside world perceived them—they were the Black trash whose very existence W. E. B. Du Bois and his ilk lamented for tarnishing the larger image of the race. Leading figures like Mary Church Terrell, acting in her capacity as the president of the National Association of Colored Women, bemoaned the fact that "the entire black race is compelled to suffer for every crime of its component individuals. The fault of the one becomes the scourge of the many." But we can't lay it all on Du Bois or Terrell. In fact, Terrell was among an early group of Black activists decrying peonage and convict leasing. And we can't pretend that Black reformers didn't have a point on some level either. Black criminals were held up as proof positive of the race's inherent degeneracy. Plus, white Philadelphians also traded ugly insults about the women who lived there—those who were especially wanton and reckless, and those who were not. Hurling such insults, however, did not deter them from daily visits to the place in search of alcohol, gambling, and illicit sex. Black men, too, sought out the ladies who worked the corners and lingered on stoops and in doorways. Some of the women were unemployed and too addled with drink, some were well-known hookers and thieves. Some of the women were brawlers.[6]

Ida Payton (alias Ida Gibbs, alias Ida Burton) was no stranger to combat, or to strong drink either. And she was well acquainted with the opposite sex. At twenty-four, she was only a year or two older than her victim, Samuel Jackson of 511 Gillis Alley.[7] Ida reportedly lived on 318 Trout Street but seems to have maintained a space at 513 Lisbon Street, in Blackston's resort. This is where she was on the night in question—when she encountered Samuel.[8] Samuel and Ida had something fiery between them. She was rumored to have been sweet on him at one point, though word on the street lately was that he had given her "the shake." Whatever their affiliation, they had an explosive argument in her room—as his two friends would later testify. Some accounts said he insulted her and slapped her face. Then she hit him over the head with a blackjack.

Others would later say that she struck him with the blackjack but that "it was only in fun." Ida herself testified that she used a "whip handle in self-defense" after he hit her first.[9]

While the start is debatable, the result is not. All parties affirmed that Samuel then flew into a rage. With the din of laughter and craps games, tobacco smoke and fumes of beer and whiskey likely serving as the backdrop, Ida survived a punishing assault. Samuel "pitched into her" before he threw her down and "beat her head against the floor." Edward Miner and Jacob Lewis, the two other men who had been hanging out with Samuel, intervened. They pulled Samuel off Ida and forced him out of the house. She warned him not to come back. An officer would testify that he overheard Ida say, "If the —— comes back I will shoot him."[10]

The same policeman, William J. Holland, had encountered the men as they hung outside afterward at the corner of Hurst and Lisbon. He listened to their conversation, as Samuel grew more riled up about having been struck with a blackjack. Samuel wanted "satisfaction" for the affront. Officer Holland advised him to go home. He did not—Edward headed back inside to borrow a bottle to put whiskey in, and Samuel would soon return to the house as well. Edward cautioned him that Ida had a gun, to which Samuel replied, "Well, let her have the pistol in her hand."[11]

Another coarse dispute between Samuel and Ida ensued. Ida declared that it "was all over with him." Edward and Jacob worked to separate the pair again, with one nudging Samuel to the door while the other coaxed Ida toward the stairs. During her trial, witnesses testified that she was standing on the third step when Samuel insulted her for the last time. It was then, after Samuel Jackson "called her a name," one that could not be printed in the papers, according to Jacob, that she turned and said, "I'll mark you for that." Edward's testimony concurred: "Then Jackson called her a name and she let him have it." All testified that it was an "ill name." From her staircase perch, Ida took aim and fired over Edward's shoulder, and the scene dissolved into smoke and confusion.[12]

We should step back for a moment and carefully consider the sequence of events to be clear about what Ida did *not* do. Ida didn't try to retrieve the gun and fire in the immediate aftermath of the beating. Ida did not fire on Samuel when he returned to the house, per her original threat. Even as the embers of the first row quickly reignited, she did not shoot. Both parties were retreating. The parting dig, the ill name, the vile affront—that was the final straw. She stood on her honor and ultimately shot Samuel dead.

During her trial, however, Ida rested on something else. The defense first tried to blame the shooting on Edward, particularly as he had priors and had left the city in a rush upon learning of Samuel's demise. For her part, Ida's story was that there was so much commotion in the residence that she did not know what happened to Samuel—that she had gone upstairs and couldn't see how he was shot. The jurors did not buy it. Edward's version of events had been corroborated by additional eyewitnesses, such as Robert "Grandpop" Edwards, a youth who had been hanging around the parlor that day. And later, another patrolman, a police sergeant, and a doctor who treated the victim all testified that before his death, Samuel said Ida was "the one who had done the shooting." Ida was convicted of murder in the second degree and sentenced to twelve years on November 1, 1893.[13]

Once behind bars, she would find herself among other Black women who also answered similar offenses with violence. Women such as Ida Howard, who had stabbed a man to death in 1891 at the corner of Lisbon and Hurst after he rudely stared and cursed at her. She was not in immediate mortal danger and was, according to the *Philadelphia Inquirer*, "muttering something about his calling her a bad name" when she struck back with deadly fury. The same was true of Ida Payton, who could have walked away from her argument with Samuel. Black women like Ida were afforded so few courtesies, so little consideration. They simply could not countenance disrespect. As fraught as such responses may be, there was something radical about the actions too.[14]

Ida's decision to pull the trigger suggests that she was grasping after ideals and protocols typically reserved for men, and generally elite white men at that. Even as duels waned significantly after the Civil War and would increasingly be policed, the deadly contests sporadically took place in the late nineteenth century, and not just in the South. Pennsylvania's own state representative, Robert Adams Jr., who will be discussed in more detail shortly, had himself participated in a duel with a fellow member of the First Troop Philadelphia City Cavalry on April 10, 1880. Robert especially was a member of the wealthy "old families of the Quaker City," but both men were regarded as "not only highly respectable but very well known in the best society." Early accounts reported that an argument over an unnamed woman lay at the heart of the matter. Robert charged that "Dr. White's course in the affair had been very cowardly." For this, "Dr. White called him a liar and slapped his face. The usual regulations followed, and the journey for the dueling places made." Indeed, the fight found the men standing back-to-back with "nine-inch rifled pistols of regulation dueling size" in hand. The two marched the requisite paces, though accounts vary between ten and fifteen steps, and then fired. No one was injured. Robert Adams fired at his target, "without effect." Dr. White fired in the air. Rather than firing for a second round, the parties agreed that "ample satisfaction had been given." Their showdown was held in neighboring Delaware, where the law permitted men like Robert and Dr. White to violently avenge dishonor.[15]

Yet in the face of far more vulgar and violent indignities, Black women were expected to swallow their pride and shoulder on. Masses of Black women did—but vengeance feminists couldn't.

Even as Ida's decision to pull the trigger was an intensely personal avenging act, it still challenged the notion that honor and its restoration were the province of white people, and

31

men in general. Ida delivered a blistering rebuke of her demor-
alization. And in that chosen course of action, she was not
alone. Annie Cutler found herself in the throes of a similar
kind of rupture in 1885. Originally from New England, she
had left home for a boy. William Knight had stolen her heart.
He relentlessly wooed her and persuaded her to follow him
to Philadelphia. She did, as the two planned to wed. Despite
the bigotry and poverty and daily perils, owing to the ample
and growing size of Philadelphia's Black community, it was a
city where folks could breathe a little. There were parties and
dances and outings to the shore. There were churches and jook
joints and restaurants where they could buy oysters and tote
away pails of beer if they wanted. It probably seemed like the
future. For a while, it was. William worked as a waiter, and
Annie worked as a cook for the Mettlers, who owned a saloon
on 835 Race Street.[16]

Annie was hopelessly in love with William. And they had
sex—they were practically married, after all. Except they
weren't. Despite William's promise to make her his bride, he
had been stepping out on her and married the other woman
instead. But that was only part of the problem. The other part
is that he did not tell Annie anything about it. For months. In
all the time he was a newlywed, he had still been visiting her
regularly. When Annie found out, she was beside herself with
grief and shame. And rage. She had given him everything—her
time, her money, her affection, and her body. Not only had she
turned over money to him, expecting that he was preparing a

home for them, but so, too, did her mother. Mrs. Emily Cutler "also bestowed many gifts and considerable money upon Knight for the same purpose."[17] Annie lamented the fact that she had been ruined by him. She tried to talk to him, but he was done with her. And when she couldn't let it go, he roughed her up to make her understand the point.[18]

Annie mourned the loss of her virginity, and what happened next gestures to the intricacies of vengeance feminism and its relationship to respectability and honor. She had been invested in the prospect of marriage. Yet she still engaged in premarital sex, probably in the hope that it would result in a proposal. When that failed, her actions blended honor and vengeance as she unleashed fury on the man who betrayed her.[19]

She purchased a secondhand pistol and tested it to make sure it worked. Despite drinking a lot, she managed to write two letters to loved ones days before her fateful encounter with William. One was to her mother. She forewarned of her actions and instructed her mother to bury her in a plain white box when they found her. Annie apologized for letting her down and for bringing shame upon them. A similar letter was sent to the Mettlers.[20]

Annie waited for William after he got off work. When he attempted to walk past her, apparently without even acknowledging her presence, she pulled the trigger, twice. One bullet struck him under his left eye and exited the back of his skull. The second bullet went to his heart. Passersby disarmed and detained her. One wonders about Annie's physical state as she fired. If a surge of adrenaline made her body tremble, it didn't obscure her aim or diminish her resolve.[21]

The Samaritans who intervened would later testify that she fought with them, entreating them to let her make certain that she had finished the job. Reportedly, she cried aloud, "I hope to God I have killed him. I could kill him twice for the wrong he has done to me." On the face of it, hers should have been an open-and-shut case. It would be anything but.[22]

Robert Purvis, the legendary Black abolitionist, is probably the last name that would come to mind in relation to vengeance feminism, but in the Cutler case, his is a name that would feature prominently in the court of public opinion and the discourse itself. Born of mixed ancestry in South Carolina in 1810, Purvis's father, a white man of considerable means, moved his family to Philadelphia so that his three boys might be educated and enjoy a better quality of life. They did. Robert was well educated and considered quite handsome. He was six feet tall, with dark, wavy hair and thick sideburns, fashionable for his day. Though he could have easily passed and was mistaken for white, he clung to his Blackness. As his biographer noted, Robert's "identification with his grandmother's race was perhaps the strongest element in his sense of self." Dido Badaracka had been captured in Africa at twelve years old and sold on the block in a Charleston slave market. Robert revered her beauty, "crisp hair," and regal manner.[23] When he came of age and wed, it was Harriet Forten who had stolen his heart—the "dark, beautiful, and talented" young woman who was six months his senior. They married in 1832 and remained so until her death in 1875. Throughout their lives together, they were both abolitionists and among the Black elite, as her own father was the well-to-do businessman James Forten.[24]

At the time of the Cutler case, Robert Purvis and his family lived on an affluent, predominantly white block in the city, at 1601 Mount Vernon Street. Far removed from the likes of Lisbon Street—and Race Street, for that matter—the home was a large, stately corner building. Robert owned $43,000 in real estate and possessed $50,000 in personal assets. These sums would be roughly $17 million and $20 million, respectively, by today's standards. Moreover, he was highly respected for his renowned work on abolitionism and suffrage.[25]

Typically mild-mannered with family and friends, Robert was a militant opponent of racism and enslavement. His home, horses, and carriages were all put in service of the Underground Railroad, along routes he was instrumental in pioneering—particularly helping those traveling through Pennsylvania to Canada. He is believed to have shepherded multitudes of enslaved women and men to freedom; his activism helped free renowned author Harriet Jacobs, whose wrenching autobiography, *Incidents in the Life of a Slave Girl*, remains central to understanding the impact of enslavement and the sexual exploitation of Black women, but also enslaved men. Her account of the sexual violation of an enslaved man named Luke, who was left half-clothed and chained to his master's bedside, is one of the few accounts that attests to these kinds of atrocities.[26]

Robert's radicalism incorporated progressive stances on women's rights as well. He routinely voted in favor of including women on governing bodies in abolitionist organizations, and in 1869, when the American Equal Rights Association split over supporting the Fifteenth Amendment, which gave the franchise only to Black men, Robert was the only Black man to stand in opposition. He made it known that "he would rather that his son should never be enfranchised, unless his daughter could be also, that, as she bore the double curse of sex and color, on every principle of justice she should first be protected."[27] Those were not idle sentiments either. He held a deep commitment to the protection of women and was sensitive to the kinds of discrimination and vulnerabilities that plagued them.

In 1885, he was—and had been for some time—an active member of Philadelphia's Citizens' Suffrage Association, a body that comprised women and men dedicated to equal access to the vote. But increasingly, Robert Purvis's layered view of race, gender, and politics would gestate deep divisions in the organization. It started with his support for proposed changes to the laws on wife beating.[28]

Robert Adams Jr., the aforementioned gentleman dueler, five years later, acting in his role as an elected Republican state representative for the Sixth District in Philadelphia County, proposed a new bill that would reestablish the pillory and whipping post for men who beat their wives. The bill's creation was in response to the growing instances of intimate partner violence in the city and the state, and concern that the current punishments were too lenient, as discussed in a *Philadelphia Inquirer* piece on January 24, 1885:

> Wife beating has become so common an offense as to be regarded with comparative leniency by the courts, and the sentences imposed upon offenders are apparently no discouragement to those gentlemen who indulge in the occasional luxury of breaking a chair or a stove plate over the heads of their defenseless wives. The present law being inadequate to convince wife beaters that they should not beat their wives, that it is a brutal, cowardly and demoralizing thing to do, and that it frequently leads gentlemen who merely wish to chastise their conjugal partners to kill them outright, owing to an exaggerated fervor of correction, it should be changed, and it has naturally been suggested to the author of the bill in question that if the wife beater were made to understand the cruelty of blows by baring his own back to them, that he would be reclaimed and society have restored to it a human being in place of a wife-beating brute.[29]

The writers gave their support for the construction of a new whipping post, ultimately believing that once built, it would never actually be used because "the mere exhibition of it would so terrorize the tribe of wife beaters as to make them forego the luxury of breaking the bones of their spouses."[30]

The local judiciary roundly criticized the proposed changes as barbaric and retrograde—the nation had moved away from corporal punishment in large measure following the Revolutionary War. Still, Adams managed to get the bill on the calendar to at least be debated. He discussed being in receipt of letters from across the state and the nation in support of the measure—women especially who had been brutalized spurred him on in what was admittedly an uphill battle. He himself could understand how the proposal seemed like a step backward but insisted upon the reinstatement of the whipping post because "there is no way to punish the hounds who beat women. For such men there is no terror in a warm, comfortable prison, and while bad husbands are kept in the jails their wives, perhaps, are suffering additional woes from being deprived of the usual support." Officials from organizations such as the Guardians of the Poor, along with several judges and lawyers, expressed support for the bill; as one judge explained, "Husbands who had been brought before him were generally men who could be reached only with the lash." Indeed. However, opposition was equally impassioned.[31]

Other lawmakers felt that since in such cases the husband is nearly always presumed guilty until he can prove otherwise, the probability was high that too many wrongly accused would be punished, and that "to disgrace a man unjustly by whipping him with a lash would be so terrible a wrong that the risk should not be taken." Democratic state senator Joseph P. Kelly, who served on the judiciary special committee, took the extra step of offering some counsel to Representative Adams. He advised Adams to take a wider view of the matter, as "Adams, who, being young and unmarried, might in putting this bill through, be subjecting himself to danger of future pain and embarrassment." Reporters at the *Times Philadelphia* delighted in recounting the exchange as the barb seemed to have struck a nerve. While Adams recovered and suggested that "Mr. Kelly would do better to look to his own matrimonial future," he did so with his face flushed as he choked back anger. The bill made it to the calendar by a vote of 32–16 but would be defeated in the state senate in late February by a vote of 16–24. As one report lamented:

> On the same day and about the same time the bill was defeated in the Senate a married woman named Fanny Murphy died at the city farm near Pittsburgh from the effects of a terrible beating inflicted by her husband, Martin Murphy, three days previously. The bill, even if it were an existing law, would not of course cover Murphy's case, which can only be adequately avenged by the hangman's rope, and we merely mention this as an aggravated instance of a crime which is becoming very common, and which the defeated bill proposed to punish in summary manner.[32]

The bill lay at the heart of a complicated set of realities about women's lives and the ways that the state and the justice system had fallen short. Even though the courts had repudiated "marital chastisement," in the late nineteenth century, the legal system continued to treat wife beating differently from criminal cases of assault and battery. Even as "authorities denied that a husband had the right to beat his wife, they intervened only intermittently in cases of marital violence," often bestowing formal and informal immunity from prosecution in the name of protecting the sanctity of families.[33]

The discourse reveals how widespread the debate had become. It also exposed the breadth and intensity of the divisions. Before the bill's defeat, in early February 1885, Robert Purvis rankled some sensibilities when he suggested "that the association pass a resolution commending Representative Adams for introducing a bill of such a nature into the State Legislature."[34] A devout Christian, Robert Purvis was clearly one for whom the arc of justice bent toward the Old Testament, rather than those scriptures advising the turning of the cheek. Edward M. Davis, another association member, immediately called for a postponement, as he considered the proposed action to be "beneath the dignity" of the organization.[35]

Edward was among white Philadelphia's storied elites. He was himself an avowed abolitionist and Civil War veteran. He was married to one of Lucretia Mott's daughters and attended the National Woman Suffrage Association meetings regularly.[36] He sponsored a lecture by Susan B. Anthony at the Philadelphia Radical Club, of which he was president, though he disagreed with Anthony and Purvis on the question of Black men's suffrage. He supported the passage of the

Fifteenth Amendment, believing it necessary for Black men of the South to stave off racial violence. That position helps give a window onto his narrow view of racial tyranny and perhaps a naivete about the quotidian, violent degradation Black women suffered. Still, his objection in that suffrage meeting was successful. But even as Edward tabled the action, as it turns out, many of the other suffragists agreed with Robert's position. The tensions in the group came to a head. Annie Cutler's case would be the proverbial straw.[37]

On Wednesday, May 6, 1885, Robert presided over the group's meeting. Gathered at Ninth and Spring Garden, their room featured a card prominently displayed with the epigraph "Taxation Without Representation Is Tyranny." At the helm, Robert wasted little time discussing support and advocacy for the whipping post for wife beaters. "Several of the ladies were of the opinion that the bill should be approved by the association," but the debate was derailed, as was the remainder of the day's agenda, by a spirited discussion about the court proceedings in Annie's case.[38]

Mrs. Emma A. Rhoads, a passionate member of the association, declared, "I hope she will be free."[39]

Emma added, "I think I would be almost glad . . . if more of our women so treated would do the same thing." It was a surprising disclosure on the part of an otherwise decent, law-abiding, married, Christian woman. And it's important because it gives us a sense of how often vulnerable Black women like Annie had been deceived and disgraced. We need to understand this dishonor would have grave consequences for the women. It hobbled their marriage prospects going forward, which had implications not just for their social and emotional well-being but for their economic survival as well. Then as now, Black women were among the lowest paid workers. Not having a partner could mean a lifetime of crippling, abject poverty. It was a serious thing that Emma was reacting to. And she did not stop there. She suggested that the association get involved and investigate further.[40]

Discomfort and general shock must have washed over the room. As practiced a diplomat as he was an activist, Robert conceded that it was "hard to conceive of the approval of murder by a Christian. There are, however, circumstances in which people may be driven to desperation." He talked about his own advocacy for "peace principles," and yet admitted that he, too, had carried murder in his heart.[41]

Given his stature in the community and the nation, the group must have been riveted. One can imagine a hushed awe, with all eyes focused on him. And he went further. He talked about his own feelings of rage when a racist schoolmaster threatened his children. Fury overtook him. Robert swore that he would kill the man if he harmed his son and believed that he had that inside himself. And as if Robert's story was not already a stunning admission, he had even more to say.[42]

He turned his attention back to Annie and said, "I think she is a hero in a true sense of the word and has rid the world of a villain."[43]

The association resolved to start visiting Annie and exploring other ways to offer their support. Robert, Emma, and a Mrs. L. P. Danforth all agreed to go. When Annie was sentenced to hang for her crimes, the group together with some of the who's who of the city mobilized to pressure the courts and the Board of Pardons. Even members of the clergy had begun to lobby on Annie's behalf. Most of the supporters opposed the death penalty outright, but others also affirmed a Black woman's right to defend her honor, even if somewhat backhandedly. On October 17, 1885, the *Evening Bulletin* described Annie as a "poor, ignorant colored woman who killed a scoundrel who had betrayed, ruined, deserted and abused her." The piece went on to add that while in the eyes of the law she was a murderer, "in the eyes of the Higher Law, the retribution that followed the original crime against all humanity, at the hands of a wronged, outraged, desperate woman, will surely be viewed with a justice very largely tempered with mercy." Others sent in affidavits attesting to her being a "very truthful, kind, affectionate and industrious girl." Annie was a woman who had been wronged by an unscrupulous man. It was a stunning turn of events in every sense of those words.[44]

Even so, there were other voices.

Rumors surfaced that Annie was not the woman she pretended to be. These accounts depicted Mettler's saloon and concert hall as a sinful haven with illicit parlors and seamy activities taking place. An opinion piece lashed back at the outpouring of support that she received. "False Sympathy for a Murderess" acknowledged that hanging anyone was a difficult task, especially a woman, but that if a woman committed a crime for which death was the penalty, she should "suffer the same penalty that would be inflicted on a man." After deriding Annie as "not an innocent girl, but a mature woman of bad character and low associations," the unnamed author concluded: "It is time to give up the sentimental idea that a woman is not a responsible being. Even a common negro woman knows enough to abstain from murder; if she does not, she should be taught by stern example."[45] This was a curious line of reasoning; most held that women, especially Black women, were not responsible enough to vote or hold office, yet they had no compunction about holding them to the same standard of punishment as those who were.

The contempt for those sympathizing with Annie was not confined to op-eds. Growing support and agitation on Annie's behalf deepened the wedge forming in the Citizens' Suffrage Association as well. Edward resigned over it.[46]

The fracture and its origins mark a weighty juncture, certainly in the history of the organization, but for our purposes as well. Annie Cutler's actions, and those of other Black women like her, churned up the ugly bits about misogynoir and sexist double standards, and sex and integrity, violence, and the limits of Black women's protections. Yet her plight coerced a rare reckoning, a kind of widespread acknowledgment of a Black femininity once possessed of purity; virtue that many felt she had the right to safeguard and avenge. It also touches on the raw emotions and interiority of Black women. In the end, Annie was sentenced to eight years at Eastern State Penitentiary, where she refused male visitors. She was apparently done with men.[47]

Mary Crawford seems to have reached a similar conclusion in 1890, though she came to it too late to avoid calamity, the ravages of which had been inscribed onto her flesh, when the man she loved "whipped her."[48] His name was also William. We don't have many details about the beating itself or whether she was actually struck with a whip, but what we do have suggests that the resulting devastation haunted her. At twenty-two years old, she might have tried to heal and move on somehow, but trauma, resentment, and fury seemed to have firmly taken hold. In the days before her arrest, she had gone about making arrangements, deliberately and with precision.

On Sunday, she "gave away all her clothing." She paid off her debts too. William lived in a house at 248 Duponceau Street, in the Seventh Ward, Philadelphia's largest Black neighborhood. He had a good job. He was a machinist.[49] Mary approached in the evening as he sat eating his supper. His table was near the window. She timed her attack perfectly. After taking him in, seated and dining, she raised her arm with the pistol in hand. Mary fired five shots through the window. She was not a practiced shot, however. Physically, William's injuries were minor. Less is likely said about his nerves, as he resigned to move from the place where he had come so close to losing his life.[50]

The burst of gunfire drew Philadelphia's patrolmen, men keenly attuned to the crack of a bullet exploding from the chamber. In short order, as Mary fired, they came running. Arresting officers Addis and McGlinchey gave chase and wrested the weapon from Mary's hands. Mary told the officers that she had "no reason to live" after he beat her. One wonders what else might have been lost in that assault. Something she could not regain but resigned to avenge. Upon her arrest, she informed the authorities that she was not sorry. She was brought before Magistrate Milligan and charged on the oath of Officer Addis with assault and battery with intent to kill.[51] By the time of her hearing on June 9, she had racked up more charges—in addition to the varying assault crimes, she was indicted for carrying a concealed weapon and for "playfully pointing a pistol." She pleaded not guilty just the same.[52] "Neatly attired" in a black dress and "wearing gold-rimmed glasses," Mary was indicted and found guilty. True bills having been handed down on all counts, she was ordered to pay a fine of one cent, court costs, and to confinement at the Philadelphia County Prison for three months.[53]

All things considered, it wasn't the worst outcome. Perhaps in the years following the high-profile case of Annie Cutler, and in the aftermath of wider discussions about the prevalence of violence against women, jurors and justices in this instance considered the precarity of women in the city, even a Black one.

IDA, ANNIE, AND MARY COMMITTED EXTRAORDINARY acts of violence, especially among Black women arrested in the city. The vast majority of those who were placed under arrest at the time were charged with larceny and other associated crimes against property. Ida, Annie, and Mary therefore stood apart—their violence spoke. It snarled at their dishonor. It also wailed in a register midway between madness and rage. It was an agonizing dialect, a guttural language that found surprising purchase in the most unlikely of spaces. It prompted impassioned discussions about their womanhood and their honor. Annie's killing of a man in broad daylight struck a nerve among women and men across the city—across race and class strata too. It cast a light on the rupture between notions of integrity, justice, and Black women's lived realities. Hers also spotlights how Black men like Robert Purvis connected the dots. He, and many of the members of the Citizens' Suffrage Association, recognized that their campaign for the female vote was ultimately connected to women's rights in a much broader sense. Robert's passionate embrace of women getting the franchise and also his support for violently punishing men who beat women evidence this. At the same time, the stunning levels of brutality against women are rendered in a layered sense—Representative Adams's abortive bid to bring back the pillory and whipping post as a deterrent attest to this as well as the inability of existing law enforcement to effectively intervene.

Ida's and Mary's beatings unearth the spectral range of the violence rained down on Black women—the first providing a graphic window onto just how punishing the assaults could be, while Mary's offers a portrait of the lingering wounds. How they festered, rotting her from the inside out. The women found their breaking points at different junctures in their respective sagas, but their fury and need to lash back in defense of their honor and selfhood links them. It whispers, too, in disorderly murmurs and profane outbursts about what it was that vengeance feminism was bent on defending.

TWO

THEIR HISTORY

Lawlessness and Black Womanhood

What makes your crime more aggravated is that you held a position of trust in the family. A person who would commit a crime like this deserves no mercy.

—JUDGE FRANK BREGY, 1890

Let me in, the cops are after me.

—SARAH WARD, 1895

"YOU DONE STOLE MY JOHN." WITH THE CHARGE announced, Sarah Ward retrieved a revolver from her pocket to deliver the verdict. Sarah, who sustained herself on a servant's wages, reputedly feared that her razor had grown "too dull" to execute the sentence she unilaterally handed down—the "cheap double-action" pistol would have to suffice.[1]

The crime her nemesis, Laura Anderson, committed was to spend the afternoon with the young man that had stolen Sarah's heart. If accounts of their relationship are to be believed, John and Sarah had danced at a bevy of parties and balls and made appearances at all the local cakewalks. Sarah made it clear to any young ladies who may have had designs on the man that she and John were exclusive. John, it seems, did not get the memo. He invited Laura to accompany him as he joined a group of friends on a day trip to Atlantic City, New Jersey. The shore was a popular destination, and the pair would have enjoyed themselves like so many other young people, frolicking against the backdrop of frothy waves, their skin and hair whipped by salty air as they elected to "shoot the chute" in the waning days of summer.[2]

When Sarah learned of the excursion, she felt that "her lover had played her false." She was not the type to suffer in silence or to tolerate any perceived disrespect. Rather than wallowing in sorrow, she "resolved to be avenged." Her anger suggests that she and John had been more than spirited dance partners during those evenings at the parties. Court records listed Sarah as having been a married woman. Maybe she was an adulterer, too, but it's equally possible that the press had it wrong—perhaps John wasn't a lover but her spouse. The latter might explain why she went after Laura so violently.[3]

In the apartment at 414 Ratcliffe Street that Laura shared with Mamie Brooks, Sarah made good on her intentions by drawing her weapon in the early hours of September 5, 1895.

Laura, still in the fog of her slumber, managed to pray as she hugged the wall, probably hoping it might act as a shield. Whatever Laura prayed for, it seems to have been answered, though in a manner she probably did not expect. Sarah pulled the trigger, the hammer made an audible click, but the dreaded blast of a report did not issue.[4]

The gun misfired.

Once. Then twice. Sarah's chosen method of execution had failed. Taking stock of their situation, Mamie advanced on Sarah. The two locked in a fierce struggle.[5]

Laura seized on the commotion and shouted, "Murder!" at the top of her voice.[6]

The police were already within earshot. Laura and Mamie's apartment was nestled among the densely packed quarters of houses lining Ratcliffe Street, a cramped alleyway that ran between Minster and Lombard Streets. Since Minster had a reputation as one of the roughest streets in the Seventh Ward, it's probably not a shock that the cries and tumult drew the attention of nearby Officer Joseph Zintl of the Nineteenth District. In haste, he burst onto the scene and arrested Sarah. On Zintl's oath, Sarah was charged with assault and battery with intent to kill.[7]

There is an irony in the way that law enforcement intervened, given how Sarah gained access to Laura's apartment in the first place. Normally, an unexpected rap on the door late at night would not lead to successful entry, especially given the nature of the area. Moreover, in light of their rivalry, it's

unlikely that Laura—or her roommate, for that matter—
would have unlocked the door under ordinary circumstances.
But Sarah must have been confident in her plan, because she
would have traveled roughly half a mile through narrow corridors and dangerous alleyways against a black sky if she traveled
from her home at 633 Barclay Street. To be admitted, Sarah
had only to invoke a distress call that most African American
women felt a duty to answer:

"Let me in, the cops are after me."[8]

That plea led Mamie to move swiftly to help; she believed
she was aiding a distressed Black woman to "escape from the
police." That it was a ruse for a failed ambush was probably
inconceivable. Still, that betrayal might explain what followed.
Even though mistrust of the police and the justice system was
such that many Black women put aside their differences in the
face of its tyranny, both Laura and Mamie cooperated with
authorities and appeared as witnesses against Sarah. Yet the
ultimate outcome of the case probably reified any doubts about
the justice system that the victims harbored.[9]

Sarah would be indicted on two criminal counts on September 12, 1895, but after being released on bond, she was not
actually tried until four years later, on September 25, 1899.
Such a delay was highly unusual for the period and likely
related to the fact that on October 3, 1895, the bill of indictment noted that "Recognizance of Defendant and surety
forfeited." It seems that the $1,000 bail posted by a consta-
ble, Samuel G. Maloney of 811 Lombard Street, effectively

allowed Sarah to evade trial. By the time she faced the music, she received a same-day acquittal for the assault and battery charge. As for the second indictment for "playfully pointing a pistol," that, too, was resolved with a same-day acquittal.[10]

Despite the violent nature of her conduct, Sarah's attempted vengeance is not actually the primary focus here, as her actions were not avenging misogynoir. Rather, it is Laura and Mamie's inability to obtain justice paired with how Sarah gained access to their home that help display Black women's vexed history with the lawlessness pervading not just local jurisprudence but also the country's legal system in a broader sense. It underscores a larger pattern of state negligence when it came to Black women's safety. But while it starts to frame Black women's—and by extension the Black community's—fear and lack of faith in the law, it does not explain its beginnings, nor does it map the true extent of the harm that the legal system has caused Black women. Vengeance feminism is as much about Black women's contentious relationship with American justice as it is about Black women turning to violence and mayhem for revenge against racist and misogynistic wrongs. The start of this rupture stretches much further back.

Before the nineteenth and twentieth centuries, before the nation's inception, down to its colonial foundations, Black women were property. Early laws governing enslavement jeopardized Black women, disallowed for their protection, and effectively criminalized their self-defense; all while society maligned Black women as immoral and unchaste. As this chapter will show, these laws, legal practices, and legacies shaped Black women's experiences of policing and incarceration long after slavery's end, forcing African American women to contend with the consequences of this history at every stage in the judicial process. It is vengeance feminism's origin story.

EVEN BEFORE ENSLAVEMENT PROVIDED EUROPEAN explorers with a financial interest in dehumanizing Africans, they harbored a deep mistrust of Blackness and the darkly pigmented skin associated with it: "White and black connoted purity and filthiness, virginity and sin, virtue and baseness, beauty and ugliness, beneficence and evil, God and the devil." They took a particularly harsh view of African women, whom they regarded as hedonistic, licentious, and dangerous. Not only because the women's shapely and robust figures were bathed in richly black and brown hues but also because the women wore less clothing—European men cast their nudity as crude solicitation, rather than as a cultural difference appropriate for the climate. They told tall tales of the women pouncing and sexually coercing them, in many ways likening African women to the succubae of night terrors. And yet, in the face of such unfathomable peril, white men could not stay away.[11]

By the 1660s, so multitudinous was the rape of enslaved African women that colonists had to create a new law to address the growing and worrisome presence of "mulattoes." Under customary English law and traditions, the status of a child followed that of the father. But as increasing numbers of brown babies dotted the landscape, legislatures moved decisively to stem the tide. Virginia led the pack in 1662, with an "act that defined all children born of the bodies of black women as slaves, even if their fathers were free and white." To make it plain: if your mother was a slave, you, too, would be enslaved from birth for life.[12] And so it began.

As other colonies quickly followed suit, the legal changes effectively incentivized rape and other forms of sexual coercion, such as forced breeding given that enslaved women's offspring served to enhance enslavers' wealth. Few expressed any concern about the plight of the women or their condemned children. As far as white men were concerned, as the *South Carolina Gazette* noted in 1736, African women could serve lovers "by Night as well as Day." And, according to Johann Schoepf, they counted "it an honor to bring a mulatto into the world."[13]

The staying power of such myths was reinforced by the very nature of enslavement. For example, in addition to rape and forced breeding, Black women were often immodestly clothed and routinely stripped in public as they were beaten. Formerly enslaved women's and men's accounts are rife with scenes of Black women's exposed "naked quivering flesh." Henry Bibb lamented the conditions: "Licentious white men can and do enter at night or day the lodging places of slaves, break up the bonds of affection in families, destroy all their domestic and social union for life; and the laws of the country afford them no protection." Worse, planters like "Big Jim" McClain in Virginia, "entertained his friends by allowing them to rape the enslaved women he owned while their loved ones watched."[14]

This revolting sadism was echoed in myriad rulings such as the *George v. State* verdict in Mississippi in 1859, which overturned the conviction of an enslaved man who sexually assaulted an enslaved girl. As far as the law was concerned the "rape of a female slave under the age of ten by a slave was not a crime." It was as his attorney argued: "The crime of rape does not exist in this State between African slaves . . . their sexual intercourse is left to be regulated by their owners." He added, "their intercourse is promiscuous, and the violation of a female slave by a male slave would be a mere assault and battery."[15]

Such denigration was widespread, and the Quaker City was no exception. Even as the region had a history of abolitionism early on, it nonetheless countenanced slavery. The practice had been occurring before the arrival of William Penn in 1682, and it continued in a de facto sense, with the status of owned Black people being ill defined. For example, even as they were considered as separate and below whites, an enslaved woman named Prudence, who was summoned to court in 1687 to answer "all such Complaints as shall be layd against her," went before the same court as whites. However, beginning in the 1700s, Pennsylvania followed colonies such as Virginia, South Carolina, New York, and Massachusetts by "legislatively and judicially sanctioning racial slavery within its borders."[16]

Dehumanizing rules and mandates sprang up in the after-math, underscoring an unfortunate and enduring truth: the legal system has always failed Black people, and it did so right at the start.

Even if we put aside its sanctioning of lifelong racial enslave-ment in the 1640s and its wholesale disregard for Black wom-en's and girls' bodies, historically it consigned Black people to separate, unequal systems of criminal justice. To begin with, enslaved Africans were subject to whatever punishments enslavers and overseers cared to dish out. If enslaved or free Black people were involved in incidents that rose to the level of the local judiciary, most could not offer testimony against whites, rarely did they have counsel, and they were usually sent to separate "Negro Courts" like those adopted in Pennsylvania after enslavement was codified into law. These "courts," which would be made up of two justices of the peace and a handful of freeholders, were designed with the needs of white enslavers in mind—they could be called together quickly to hear cases to avoid depriving whites of their free laborers. The punishments were overwhelmingly corporal, as opposed to fines or inden-ture, and despite the nature of the origins, both enslaved and free Black people were tried in them.[17]

Across the burgeoning country, Black people, whether enslaved or free, faced a biased and unequal justice system. Key bedrocks of American jurisprudence, such as a trial by one's peers, were denied to Black people for centuries, as historian

Nikki M. Taylor notes, "In fact, it was not until 1860 that the first African Americans were impaneled to serve on juries in the United States."[18]

Rape laws further cemented the racialized hierarchy by simultaneously placing Black women and girls in jeopardy while subjecting Black men to unequal discipline. Statutes that laid out specific, harsh punishments for the rape and attempted rape of white women and white girls also took pains to define the severity of the sentences in accordance with the race of the perpetrator. In Pennsylvania, for example, a Black man would face the gallows for rape, while a white man would be publicly whipped and subject to seven years of indentured service. These same laws made no mention of any punishment at all for the rape or attempted rape of Black women or Black girls, by either white or Black men. As a consequence, Black men faced grave punishment even as Black women were deprived of legal redress altogether.[19]

Lacking recourse in a legal system that operated wholly against them, enslaved women resisted extralegally. They damaged property, feigned illness, and took flight, and scores of enslaved women turned to arson or poisonings as they resigned to kill cruel enslavers. Some even targeted the enslavers' kin. Such was the case of Cloe, an enslaved teenager executed in 1801 for murdering two of her enslaver's three daughters in Carlisle, Pennsylvania.

By all accounts, the mistress of the house, Mary Carothers, was exceptionally brutal toward Cloe. She meted out vicious discipline for small infractions, and her daughters routinely informed on the girl, which led to more violent punishments. Cloe drowned four-year-old Lucetta in a nearby creek in late January. When the child's body was discovered, the assumption was that she had fallen victim to a tragic accident. It was not until the second death, that of six-year-old Polly, that Cloe's actions would be uncovered. Cloe explained that almost immediately after the funeral for Lucetta, Mary "made me strip off my short-gown and gave me a severe whipping, with a cowskin." After that beating, Cloe was beaten again on Tuesday and again a few days later on Saturday. It was then that she decided to take "further revenge" on the family by murdering Polly.[20]

Cloe's case foregrounds enslaved women's own sense of justice and the lengths to which some would go to enact violent retribution. Further, amid nearly insurmountable odds, they passed fierce lessons down through the generations. Cornelia, a formerly enslaved Black woman in Tennessee, said as much when she recalled her own enslaved mother's survival stance: "The one doctrine of my mother's teaching which was branded upon my senses was that I should never let anyone abuse me. 'I'll kill you, gal, if you don't stand up for yourself,' she would say. 'Fight, and if you can't fight, kick; if you can't kick, then bite.'"[21] Countless enslaved women adopted and practiced a similar credo, as historical accounts teem with details of their efforts to fend off rapes and other forms of sexual violence. This legacy of systemic lawlessness begets, in part, the history of Black women finding ways to defend themselves.

They paid the price for it too.

As one formerly enslaved woman bitterly recalled, "My young marster tried to go with me, and 'cause I wouldn't go with him he pretended I had done somethin' and beat me. I fought him back because he had no right to beat me for not goin' with him. His mother got mad with me for fightin' him back and I told her why he had beat me. Well then she sent me to the courthouse to be whipped for fightin' him." An enslaved woman named Celia was hanged in 1855 in Missouri for killing her rapist enslaver. Her case struck at the core of Black women's subjugation as her defense tried to argue that enslaved women "were protected by law from sexual exploitation by white men." The prosecution, court, and jurors disagreed. Celia's fate mirrored that of so many other Black women confronted with American justice: it failed to protect them when they were victims and wielded the worst punishment against them when they were convicted.[22] Despite the wholesale cruelty, violence, and rampant sexual assault, Black women and girls were regarded as *unrapeable*. It's impossible to overstate the damage that this had on their lives and that of their descendants.

It's also impossible to overstate how deep-seated the stereotypes about Black womanhood were in American and European culture. Characterizations of the wanton wiles of *Sable Venuses* piled up over the course of the eighteenth century. One notorious ode penned by Isaac Teale "climaxes with a claim that because of the beauty of the 'Sable Venus' it is the author's duty to sexually abuse any black woman in the slave Diaspora he can get his hands on." And as Regulus Allen explains, "Like many depictions of African women, the Sable Venus poem and painting attempt to rationalize white men's attraction to black women by situating it in the realm of base desires instead of idealized beauty and by insisting that these immoral urges originate in the African woman." American and European history is littered with white people projecting onto Black women a host of purported, craven sexual proclivities.[23]

But it was not Black women's seductions that corrupted white men, rather the men had been despoiled by their own unrestrained power. White women, too, were irreparably tainted by the barbarism of enslavement. With her dark hair parted down the middle and smoothed on each side, a dour-faced, alabaster-skinned Mary Boykin Chesnut took sober stock of her world when she penned these words on the eve of the Civil War: "Like the patriarchs of old, our men live all in one house with their wives and their concubines; and the mulattoes one sees in every family partly resemble the white children." Yet even as she wrote, the daughter and wife of South Carolinian senators also likened enslaved Black women to prostitutes jeopardizing white female purity.[24]

These ideas didn't stay confined in some distant past either. What we need to understand about this history is that the ramifications have endured for centuries. Few cases of rape against

African Americans were prosecuted, especially when their assailants were white men. Indeed, one of the first instances of a successful prosecution doesn't occur until 1959, after a group of white men were convicted and sentenced for the gang rape of Betty Jean Owens. In that instance, she was found bound and gagged in the men's car by an officer whom her friends had flagged down and begged to rescue her. Flagrant a violation as it was, actually summoning the courts to respond required the mass mobilization of the Black community nationwide, with civil rights figures from Ella Baker to Malcolm X weighing in, and to her own peers at Florida A&M University protesting en masse for justice.[25]

More recent history bears the weight of this legacy. The serial rape and sexual assault of over a dozen Black women by an Oklahoma City police officer, a white-and-Asian man named Daniel Holtzclaw, did not rise to the level of national news until he was convicted. Even then, the coverage seemed less concerned with the victims and more stunned that someone would actually be punished for it. In 2015, he was convicted on eighteen of thirty-six counts and sentenced to 263 years in prison. That outcome is a testament to the bravery of the victims who came forward and the local activism of Black feminists determined to see some measure of justice served. The rarity of that verdict summons the stark contrast to the ways that the justice system, and white mobs, historically have responded to alleged sexual assaults on white women by Black men. Few of the accused ever saw the inside of a courtroom;

rather, they would be removed from jails, brutalized, and lynched—sometimes set ablaze as well, and routinely to the glee of lawless white crowds.[26]

Meanwhile, damning popular notions of libidinous, immoral Black women proliferated. The reach of the ideas animating them can be hard to imagine, yet they were and remain everywhere. The Rolling Stones' "Some Girls" lyrics in 1978 might as well have been straight out of the eighteenth century's greatest hits: "White girls they're pretty funny, sometimes they drive me mad / Black girls just wanna get fucked all night, I just don't have that much jam."[27]

Sexual exploitation, the lack of protection paired with the denial of self-defense, and the ruinous myths about Black women's desire congealed and endured across time and territory, well beyond enslavement. The injurious impacts converged on Black women whenever they had to interact with the state. It met them when they were detained and charged. It harmed them when they stood before magistrates, justices, and jurors. And it haunted them when they disproportionately languished in filthy cells in the Northeast or in vile work camps in the South. The assemblage of these dynamics amplified Black women's vulnerability to all manner of assault while simultaneously finding them living and laboring under extreme surveillance—by employers and state authorities, all of which left them disproportionately susceptible to criminalization.

After emancipation, Black women migrated to mid-Atlantic and Northern cities in droves hoping to escape the predations of former enslavers and the slavery-inflected legal system that continued to enable their abuse. Many of those hopes would be dashed. This was certainly so in Philadelphia, in 1886, when Mary Jackson worked as a servant for the Eldridges, a wealthy white family. The seventeen-year-old Mary learned about a ball being held at Musical Fund Hall and dutifully asked for and received permission from Mrs. Eldridge to attend. Then, when it was time to get dressed for the event, she *borrowed* a few items from work. Specifically, she selected some of the Eldridges' daughter's finest garments—a gorgeous, heavy black silk dress and a plush cardinal-red coat, items valued at roughly $125. As a point of comparison, Mary would have needed to work full-time for over a year to amass such a sum. She probably felt like a princess, and she must have been the talk of the gala. Maybe she caught the eye of someone special. She danced until the wee hours and was presumably returning to the Eldridges' house when she caught the attention of Special Officer Murray.[28]

Murray and officers like him were a part of a series of changes to the city's police force as it evolved from horses and buggies and call boxes to telephone lines and motor patrols and police boats. As the size of the African American community doubled in the two decades after the Civil War, growth largely driven by Southern migration, the number of patrolmen grew from roughly 1,200 in the 1880s to nearly 4,000 in the early twentieth century. The force also employed a cadre of special officers who aided detectives and engaged in a kind of muscular surveillance, aimed at rooting out members of the dreaded "crime class"—this group reputedly consisted of recidivists and Black and Indigenous women and men, groups deemed inherently degenerate as espoused by the era's criminologists. Special officers camped out at bus depots and railway stations, aiming to spot and detain "professional thieves" as soon as they touched ground. New policies allowed police to detain "habitual criminals" for up to ninety days on mere suspicion of a crime. Even when the streets were "almost free of beggars, vagrants, and panhandlers," a special surveillance detail remained in place due to concerns about "a steady influx of such undesirable characters from other cities."[29] As the chief of police boasted in his 1885 annual report, Philadelphia officers had inspired "a wholesome dread" in the criminal classes through "a number of judicious arrests, even before they had committed any specific offense." Further, policing manuals directed officers to detain any persons they suspected to be from out of state without "visible means of support." That 1897 manual and mandate continued to be used for training up until 1915.[30]

Under the circumstances, African Americans moved about the city with a target on their backs, and it wasn't just those who looked broke that set off red flags. Officer Murray took in the resplendent young Mary Jackson coming down the street adorned in a gorgeous silk dress and wrapped in striking cardinal. He immediately suspected her of a crime. He believed she "had stolen the valuables" and detained and questioned her.

She told him she had permission from her employer to attend the dance and wear the items. Officer Murray arrested Mary on the spot and contacted Mrs. Eldridge. Before Magistrate List, he stated that Mrs. Eldridge affirmed his suspicions, Mary did not have her permission to wear the items, and further, she "believed Mary proposed of disposing of it." Mary Jackson was held over for trial and was initially sentenced to six months in the county prison; that sentence was reconsidered and reduced to three months.

Mary crossed the line by sporting the gear without asking, but since she obtained permission to attend the party, Mary probably intended to sneak out in the items, show off, and then return them before her boss was any the wiser. Instead, the seventeen-year-old was arrested and fed into the legal system. Had she been a young white woman strolling "gaily attired" in expensive apparel, Murray probably wouldn't have batted an eye, and she would have been able to return the items without notice. In this sense, hers mirrored the experience of countless African Americans who were routinely detained and taken into custody on scant evidence and in violation of their Fourth Amendment rights. Once in custody, African American suspects were beaten and threatened; some later reported that they were compelled to give false confessions. For example, in 1904, Henrietta Cook, arrested for infanticide, testified that she had essentially been forced to sign a false confession. Six years later, another African American woman would testify that masked officers all but threatened rape if she did not sign a confession for the stabbing death of a white man who had sexually harassed and assaulted her on a streetcar.[31]

I want to be clear here: I am not suggesting that each woman was innocent. I think Mary Jackson probably did use the Eldridges' clothes without asking, in much the same ways that today's seventeen-year-olds might "borrow" gear or the car without asking for a night out to impress their friends. Rather than arguing innocence versus guilt, my larger point is that the legacies and topic of lawlessness that haunted Black women and girls contributed to a kind of policing and state surveillance that always left them more likely to be searched and harassed, in ways that white women and girls never had to contend with; as Nicole Hahn Rafter explained, "Chivalry filtered them out of the prison system, helping to create the even greater racial imbalances among female than male prisoner populations."[32] Nationwide, the numbers bore that out: in the South, where African Americans accounted for 36 percent of the population, even as Black men represented as much as 72 percent of the male prison population, Black women represented 86 percent of female prisoners in the region in 1880. In the Midwest, those numbers were 12 and 29 percent, respectively, and in the West, Black men accounted for 18 percent of male prisoners while Black women represented 20 percent of females. At that time, African Americans accounted for less than 1 percent of the overall population in the West and roughly 2 percent in the Midwest. African Americans actually fared a little better in the Northeast, where Black people counted for 2 percent of the population. There, Black women were 7 percent of female prisoners, while Black men were 8 percent of male prisoners. Though by 1904, those numbers would change, with Black women accounting for 18 percent of female prisoners, while Black men accounted for 12 percent of the males.[33]

Indeed, while whiteness operated as an off-ramp, Blackness was a liability to be navigated at every stage of the judicial process. When juries were being impaneled in Black women's trials, it was not uncommon for prospective white jurors to state during voir dire, as one did in 1908, that their "morals are not as good as those of white people. I have a natural prejudice against them." He was hardly alone. Overwhelmingly arrested for larceny and usually on oath of the white employers and little corroborating evidence, Black women with no priors could be accused, arrested, charged, convicted, and sentenced within the span of a few hours.[34]

Moreover, caricatures of their comportment operated like a malignant fun house mirror, casting deformed images of African American women far removed from mainstream ideals of femininity and humanity. Within these narratives, Black women "disturbed the dignity of the court" with their crass lasciviousness. And press accounts delighted in exaggerating dialect and depicting cases that lampooned them. Covering a case involving an altercation between two Black women, the article, "Magistrate Smith Blushed," mocked the victim,

Annie Davis, as she offered to show the judge "de tooth marks on me breast, too" as proof that she had been struck and bitten. Mortified by the lewd and classless offer, the judge demurred, "'Oh, no,' remarked his Honor, as he raised a piece of paper to his face and blushed behind it, 'we will take your word for it.'" Annie then reiterated that she was more than willing to do so, to which he replied, "Now, that's enough, Miss Davis."[35] Her reported attempts to scandalize the magistrate harken back to those earlier claims about lustful African women—women blamed for their own kidnap and trafficking; while the jocularity entirely diminishes the gravity of the assault Annie sustained.[36]

Such accounts infuriated Black women. They knew all too well where these stereotypes came from and how they contributed to their current vulnerability. It dogged them in the South, as one Black woman lamented in 1902: "A colored woman, however respectable, is lower than the white prostitute. Southern white women will declare that no negro women are virtuous." Whereas Black men were being lynched on the barest claim of sexual impropriety with white women, Black women were raped with impunity; some were even lynched for fighting back against their attackers.[37]

It was a contemptible situation, and Black women of the time recognized it as such. Addie Hunton, an early-twentieth-century African American reformer, decried the hypocrisy in a simmering commentary:

Whence come these base aspersions to blight and dwarf the spirit of the Negro woman? Who in all this land can be so forgetful of her service and servitude as to seek to crush her already wounded and bleeding soul? Wounded by the violence and shame forced upon her in times when she had no voice to speak her woe; bleeding because of the constant irritation of these wounds by those who, while spending their best energies to vilify her to the world, are at the same time ever secretly seeking to make these vilifications true; she asks, Whence comes all this talk about the immorality of the Negro woman?[38]

Once Black women were behind bars, the rot in the justice system was even more inescapable. Administrators routinely denounced them as black and ugly, thoroughly bad, and vicious. Or, perhaps even worse, others used their positions to ogle the Black women in their custody, as did the warden of Eastern State Penitentiary when he described Sarah Scott as a "young, muscular finely developed woman weighing 218lbs 5ft 8 inches in height clean and straight without any superfluous flesh." Some of these women turned up pregnant, despite having been confined for years, further demonstrating how state apparatuses fomented Black women's rape and sexual exploitation.[39]

THE LAW AND ITS ADMINISTRATORS, LIKE MOST OF THE society, principally served and valued white life—and when

Black women were seen as a threat to those lives, the punishment was steep. Judge Bregy did not mince words when he sentenced a Black domestic named Martha Davis to ten years: "What makes your crime more aggravated is that you held a position of trust in the family. A person who would commit a crime like this deserves no mercy." Before the crime, Martha had been working for a white family named the Ervins. One day, she was informed that she was going to be let go for staying out too late, too often. Two days later, Anthony and his wife, Ida, along with their two young sons, Edwin and William, and "another colored girl, who was a servant in the house" all became violently ill after drinking coffee with their breakfast. Martha and the Ervins' fourteen-year-old daughter, Blanche, had not drunk the coffee and as a result had displayed none of the symptoms affecting the others. A merchant testified to having ground the coffee and freshly packaging it, and his delivery boy attested to this as well. A physician analyzed the coffee in the wake of the family's mass illness, and upon its positive test for arsenic, authorities homed in on Martha and eventually put her away for "administering poison with intent to kill."[40]

Martha's case operates as its own kind of vortex. Seated along the space and time continuum of what was and has been Black women's experience of life and work, it's a maelstrom of unfairness, erasure, and bitterness. It smacks of the myriad ways African American women were railroaded and underserved by the legal system. Blanche's race and gender effectively took her out of the running for suspects altogether. Equally instructive is that while accounts noted that another Black servant (presumably another Black woman) in the household was also stricken by the poisoning, the charging documents only acknowledged the white victims: Anthony, Ida, Edwin, and William.

Maybe Martha really was angry enough at the decision to give her the boot to pour a near-lethal amount of arsenic into the Ervin family's coffee and watch them drink it. Perhaps watching them writhe in pain afforded her some satisfaction. Maybe she believed that they deserved it. Maybe this vengeful, malicious, and dangerous response was her way of mediating the crushing weight of lawlessness.

That lawlessness, that toxic system of racial violence and corruption erected and maintained by laws and policing practices, upheld some of the basest inequities. It disallowed Black humanity while it permitted sexual violation and the commodification of Black women's bodies. It sanctioned Black women's rape and then cast them as immoral for it. It left them vulnerable to the vicissitudes of grinding poverty rooted in racial discrimination but swiftly punished them on the flimsiest of evidence. Police, magistrates, judges, and jurors were all primed to believe the worst about their character. Whether guilty of crimes or not, the overarching conditions made it nearly impossible for Black women to avoid criminalization.

This fraught history and the ongoing biases stemming from it ultimately engendered in some Black women a profound fury and the need for revenge in place of unavailing justice. The other lesson some learned from its legacies and present circumstances was that when they were in danger, it was best to take matters into their own hands.

THREE

THEIR WEAPONS

Danger and Survival, on Multiple Fronts

The woman claims that she stabbed Campbell in self-defense.

—*PHILADELPHIA INQUIRER*, SEPTEMBER 26, 1900

She is above the average in intelligence among her class, and I think that after her arrest she evolved several ways of exonerating herself.

—*TIMES PHILADELPHIA*, JUNE 15, 1901

PAIN GRIPPED WILLIAM CAMPBELL. HE MIGHT HAVE heard the scrape of a heel, a footfall, or some other tell that forewarned of danger, though accounts charge that his partner, Lillie, had crept up stealthily. Surprise came in a flash, the agony and horror of thick fluid running down his shirt; his adrenaline would have risen like a cresting wave to meet the "large butcher knife" buried in his chest.[1]

Tensions had boiled over Monday evening, September 24, 1900. William and Lillie spat ugly words at each other hours earlier, words that didn't stay confined to the borders of the room they shared at 619 Lombard Street. Their vitriol intruded on their housemates in much the same way that noxious odors might waft through a crowded row home—the rancor of rotting meat, sewage, and musty clothes seeping through dilapidated walls and crevices. William had stormed out after that initial argument but returned to the house, touching off a second round, one he would lose.[2]

William's anguished screams summoned his clamoring housemates into the dining room where he collapsed. As his blood soaked the floorboards, Lillie slipped out of the house. Perhaps the sight of William with a knife sunk into his breast was enough to dissuade the others from stopping her. No neighbors appeared to give chase. The darkened corridors of the Seventh Ward enveloped her as if its streets were pockets in the night sky.[3]

When Special Officer Ritchie of the Eighth District arrived on the scene, he arrested all the witnesses. William was carted off to Pennsylvania Hospital, one of America's oldest medical establishments. The brainchild of Dr. Thomas Bond, the institution had received its charter in 1751, thanks to the lobbying and fundraising efforts of men such as Benjamin Franklin and Dr. Benjamin Rush. Wealthy patients could afford private doctors, so Pennsylvania Hospital opened its doors to care for the mentally ill and the poor. The facility was expanded many times over the centuries that followed to "increase its capacity to care for the ill and wounded." William's injuries were so grave that he expired in transit, and his corpse was diverted to the morgue instead.[4]

Lillie's flight would also be rerouted. Lieutenant O'Brien, of the Second District station, discovered her hiding in an "outhouse connected with a colored tenement house in the rear of No. 715 Hutchinson street." Disbelief and fear probably clung to her like the foul odors of her hiding place, but the police and the jailers carried out their duties, undeterred by her condition. On September 25, 1900, before Magistrate Kochersperger, Lillie was charged with the murder of her partner, and less than twenty-four hours after sinking a knife into William's breast, "she was committed to jail without bail to await the action of the coroner."[5]

It was only the beginning for Lillie Fisher. She would have to mobilize every survival instinct she'd ever had to wade through both the violent altercation with her partner and what passed for justice in its aftermath. Her story is not unique and exemplifies the weapons Black women deployed when confronting existential crises—whether the threats came from partners or the legal system itself. Alongside the story of Mary Wright, accused of murder in 1901, the diversity of tactics reveals how Black women marshalled everything from their fists to knives to their keen intellect and organizing tactics to survive physical attacks but also to preserve and avenge their dignity.

As William Campbell's corpse lay cold in the morgue, two stories emerged about how he ended up there. The one that seemed to have the support of his neighbors alleged that after a contentious dispute on Monday afternoon, a fed-up William left the residence for several hours—presumably to cool off. He returned only to collect his clothing and other belongings, as he was intent upon leaving Lillie. The whisper was that William had fallen for another and would be soon joining her. Lillie Fisher—"alias Campbell," as accounts made sure to note—did not exactly cotton to this new plan. She allegedly seized a butcher's knife and snuck up behind William as he packed his clothes in the dining room. She stabbed him three times, with the fatal blow piercing his heart, then bolted. This story of a heinous murder following a breakup proved compelling to arresting officers.[6]

The second version of the story was Lillie's own, and it contained important distinctions from the tale her neighbors had spun. She held that William had been drinking heavily before he began to quarrel with her. Well-spiced words passed between them. He stormed out, but not to cool off, since he returned even more fired up than before. This time, however, he returned armed. As Lillie told it, he entered their abode brandishing a knife and threatening to kill her. They scuffled, and she managed to wrest the deadly blade from him. Refusing to be bested, he allegedly grabbed a heavy chair and attempted to "brain her with it." Fearing that a blow from the chair might be the death of her, Lillie tried to shield herself before finally stabbing him with the knife. She struck him with it, yes, but she never intended to kill him. As the *Philadelphia Inquirer* dryly noted, "The woman claims that she stabbed Campbell in self-defense."[7]

Two months had passed since William's death by the time Lillie got the chance to utter those words in court. She had spent the intervening time sitting in the county jail, where she may have been privy to the newspaper coverage of her own case. Articles appeared between September and December that described William Campbell as a man with an extensive support network. Even though he had been a gainfully employed waiter, he died with little money, and his friends pooled resources to cover his funeral and burial expenses. Such a sizable crowd attended the service on Monday, October 1, 1900, that a squad of Third District officers "was detailed to keep it from blocking the streets." A procession of carriages a "quarter of a mile long" followed his coffin to William's final destination: Mount Lebanon Cemetery, in the southwest section of the city.[8]

These notably well-attended services distinguished William as a man with dimensions. He may have held a decent job, but he was also a member of the Seventh Ward's "Grant Club and the Smith Social, on De Lancey street" as well as the

J. McConly Republican Club of the Fifth Ward. Political clubs like these were notoriously associated with an often-seedy tangle of bribery and corruption, as local ward bosses wielded all manner of vice to drum up votes for the support of various party candidates. Such clubs abounded in Black and white wards throughout Philadelphia and were usually financed in part by ward bosses who helped a dozen or so men rent local spaces. These became gathering places for raucous drinking, gambling, and prostitution—along with occasional political networking.[9]

As W. E. B. Du Bois explained in his study of Black life in Philadelphia at the turn of the twentieth century, "the business of the club is to see that its precinct is carried for the proper candidate, to get 'jobs' for some of its 'boys,' to keep others from arrest and to secure bail and discharge for those arrested."[10]

Though clubhouses hosted daily scenes of debauchery, members boasted that they were largely untouchable because they could "get bail for any amount." As much as Du Bois personally despised the outfits and their "deplorable" influence on Black youth and newly arrived Southern migrants, he could not deny that many club members did indeed appear to "have powerful friends at the Public Buildings."[11]

There were certainly some political clubs that operated more honorably than others, but the dodgy reputation of these organizations was generally justified by the crime and corruption many contributed to their surrounding communities. Club buildings were reliably encircled by drunken loafers and streetwalkers hovering near groups of men throwing dice and carousing, and even when these spots were raided, few members saw the inside of a prison cell. In one instance, a raid on one of the spots run by a well-known hustler—a figure that, according to Du Bois, even "schoolboys" knew was as "guilty as sin"—failed to result in any charges due to a "lack of evidence." The seeming immunity of these clubs also served as a reminder of the corruption that fueled the Black community's skepticism of law enforcement. Officers were themselves implicated in running speakeasies and working in tandem with known thieves and scofflaws. The cozy relationships between police and ward bosses only reinforced the community's mistrust.[12]

Philadelphia's 1911 election of an anti-corruption, anti-vice mayor, Rudolph Blankenburg, put the problem in stark relief. By attacking police corruption, Blankenburg disrupted crooked politicians' ability to pay for police protection, which opened the field for a wider array of candidates, because: "Without their surveillance and strong-arm tactics at polling places, Republican candidates would be vulnerable to challenges by Democrats and reformers."[13]

Police corruption wasn't limited to political clubs. The same officers suborned all manner of crime and vice in Black neighborhoods, either standing idly by while crimes occurred or going so far as to take a cut from the criminal enterprises around them. Patrolmen, ward bosses, and political titans of the city were so thoroughly implicated in its lawlessness, a Black woman like Lillie must have felt profoundly vulnerable.

Conversely, politically connected men like William probably felt untouchable—at least when it came to attacks on Black women. But now, he would feel nothing at all as Lillie went on trial for his murder.[14]

Lillie Fisher faced a perilous fight—against racist police and prosecutors, but also against the widespread assumptions of Black women's guilt and general unworthiness. Reporters cast her as a jealous woman who lashed out after her partner spurned her, and few credited the notion that Lillie had faced any jeopardy before the fatal stabbing. No local cavalry nor any groundswell of community activists rushed to Lillie's defense. That her victim was a Black man certainly played a role, and his affiliation with political clubs likely tainted him in the eyes of the court. William's widely publicized club membership probably made it easier for the jury to believe that he was drunk and, at the very least, delivered the first blow. Lillie was acquitted and discharged on December 28, 1900.[15]

Beating a murder charge, as Lillie did, was unusual, but in other ways, her story illustrates how, where, and against whom Black women defended themselves. Tellingly, their own homes were some of the most dangerous spaces for them, which can be seen in the catalog of everyday kitchen and household weapons they used in self-defense—things like knives and hatchets, and occasionally lighted lamps. Some even went so far as to proactively purchase guns.

Despite the nation's professed commitment to liberty and self-defense as codified by the Second Amendment, historically, a wide swath of laws and statutes (never mind everyday practices) aimed to keep such weapons out of Black hands. During enslavement, most colonies, Pennsylvania among them, barred Black people from possessing firearms. This applied to those free as well as those enslaved. By the late nineteenth century, times had changed. Black women bought guns to settle disputes and guard their safety in a lawless society. Activists such as Ida B. Wells counseled all Black people to arm themselves, famously noting "a Winchester rifle should have a place of honor in every black home, and it should be used for that protection which the law refuses to give."[16]

A woman named Anna May Hubbard seems to have heeded that advice. She used her revolver in April 1920 during a domestic dispute in which her spouse, Clifford, left her certain she would be the one dead if she didn't kill him first.[17]

Outwardly, the Hubbards might have looked like a perfect, happy family. Clifford was a stout man with a good job at a steel plant, and Anna stayed at home raising their two adopted sons, Raymond, eight, and Clifford, six. A brother-in-law lived with the couple, along with a lodger. News accounts alluded to some sort of love triangle as the cause of the dispute, but this was so routinely used in cases involving Black women that it is difficult to assess its veracity. Whatever the cause, what is clear is that for Anna May Hubbard, as was the case for far too many Black women and their families, life was irreparably changed by partner violence.[18]

Another important attribute of vengeance feminism that we can see in the stories of women like Anna and Lillie is the ability to activate a variety of tactics at once. Domestically and intraracially in their own homes among friends and lovers, but also externally and interracially when navigating public spaces and, as we will see, working in white homes, Black women had to be adept at knowing how to defend their persons on the fly. That could mean seizing a secreted hatpin or razor stored on their person or being ready to disarm would-be attackers. They mobilized might and their minds in these battles—and did so in multiple ways.

We should not overestimate their rate of success, however, particularly given the odds they faced. No matter how creative these women were in summoning the skills necessary to protect themselves in an instant, their survival often came down to random chance. For example, when a Black barber named Joseph R. Barrett shot his wife twice with a revolver in 1884, she survived, miraculously, and credited her corset with having saved her life. Margaret had separated from him because of "brutal treatment" and had accepted a position as a domestic at 2018 Arch Street. Joseph stalked her, and as she did yard work at her employer's, he emerged from the outhouse and fired. Convicted of assault and battery with intent to kill, he was sentenced to one year. Whereas luck saved Margaret, Lillie used her physical strength to disarm William, and then

comported in a way that helped convince a jury her dead partner was likely the true threat.[19]

There were other factors that contributed to Lillie's acquittal. William's club membership nonwithstanding, one could
argue that the outcome reflects how little Black men's lives
mattered to the courts, which is sadly true, and it's difficult
to imagine her getting off if she had killed a white man. Black
women's skirmishes with white women were also unlikely to
go unpunished. During an altercation with a white woman
named Helen Murdock, Sarah Williams cut Helen's abdomen,
though the *Philadelphia Inquirer* reported that "the injury is
not of a serious character." Serious or not, Sarah was convicted
in short order and sentenced to nine months in the Philadelphia County Prison.[20] And there were certainly cases where
Black women heard the prison bars clanging loudly behind
them after failing to convince justices and juries that their lives
were in danger.[21]

Often the women had to be extraordinarily adept at using
any and all weapons at their disposal—and also be beneficia-
ries of incredible fortuity. The latter characteristic is nebulous,
yet it contributes to our understanding of why some women
turned to vengeance feminist tactics.

Since Black women battled direct attacks as well as the legal
system, their survival usually meant that they had to get lucky
twice. When this didn't happen, Black women advocated
for themselves following the court's judgment. For example,
after receiving a hefty sentence for three counts of assault and

battery, Bertha Richardsin appealed directly to the judge. On September 22, 1910, she wrote, "sir i [sic] want to ask a favor of you would you please take some of my time off my long sentence three years i [sic] was never in prison." Her effort paid off, as the judge reconsidered and reduced the sentence to two years instead for aggravated assault and battery.[22]

Those Black women who managed to successfully fend off convictions for self-defense were usually incredibly tough and savvy, and even so, many still needed providence on their side as well as the support of the wider community—even more so if they found themselves charged for harming whites. The overall social status of victims and perpetrators has always played a mitigating factor in the administration of justice, and because of their station, Black women routinely found themselves outmatched in court—particularly when white employers were involved. This would certainly be an apt description of the circumstances in 1901 for Mary Wright, who started the twentieth century much like Lillie Fisher a year earlier: under the judicial threat of death.[23]

Mary was a young woman, with smooth, dark chocolate skin and almond-shaped eyes ringed by long lashes. She had a straight nose and full mouth, and she wore her close-cropped hair pulled and swept back on her head.[24]

Like most Black women, she worked as a domestic servant for a white family. However, her position was unique. Because her employers were among the upper classes, she worked in their stately four-story row home in West Philadelphia and

MARY WRIGHT.

Mary Wright, *The Philadelphia Inquirer,* June 7, 1901.

spent vacations with them at their seaside home on the New Jersey shore.[25]

Even as she worked hard for her mistress, the matriarch of the family, the long-widowed Mrs. Sarah Haggenbotham, Mary managed to sneak off and frolic with friends. She enjoyed evenings out—especially when her work took her with the family to Somers Point, New Jersey. After work, she drank and caroused into the wee hours. Those balmy nights could have included gallivanting with other young men and women—likely other servants who also accompanied their employers on vacation. Mary's escapades may have included taboo meetings with someone a little closer to home. Sarah Haggenbotham had two sons, William, forty-one, and John, thirty-seven—the latter had begun making a name for himself among those summering on the shore since he had bought the storied Anchorage Hotel.[26]

Established in the eighteenth century and incorporated as a borough in 1886, Somers Point served as the port of entry for Great Egg Harbor well into the nineteenth century. In addition to local homes, it hosted taverns and hotels. The town witnessed well-to-do white tourists converging during the summer months, with some from Philadelphia, and others making the trek from New York. Tourists sunbathed, swam, fished, drank, and danced. The location was predominantly white, yet African American domestics, cooks, butlers, coachmen, and the like created their own distinct leisure and social scenes—away from their employers' gaze and usually long after their bosses had retired to their beds. It was a way for weary Black folks to enliven and satiate their senses. They had seen the good life—up close and personal—and found ways to take hold of it. But their nocturnal activities were not without consequences.[27]

Despite her efforts at discretion, Mary's mistress, a true taskmaster, caught her trying to sneak back in after partying in nearby Atlantic City one night. After she got an earful from Sarah about her late nights and intemperate conduct, Mary was warned that soon her services would no longer be necessary, as Sarah intended to hire another. Whether such admonition was part of a routine as they visited the shore (sources suggest Mary had worked for the Haggenbothams for about a year) or the final straw in a fraying employment relationship is hard to determine, though, in the months ahead, the course of Mary's life would ultimately depend on which scenario could be proven.[28]

The hourly demands of most servants usually precluded any sort of vibrant social life, but Mary bucked the trend. By the time the family returned to Haggenbotham's home at 3216 Chestnut Street on Monday on June 3, 1901, two gentlemen callers had already stopped by looking for Mary earlier that day. Later that evening, Robert Caldwell, a friend, paid her a visit as well. They stayed outside on the stoop talking before Mary went to bed.[29] With darkness gathering, perhaps only disrupted by the glint of stars in the sky, Mary settled into what was likely the last restful night she would have for a while.

The morning started off much like any other. Mary made and served breakfast to Sarah and her son John before he headed off to work. Sarah then returned to her quarters upstairs. The peace of her midmorning repose was shattered, however, when a thick red brick careened past her head. It crashed violently into her bureau, thudding loudly as it landed. The unfamiliar sounds drew Mary's attention, and she went up the stairs in time to see a "man's heels just going in the parlor door." She went to the window and observed the stranger as he walked outside on the grass. Mary checked on Sarah, who met her with brick in hand. Sarah told Mary that the man had thrown it at her and said "if she had had her back to him he would have killed her." Sarah was already a jangle of nerves because, as Mary first told it, she had earlier discovered that some attic trunks had been opened and rifled through. Had they been robbed as well? It was all deeply unsettling. For Mary, as a housekeeper, any suggestion that household goods had gone missing would have sent up red flags—how long before she might be accused? How long before she might be hauled off, forced to plead her innocence before a magistrate? This on top of a dangerous intruder, it was all simply too much.[30]

Both women's anxieties were surely still riding high an hour or so later, when John Haggenbotham stopped by the house with a gentleman who was doing some work for him. Mrs. Haggenbotham excitedly recounted the events. She was a cultured woman, and we can imagine how the white-haired septuagenarian must have sounded as she spoke hurriedly, perhaps in staccato tones, her hands flailing to animate her words as her white blouse ruffled and she nervously paced the floors. She debated whether to contact the authorities. It was a move her son discouraged. As Mary later told Henry Gardner, a Black cook who worked next door, John "came in and laughed it off as foolishness and I did not get any policeman." Sarah demurred to her son's reasoning and went upstairs to her bedroom for a nap. John claimed to have taken a nap as well before getting something to eat and walking back to his office on Fifteenth and Chestnut Streets, where he designed store windows.[31]

Back at 3216 Chestnut Street, all was hardly well. Mary, seemingly spooked by strange noises and fearful that the brick thrower had not yet finished his work, remained on edge. Yet a quiet settled over the house after John's departure later that afternoon, when Sarah had gone to rest. The tale gets murky after that. In initial interviews, Mary told the police that she had gone next door to find someone to stay with Mrs. Haggenbotham. She returned with another servant who worked next door, a waiter at the Luray Apartment House, Samuel Moore. The two went through the house, heard moaning, and climbed the stairs to investigate. They found Sarah lying barely conscious on the floor in the doorway. Her body was halfway between the bedroom and the hallway, a halo of blood crowning her dented skull, one of her ears nearly shorn off. A broken bottle littered the room, with bloodied shards glistening on the floor together with splintered wood from a cane.[32]

Mary screamed. Medical help and the authorities were summoned, and a very fragile, grievously injured Sarah Haggenbotham was rushed to University Hospital. Authorities contacted John immediately, as well as his two siblings. William received a telegraph in New York where he worked, and officers reached out to May Haggenbotham, a local socialite well known for breaking new ground for women in education. She had been among the first women to serve as an assistant to the superintendent in the public school system and would subsequently serve as a lecturer at the Drexel Institute, now Drexel University. The family's overall standing and social stature

SERVANT BAFFLES POLICE IN HAGGENBOTHAM MYSTERY

MARY WRIGHT ALIAS MARY RIDER

THE HAGGENBOTHOM HOME

WHERE MRS HAGGEN- BOTHOM WAS FOUND

Haggenbotham crime scene, *Philadelphia Inquirer*, June 6, 1901.

guaranteed that the vicious attack would give way to a press feeding frenzy. At the center of it all was Mary Wright, whom the police now took into custody.[33]

Held in Woodland Stationhouse, Mary told authorities about the strange episode with the brick earlier that day and also about a strange man she'd encountered—a man with a paintbrush who'd made a quick escape through the parlor window. Under questioning and likely terrified, Mary wove a disjointed tale. It did not help her case that her clothes appeared to be stained with blood. She told investigators that she had picked up the bloodstains while trying to render aid, though there was no one to corroborate that part of her story.

Beyond what she initially recounted, Mary remained largely tight-lipped.[34]

She did, however, repeatedly ask to speak with John Haggenbotham, and John, as it turns out, was equally anxious to speak with her. The detectives investigating declined both requests. Yet all took note.[35]

Moreover, even as authorities locked onto Mary Wright as their prime suspect, John's increasingly erratic behavior drew public attention. A day after the assault, he jumped from a parlor window in the Luray Apartment House and ran barefoot and shirtless down Chestnut Street. His alarming state prompted the family physician, Dr. W. D. Carter, to sedate him. Reporters attributed the wild episode to worry and grief over what had befallen his mother. Yet he and his business associate corroborated the first part of Mary's account—that a brick had been thrown at his mother and that he had largely dismissed the possibility of any real danger. Perhaps this was the behavior of a man racked with guilt.[36]

Mary's situation went from bad to worse, when Sarah Haggenbotham died from her injuries on June 8, 1901. Though Philadelphians rarely exercised the death penalty, a Black woman found guilty of savagely beating her elderly white employer to death had a good chance of having her "neck stretched," in the day's parlance.[37]

The autopsy results painted a grisly portrait of Sarah's injuries. Dr. William S. Wadsworth, the coroner's physician, would testify that in addition to large bruises and severe lacerations to Sarah's head and face, which included a fractured skull and cracked orbital cavity, several of her ribs had been broken and cracked in multiple places. The catalog of carnage reflected a withering, sustained beating.[38] In the end, he concluded that the cause of death was a combination of sheer exhaustion from the wounds, which were compounded by a hemorrhage she sustained as a result.[39]

The nature of the injuries pointed toward something intensely personal, venomous, relational in some way. Could the housekeeper be possessed of such rage and savagery? Certainly, there was precedent for it. Stretching back to the days of slavery, countless Black women had met their deaths under charges of having poisoned, bludgeoned, stabbed, dismembered, and burned white masters and families that owned them. Even after enslavement, presses often covered wage disputes gone wrong—and while the servants were usually on the losing end of those contests, in the white national imagination, they were somehow at the mercy of lazy, deceitful, untrustworthy cleaners. Local papers published routine accounts of servants using arson to conceal thefts, but this case didn't fit the mold. Something was not adding up.[40]

Meanwhile, Mary recognized that her circumstances required a change in tactics. She would have been keenly aware that she was at a monumental disadvantage, certainly in light of her race and gender, but also with respect to the kinds of resources and connections that the Haggenbothams could and would use against her. We have seen a handful of the kinds of weapons Black women deployed when outmatched—physical combat, household weapons, and performance to manipulate authorities. Mary adds to this arsenal a keen sense of timing and the ability to counterpunch up. In the end, the bonds of sisterhood and community, too, would mark the difference between life and death.

Mary revised her original story. She needed to point officers in the direction of another fairly obvious suspect, John Haggenbotham. But she needed to proceed cautiously. Any accusation she leveled against a wealthy white man would have to be tempered with a high level of racial deference—doing so would signal that she knew her place, perhaps boosting her credibility with race-conscious police.

She expanded upon her original story. On June 10, 1901, she now explained that there had been a strange man in the house in the morning and also in the afternoon. He came down to the cellar with two bundles and a box in his pocket, items presumably stolen from the broken-open trunks upstairs. He told her that John wanted her to put the items into her trunk to take to Somers Point. She said that the clothes would not fit. The man then stashed the bundles in the cellar. When he passed her, she noticed that his hands were stained with blood. As he washed them in the sink, he told her that he'd started doing a job for John Haggenbotham but could not finish. There wasn't enough in it for him. He claimed that John struck Sarah with a bottle after she caught him carrying the items as he came down the stairs and that he himself then hit her with a cane before leaving. He left it to John and "guessed John was up the stairs putting the finish to her." He also warned Mary that John Haggenbotham was a cold soul. With that, the stranger left the house.[41]

Mary then ventured upstairs to find Sarah's body splayed on the floor—she had been beaten, badly. To Mary's horror, John stood over his battered mother. In a weak voice, according to Mary, Sarah asked John, "Why?" He said she had seen his face and that he had to finish it. That he stood over her with the brick and dropped it on her head. It struck, breaking her skin open and splattering blood on the hallway wall and her clothes.[42]

Horrified, Mary turned to flee, but John stopped her. He gave her wine to calm her nerves and promised that if she kept his secret and helped him get away, "she could have a home with him at Somers' Point [sic], as long as she lived." She would not want for anything again. She had tried keeping his secret ever since, but she couldn't live with the lie any longer. She told investigators that that was why she wanted to speak with John on the night of her arrest. She was fond of him and didn't want to hurt him, but she intended to tell the truth, and she wanted him to know. Her words swiftly made their way from the officers who interrogated her into the press.[43]

The revelations sent shock waves through the city. Could the son of one of the city's well-to-do families be guilty of matricide? It was a stunning allegation. And yet even more confounding charges would follow.

The authorities arrested John and presented him to a magistrate with all due haste. His court appearance was beyond bizarre. He rocked back and forth moaning Mary's name over and over, mumbling aloud, "Oh, Mary, Mary. How could you." His mantra underwent slight variations, denouncing her as awful to again pondering how she could say such things. At one point, he reportedly fixed "a maniacal gaze on the accused girl and whispered pleadingly: 'Mary, Mary, Mary, come to me.'" His fiancée, a Miss Clara Ferner, aged thirty-eight, sat by his side. On the other side, the reliable family physician, Dr. Carter.[44]

John was taken into custody, though his keepers expressed serious concerns about his physical and mental state. To some, he seemed to be in the midst of a full-blown mental collapse. To others, he looked to be suffering the ill effects of *something else*.[45]

Just as reformers in the city decried the harmful effects of alcohol and pressed for temperance, there were growing concerns about the use of opium and morphine. Illicit dens and dives, as they were then called, had long found purchase in the grid-like cobblestoned streets of Philadelphia. It always had been a city full of vices. During the colonial era, its docks were especially notorious for hosting raucous drinking hovels and brothels frequented by the "lower sort." During the antebellum, its flesh parlors were so numerous and varied that little black pamphlets circulated among gentlemen's clubs mapping them and describing the characteristics of the workers inside— Black or white, young or old. In the twentieth century, some of its more wanton corridors had only grown in size and profitability.[46]

But sex wasn't the only thing on the market. Just as there were haunts that sold beer by the pail, other dives featured more illicit substances, such as opium and cocaine. Word on the street was that the victim's younger son, John, had a mammoth-size monkey on his back, and it was driving him crazy. Coroner Dugan made it plain: "We have discovered that the accused son has been addicted to the use of morphine." The jailers at the county prison recommended that John be placed in a padded cell. Dr. Thomas Andrews conceded that he had "found a half a dozen marks on the right forearm," but he was "not willing to assert that they are tell-tale traces of the hypodermic needle." Still, the good prison doctor sedated John since his family doctor was no longer allowed to administer care.[47]

Rumors about John Haggenbotham's alleged addiction electrified press accounts and no doubt captivated the court of public opinion. Out-of-state papers told of John allegedly suffering financial difficulties to the tune of $6,000—the *Brooklyn Citizen* reported that his mother confided to a friend "that he walked the floor all night and she was afraid the strain would set him crazy." Equally damning details emerged about the last seventy-two hours of Sarah Haggenbotham's life. She had returned home earlier than originally planned from Somers Point, escorted by John after Sarah and his fiancée quarreled. The women argued about everything, it seems—from décor to dinner. They did not get on, and Sarah had made her feelings clear: she did not want John to marry Clara Ferner, the woman who had later accompanied him to face the magistrate.[48]

But Sarah's death paved the way for Clara, who made haste and swiftly obtained a marriage license. She turned up outside the jail with it in hand, ready to marry John at once. She professed complete certainty of his innocence. Investigators, reporters, and gossips alike buzzed at the spectacle. Was she a gold digger or just hoping that the marriage would give her legal cover to avoid testifying against him? Meanwhile, Mary's story was gaining traction and a sizable share of press coverage and believers too. Plus, John, ashen, trembling, and mumbling Mary's name in some kind of incoherent stupor in court, had cast a worrying image.[49]

In a society accustomed to seeing white people and whiteness as inherently just, mainstream observers struggled to reconcile John's compromised and suspicious state with prevailing ideas about race and criminality. Grappling with the peculiarities of the tableau, one reporter noted, "His pale, haggard face was in strange contrast with the quaint artistic quarters of the man held on the charge of so unnatural a crime. Prints old and valuable adorned the walls, and statuettes and bric-a-brac were in profusion. It was the kind of an office in which one would expect to find a tenant of refinement and artistic temperament."[50] Perhaps, but John would be found somewhere else entirely.

At the close of the coroner's inquest, both Mary and John stood before a grand jury, charged in Sarah Haggenbotham's death. John's brother, William, like his fiancée, immediately understood the gravity of the situation, and he swung into action. He activated the family's long-standing relationship with the *Philadelphia Inquirer* and routinely gave them interviews attesting to his brother's good character, innocence, and grief at the loss of their beloved mother. He also blamed Mary Wright for the murder. Try as he might, though, he had little to go on by way of motive. To address a glaring one on their end, he publicly supported John and Clara's engagement, calling her a lovely young lady who remained by his brother's side. William also retained former district attorney George S. Graham to serve as the family's legal advisor, in addition to his brother's counsel.[51] Graham declared to the presses, "I am thoroughly convinced of the young man's innocence, otherwise I should not have taken his case."[52]

William's efforts started to bear fruit as the *Philadelphia Inquirer* began publishing supposed alibis and block quotes attesting to John's innocence. After a few days had passed, John already seemed more coherent, and he gave an interview defending himself. Under the subtitle "TALKS RATIONALLY AT LAST," he is quoted in the *Philadelphia Inquirer*, stating, "Mary Wright in desperation has made this accusation against me. If you take me to see her I'll look at her and make her tell me who did this. She's afraid of me."[53]

It was shaping up to be a David and Goliath contest. The press and the city's upper classes began to rally around the white, elite Haggenbotham, while the accused Black maid seemed poised to take the fall. "The Wright woman, in my opinion, is the guilty one," a police official opined, adding, "She is above the average in intelligence among her class, and I think that after her arrest she evolved several ways of exonerating herself."[54] To combat the latter, the authorities turned to a new character to try to squeeze a confession out of Mary.[55]

As a newly arrived migrant from North Carolina, Robert Caldwell aimed to stay out of police trouble. He hadn't known Mary for long, and one can only imagine the immense pressure he was under when he found himself swept up in the murder of a wealthy white woman, and all because of his association with her housekeeper. Caught in an impossible situation, detectives forced Robert to pay Mary a "visit," during which he asked her probing questions about the case with a detective, pretending to be a drunk arrestee in a cell nearby, listening in. They would all be disappointed when Mary "stayed true to her version of events." These efforts also seemed especially outrageous because while Mary was subjected to all manner of interrogation, the detectives had not yet been allowed to see or inspect the clothes that John Haggenbotham had worn on the day of the murder. The *Philadelphia Inquirer* had the temerity to report that John's friends (who had seen the clothes) said the items did "not bear any traces of blood."[56]

We need to linger a bit here—Mary had at this point spent days in custody subject to increasingly dubious interrogations. By contrast, John had failed to produce the clothes he wore on the day his mother was violently murdered, in a case that he was now implicated in. Is it any wonder that Black people looked askance at the police? Or at the justice system as a whole?[57]

These kinds of inequities are precisely why Black women honed their skill for interpersonal risk assessment, especially when dealing with white people. Mary may have been hesitant about how to proceed at the outset, but as things took shape, she pivoted. Plus, news of the police tactics outraged the Black community, and a "colored missionary organization" hired a lawyer for her, and Mary's congregation rallied to her defense. This, too, has been a weapon in the arsenal of Black women's survival—their ability to rescue themselves and one another. Mary would need every inch of that support, especially to steel herself for what was coming next.[58]

On June 25, 1901, John Haggenbotham entered a packed courtroom. The indictment against him contained a lengthy list of witnesses, and the hearing went on from 10:00 in the morning until 2:00 in the afternoon. Mary testified to her version of events, as did the detectives in the case. In the end, the grand jury "ignored" the charges against him. That simple.[59]

The verdict swept over the court of public opinion like a thunderclap. John Haggenbotham was a free man. William Haggenbotham declared his faith in the justice system, and

May Haggenbotham sent a note of thanks to the *Philadelphia Inquirer* for their steadfast commitment to the "impartial" reporting of the truth—every word of which was published. John Haggenbotham strode across the polished floors of City Hall, surrounded by his brother, sister, and family physician. His fiancée, the eager Miss Ferner, clasped his hand, there outside the courtroom, and again before a magistrate shortly thereafter, this time in matrimony.[60]

The verdict hit Mary hard. Bitter tears streamed down her face upon learning that John was freed, while she was indicted. I don't doubt that those tears were real, but they also helped signal vulnerability, a kind of frailty that might offset the image of a brutal murderess. She pleaded not guilty.[61] On Monday, December 2, 1901, against gathering clouds and winter's chill, her day in court arrived. She wore a calm, albeit sober expression. Detective Frank Geyer offered damning testimony. In truth, it was a confusing case with misleading clues about strange white men and flying projectiles. Yet most seemed to reach the same conclusion: it had to have been either John or Mary, as no other suspect was ever found or presented.[62]

John Durham, Mary's attorney, the former minister to Hayti, had breathed new life into her defense. Yet his greatest triumph came when he cross-examined John Haggenbotham. On the stand, John answered calmly. His overall look was much improved from his previous court appearances, but his testimony was not as persuasive. Based on the evidence and his odd conduct, some might regard it as a stroke of genius—or

John Haggenbotham's wedding announcement, *Philadelphia Inquirer,* June 26, 1901.

a well-delivered performance based on the advice of his legal advisor; maybe it was true, or perhaps it was designed to aid his accomplice? The *Times Philadelphia* recounted the proceedings: "Haggenbotham further testified that his mind was a blank as to all occurrences from 11 o'clock on the night of June 4 for many days. He did not remember anything about the proceedings at the inquest, which was held June 12, or that the defendant then accused him of his mother's murder, and that when the accusation was made, he dropped over in a faint. He had no recollection either of having been sent to Moyamensing Prison." John did assert that his "queer mental state" was not due to drug abuse, however. It was yet another bizarre development in an already perplexing case.[63]

The jurors filed out after the judge delivered his instructions on Friday, December 6, 1901. They issued their verdict the next day. Mary Wright had been acquitted.[64]

If John's "ignored" murder indictment constituted a metaphorical thunderclap, then Mary's acquittal was like lightning striking the halls of justice. Looking on from the crowd, William and May Haggenbotham were livid. Mary's supporters cried out in glee. Mary calmly thanked her attorney. She had escaped the gallows. In many ways, it was a miraculous outcome. But considering the evolution of her case next to that of John's, that she came so close to death while his highly suspicious behavior was ignored altogether shines a spotlight on the depths of lawlessness Black women were up against.

LILLIE AND MARY HAD TO BE ADEPT AT LEVERAGING their powerlessness to survive and wrest a measure of justice from a perverse system. Like so many other Black women confronting partner violence, Lillie's situation demanded that she blend a proximity to weapons with an ability to react quickly to fight when circumstances became volatile, but even then, there were no guarantees. Those women lucky enough to walk away were all too often then perp walked straight into jail cells. Going on trial was essentially another roll of the dice, but here, too, they could call upon a set of methods that helped them even up the odds.

Most people facing trials crafted personas to give them the best chance for an acquittal, but for Black women, this meant having to navigate enduring stigmas. Success required finding ways to advance their claims of innocence without ruffling white sensibilities or affirming notions of wantonness, dishonesty, or violence. They manipulated the timing of when they chose to speak once in custody and to whom—they had to stay on their guard against coerced confessions as well as self-incrimination and setups. But also, how they used their voices was of paramount importance. Unable to directly claim or have vulnerability bestowed on them outright, they had to find ways to convey it—trying to appear respectful and deferential to white authority was a delicate affair, especially in Mary's case as she had pointed the finger at a wealthy white man and drew the ire of his powerful and connected family. She had to perform her fragility, crying and praying. It isn't necessarily that she did so disingenuously; rather, on some level, Black women knew that sympathy and compassion would not easily be granted—they had to comport in ways that signaled to jurors that they were worthy.

Whatever her ultimate knowledge of or involvement in the murder of Sarah Haggenbotham, Mary managed to force an investigation into Sarah's son, when authorities did not have him on their radar. Even though John ultimately eluded indictment, he was sullied enough to engender reasonable doubt among a jury of his peers, as his shady behavior and testimony undoubtedly contributed to Mary's acquittal.

The power of Black women's collective fury was also a vital force. Church members organizing on Mary's behalf helped shift the moral tides and prompted a Christian organization to secure her a skilled attorney. This element gives us a fuller picture of Mary as well—she was a Christian girl who entertained gentleman callers and had a habit of partying and staying out late. Normally, such attributes would stack up against her, but Mary carried herself in ways that amplified her "good" characteristics—traits that theoretically outweighed or overshadowed her more dubious conduct.

But some vengeance feminists seemed to do the opposite: they embraced being bad.

They even made sport of it.

FOUR

THEIR GAMES

Black Badgers, Better Days, and the Limits of Fury

Ballinger court added fresh laurels to its already unsavory reputation last evening, when one of its colored inmates again worked the well-worn "badger" game upon an old gentleman whom she had invited to her apartments.

—*PHILADELPHIA INQUIRER*, OCTOBER 30, 1899

You will have to fight me before you can get them.

—HARRIET "BETTER DAYS" STEWART, 1900

THE ENTRANCE TO PASTIME PARK, A BEER PAVILION owned and operated by Martin Ulrich in the summer of 1890, was at Twenty-Seventh Street and Allegheny Avenue. Though it was several miles from the Seventh Ward, its proximity to the Bellevue Station on "the Norristown branch of the Philadelphia and Reading Railroad" made it accessible to a range of Philadelphians, including residents in Black sections of the city. Travelers could pick up the line at Ninth and Green Streets, and arrive at the park in twelve minutes' time. Ulrich, described as a "rough looking man" of about fifty, ensured Pastime Park's popularity by exploiting a loophole in the city's increasingly stringent liquor laws. With the aid of wholesale and bottling licenses, he had bypassed major restrictions by not selling beer in glasses but rather by pouring it from kegs into quart-size tin cups or into bottles for fifteen and ten cents a pop respectively.[1]

Word of Ulrich's hustle and low prices spread quickly, and, perhaps unsurprisingly, mayhem ensued. Mainstream whites were already hardly thrilled about the newfound mobility of Black folks thanks to the city's evolving transportation system. To the chagrin of area residents, the *Times Philadelphia* reported that the "drunken orgies" taking place intruded upon "respectable men and women who visited the park with the idea of enjoying a quiet evening." Inebriated louts cavorted on Saturday nights, and as the liquor flowed, the crowds indulged "riotous ideas of amusement." Police records and press accounts suggest that at least some of these complaints were well founded. Pastime Park became the site of several fistfights and stabbings and arrests, the result of an untidy mix of booze, bigotry, and pugnacity, which sometimes spilled over onto the train rides home.[2]

In response to the melees, officers bulked up their presence in and around the park but especially on returning trains.

Whereas many citizens viewed these efforts favorably, for African Americans, the added presence of officers cut both ways, particularly for Black women like Lizzie White. On August 26, 1890, Lizzie had attended a "colored picnic" at Pastime Park before boarding a train home. Along the way, she would find herself accused of being "excited by numerous drinks" and attempting "to stab an officer in the cars." Based on the oath of Joseph Shuck, a special officer of the train company, Lizzie was arrested and held on an $800 bail charged with "Assault with a Knife & Carrying a Black Jack." True bills would be handed down on "Assault with intent to kill" and "Carrying a concealed deadly weapon." Lizzie testified that on the railcar, what she carried in her defense could hardly be considered a weapon. As the *Times Philadelphia* reported, "When placed on the stand to defend herself the girl swore that she had only hit Shuck with a key, which she afterward threw out of the window." It's not clear whether the alleged knife and blackjack were entered into evidence. Specifics of the "disturbance" that led to Lizzie being accosted in the first place are also unclear. Still, she was sentenced to thirty days in the Philadelphia County Prison.[3]

Although it's impossible to know precisely what occurred on that train, Lizzie's ordeal echoes the ways that Black women's leisurely exploits could rapidly turn into flashpoints with white men and boys, many of whom delighted in obscenely taunting them. For our purposes, her case helps underscore the kinds of peril Black women encountered traveling, together with the attendant risks of fighting back, especially against a white man in a position of authority. It also helps contextualize the actions of Black badger thieves, those women who solicited under the pretense of selling sex to rob men—women who usually avoided criminal charges even when caught red-handed. By sketching the relationship between the two realities, that of everyday Black women's difficulties with mobility and of Black badgers' predatory scams, the following pages allow us to consider how the same ecosystem could produce both outcomes. After exploring Black badgers' conduct, in part as a vengeance feminist rebuke of the public culture of racialized sexual harassment, the lens draws back to offer a wider view of Black women and vice and the overarching brutality of that world. In the case of Better Days, proprietor of a well-heeled disorderly house, and her nemesis, Eva Dillon, we also glimpse the limits of vengeance feminism and the underside of female violence.

PHILADELPHIA WAS A CITY TEEMING WITH ACTIVITIES, shops, and industries. African American women's presence in the streets had grown significantly in the decades following the Civil War—as consumers, as passersby, but also as workers, as required by their jobs in domestic service. Not only did they travel to and from their places of employment but they also ran errands.[4] Yet walking down the city's streets put them in the path of groups of men and boys ready to dishonor them.

Day in and day out, the indignities abounded, but they didn't take the insults lying down. For example, in 1916, when Nancy Lukens reportedly asked a youth to step aside as she attempted to pass, "he yawned at her and blew the smoke of an imported cigarette in her face." That action would be the last thing he recalled before being knocked unconscious. It's hard to know how often Black women retaliated in this way. Under normal circumstances, Nancy probably could have just stepped around the young man and kept going about her day. As it turns out, an officer witnessed the incident and promptly arrested her. Nancy, who had been hoping to get to the Philadelphia Zoo that day, ended up before Magistrate Imber instead.[5]

In this way, simple outings could quickly devolve into dangerous affairs. Just being laboring women navigating public streets seemed to diminish their womanhood, according to many of the social values of the time, and their attempts to enjoy parks and other activities met unpredictable challenges. Making matters worse, whites continued to associate all Black women, whether they were selling sex or not, with vice and sexual decay. Black women regularly endured vile harassment, everything from boorish shopkeepers whispering vulgar entreaties to salesmen attempting to physically take liberties.[6]

Public transportation proved especially harrowing. Black women were jostled and fondled against their will. Even the esteemed Black scholar and author Anna Julia Cooper alluded to the "instances of personal violence to colored women traveling in less civilized sections of our country, where women have been forcibly ejected from cars, thrown out of seats, their garments rudely torn, their person wantonly and cruelly injured." Even demure attempts to escape such assaults could become explosive. When Bessie Banks and her companion exited a Philadelphia streetcar to escape persecution from a lewd passenger in 1910, their tormentor followed. The white man exposed himself, going so far as to urinate in her and her companion's direction—all while cursing her as a "Black bitch" and telling her, "I would like to ram this down your throat and choke you."[7]

Most Black women found ways to cope and to avoid those areas where they were more likely to be harassed, but even the knowledge, let alone the personal experience, of such episodes would have undoubtedly fueled Black women's fear, anger, resentment, and rage. An appreciation of those sentiments helps contextualize Black badger thieves. While they engaged in illicit behaviors, like all Black women, they faced heightened surveillance and frequent indignities; they, too, harbored fury. But rather than trying to prove notions of "virtue" or "worthiness," these vengeance feminists found ways to take advantage of the sexual stigmas to lodge their own assaults on men seeking to debauch them.

We should understand that badger theft itself was not unique to Black women. Indeed, if prostitution is the world's oldest profession, it's quite likely that badger theft is the second. Many women on the streets of Philadelphia "played the game," in which they pretended to sell themselves to rob unsuspecting customers. Sometimes opportunistic ladies of the night would take advantage of vulnerable johns, but badger thieves tended to be serial offenders. Often women would work in pairs or even in teams with men—the women being the honey and the men being the muscle. And while it is difficult to discern just how many of their victims were Black, in Philadelphia, it seems that Black badger thieves routinely targeted white men. From a cost-benefit standpoint, this makes sense. White men received the highest wages—in every stratum, whether white collar or blue collar or engaged in domestic service. Little wonder, then, that women like Georgianna Coleman would have them in their sights. But the venom in her resolve and in the actions of other Black badgers have always gestured toward something more than simply monetary gain.

Georgianna was a badger thief in Philadelphia in the 1860s. When I first learned about her crimes, roughly twenty years ago, I was surprised that even after she had been apprehended for robbing a white man of ten dollars, she remained thoroughly unrepentant. She declared that "she would rob any white man who went with her; they might send her to prison for it, but when she came out she would continue the game." Even more surprising: she didn't go to prison for it. Reportedly, the jury "returned a verdict of not guilty." When accused again of a similar theft, the charges were "ignored." As it turns out, that wasn't an unusual outcome. Whereas badgers in general received a measure of leniency from the courts, that Black women benefited at all is what makes this distinct; the irony here is that they were often able to do so because justices and magistrates took pains to castigate their victims—typically white men who breeched taboo interracial sexual boundaries. Men who tarnished white supremacy by sleeping with the lowest of the low.[8]

As far as most court officers were concerned, white men seeking sex with Black women got what they deserved. Perhaps, harkening back to the refrain made famous by prominent Philadelphia resident Benjamin Franklin in 1733: "He that lies down with dogs, shall rise up with fleas."[9] In response to one white man who brought charges against three Black badgers, the judge derided him, denouncing his shameful conduct as worthy of the reestablishment of the pillory and whipping post.[10] Moreover, even when the cases were tried, reporters poked fun at the victims' misfortune, in stories with titles such as "The Badger Game Once More: A Soap Fat Alley Siren Beguiles Verdant Man." In this instance, "a light mulatto woman known to the police as Mamie Riley" managed to entice Thomas Robb, he "having succumbed to Mamie's blandishments." Once inside, Riley's partner, a Black man named Robert "Cuff" Carter, promptly relieved Thomas Robb of his valuables—reportedly at gunpoint. Even when badgers did receive prison time, they usually received one- to two-month sentences at the county; and if they got more time, justices seemed loath to keep them behind bars. For example, after being sentenced to a year each at the House of Correction for larceny by means of the "badger game," Judge Beitler "reconsidered," and Emma Stuart and Mary Gibbs had their sentences reduced to nine months.[11]

Under the circumstances, the crime tended to be underreported. Few men wanted to admit to having been bested by a woman, let alone face the public shaming about their aims to sleep with Black sex workers. In the simplest terms, a badger thief faced surprisingly favorable odds. Men coming forward to press charges were anomalies. And Black women escaping punishment, at least for this crime, was remarkably common. The ability to bash white men and make money from it while avoiding punishment proved too seductive for some Black women to *ignore*.

Though, it's hard to pinpoint just how many Black women played this game. Because most victims accepted their losses, court and arrest records belie the full extent. This was part of the genius of badger theft—and Black women especially could take advantage of the indiscriminate immorality and sexual impropriety white men assigned to all Black women and girls. Once alone in dark alleyways or dimmed parlors, they turned the tables.[12]

By weaponizing and ultimately capitalizing on the notion that they were loose women, Black badger thieves earned sums of money that far exceeded most working Black women's wages. Between the late nineteenth and early twentieth centuries, available data suggests that their average score was upward of thirty dollars, while a servant's wages for an entire month ran between twelve and sixteen dollars. The sums were not always large, however—for example, Julia Mason only ended up taking six dollars by way of the badger game before she was arrested in 1901. Yet this was still significant when compared to what she would have earned working all week.[13]

Plus, even if their victims did screw up the nerve to bring the women before the courts, if convicted, only the most prolific of badger thieves did any significant time. Even then, a sentence to Eastern State Penitentiary was either precipitated by multiple arrests, sometimes upward of three or four terms at the county prison, or victims who had sustained sufficient injuries to merit additional criminal charges, such as assault and battery or manslaughter. Since Julia, a twenty-nine-year-old New Jersey native, was a "professional badger thief and had served several terms of imprisonment before," she ended up being sentenced to three years at Eastern State Penitentiary, adding to her rap sheet, which included a fifteen-month term at the Philadelphia County Prison, in addition to sentences in New Jersey. Such badgers also then became known to local law enforcement and thus found themselves more likely to be caught and successfully charged. Still, even after serving hard time, once back on the streets, serial Black badgers often returned to playing the game, and the city's slums and red-light districts remained ready to receive them.[14]

Philadelphia's vice districts occupied grimy alleys scented with the cloying odor of manure and cheap alcohol and peppered with rowdy disagreements, scuffles, and the not-too-infrequent sound of feet hitting the pavement as parties fled.

Likewise, the burst of gunfire was not a rarity. It was in these spaces that Black women like Eliza Jones relieved white men like Levy Munchower of thirty-seven dollars, reportedly: "Ballinger court added fresh laurels to its already unsavory reputation last evening, when one of its colored inmates again worked the well-worn 'badger' game upon an old gentleman whom she had invited to her apartments." It was where Mamie Smith and Josephine Franklin, "both colored," were "working the badger game" when they stole eighty dollars from Max Lutzner, *who just happened to be in their vicinity.* Sometimes they used sleight of hand to steal valuables, but others just jumped men and took their money. In 1904, Julia Mason, apparently back on the streets, was accused of "waylaying" a victim and seizing forty-four dollars in the Tenderloin. Badgers such as "Black Bess" were known for their size, strength, and prodigious ability to simply beat money out of men once she had them cornered.[15]

Not all serial badgers were tall, well-built women, however. At just under five feet and 140 pounds, Sarah Palmer didn't necessarily have the stature of Black Bess, but her rap sheet, together with several identifying marks, suggests that she possessed much of the requisite skill set. A well-known badger, Sarah had served five sentences at Philadelphia County Prison and two bids at Eastern State Penitentiary by age thirty. She drank and bore the telltale signs of a hard life, including a large scar that ran across her forehead, ending under her right eye. One of the last bids she served was for smacking around a teenaged white boy, whom she also robbed. This hints at another reason this crime might have been appealing, in that it also seems to have allowed Black women to exorcise some of their own demons. They could lash out at the physical embodiments of racial privilege and power, expelling some of their fury at white men and, perhaps, white supremacy in general.[16]

We can't know the intimate personal details of the lives of these women who could violently take down full-grown men all on their own, but we can credibly surmise that their life journeys had to have been very difficult. Women who could do that had to have done a lot of fighting beforehand, and it's likely that they lost a lot of battles before they learned how to win. By mobilizing fury, though, they found a way to reinterpret and invert the scene. Even so, I believe their violence also gestures toward Black women's collective fury—the lingering trauma after having suffered a multitude of ignominies.[17]

Anna Julia Cooper wrote in *A Voice from the South* in 1892 about such indignities. She noted, "With all the wrongs and neglects of her past, with all the weakness, the debasement, the moral thralldom of her present, the black woman of to-day stands mute and wondering at the Herculean task devolving upon her." But while there is a clear overlap in the commonality of their histories and assessment of their current moment, ideologically, Cooper's emphasis is on the liberatory role of Black women for the entire community. As she argued, "No other hand can move the lever. She must be loosed from her bands and set to work. Our meager and superficial results from past efforts prove their futility; and every attempt to elevate the Negro, whether undertaken by himself or through the philanthropy of others, cannot but prove abortive unless so directed as to utilize the indispensable agency of an elevated and trained womanhood."[18] Based on their social location, she boldly advanced, "Only the BLACK WOMAN can say 'when and where I enter, in the quiet, undisputed dignity of my womanhood, without violence and without suing or special patronage, then and there the whole *Negro race enters with me.*'"[19]

Cooper's early iteration of Black feminism touches on the societal violence and ongoing miseries that most Black women faced. At the same time, however, hers was an approach and reasoning clearly native to her own unique circumstances. Cooper, despite having been born in bondage in North Carolina, would go on to obtain degrees from Oberlin College and eventually complete a doctorate after having studied abroad in France. She was among a small, elite cadre of Black women intellectuals and activists. Her feminist philosophy is, as a result, deeply imbued with and shaped by her class and her educational experiences, which partly explains why she emphasized training and educating Black women, in particular, along with her larger vision for African American uplift.[20]

Vengeance feminism is ideologically adjacent to Cooper's philosophical outlook. Both systems value Black women and seek to protect and avenge Black womanhood in some way. What distinguishes it from Cooper's thought is that it is primarily rooted in the experiences and immediate needs of the

Black women who practiced it. These Black women did not have baccalaureate degrees but possessed an expert knowledge of violence, violation, deprivation, and corruption. Intimately. Black women who knew about the past and its ugly afterlives in their present.

While we are accustomed to reading feminism and observing feminist logics by women with the intellectual pedigree of Anna Julia Cooper, we need to recognize and understand the feminist logics emanating from those with vastly different circumstances too. Black badger thieves were astute at assessing the inextricable relationships between race, gender, sexuality, capital, and the legal system. At the same time, their acts were girded by a claim on agency and also a just reckoning. Similarly, they also placed little stock in mainstream notions of morality and respectability—as the white men who played a significant role in defining those notions proved to be quite often the furthest from it. Their feminism was not concerned with structural change or the wholesale liberation of Black people. That's not where these women lived. Theirs was a clout against their own debasement and against poverty, but also against men in positions to potentially exploit them. Black badgers were dealing with white men who clung to and promoted racist ideas about Black women. Those men often failed to realize that these particular Black women possessed a precise understanding about white masculinity. Financial gain may have been the optimal destination, but feminist retribution powered the engine. In a world where Black women had to be careful walking certain streets and alleyways, their attacks must have ensured that white men, too, had to be on notice, lest they be injured, humiliated, and ultimately left unprotected by the justice system.

But the violence that animated much of Black badgers' actions was not confined to would-be johns. In backstreets and seedy resorts, it frequently spilled over, with devastating, deadly results. One such eruption occurred during the early hours of March 2, 1900. The crimson glow emanating from it doesn't just foreshadow tragic events to come but also serves as a hued thematic for the denizens of vice. On that day, blistering flames burned hot and bright, scorching the walls of 1205 Pearl Street and snuffing out a life among a jovial, if raucous, group of Black women and men. The fire ended one Black woman's life, and the justice system sought to take another's for it.[21]

The domicile of Harriet "Better Days" Stewart, alias Henri-etta Stewart, alias Harriet Spencer, had witnessed deadly violence before. In 1895, she ran a popular speakeasy.[22] Bet-ter Days and other Black women like her might have oper-ated under different circumstances entirely were it not nearly impossible to obtain and distribute alcohol legally. During the 1880s, local temperance reformers effectively worked with the legislature to tighten the reins on the flow of wine and spir-its. The process for obtaining a license to sell liquor went from needing $50 and a list of references to costing a $2,000 bond on top of a "$500 license fee," in addition to a list of references. Even then, qualifying applicants underwent a rigorous screen-ing that few passed.[23]

To make matters worse, temperance and state organizations surreptitiously surveilled African American leisure spots to root out those who violated liquor laws and state mandates. The tactics were akin to tossing a lighted match onto dry kindling. This criminalization of Black taverns and the like, those formal and informal, put an already vulnerable population on course for even more routinized clashes with the state and its various agents. This is how Better Days ended up on their radar in late October in 1895.

Better Days's ever-watchful next-door neighbor, Mrs. Graham, witnessed much of the day's drama firsthand. She clocked a few men entering Better Days's parlor at around half past two in the afternoon. All seemed well for a time, until Mrs. Graham overheard the rumblings of what might be best described as a *spirited* discussion. The compact houses on their street permitted an intimate knowledge of the inner workings of one another's lives. Plus, Mrs. Graham seemed especially vigilant when it came to the goings-on at the home of her lively neighbor. She noticed that inside the tiny parlor, voices raised and evolved into hostile-sounding outbursts. To Mrs. Graham's mind, all present had been airing their "thoughts pretty freely," before once again quieting down. She did not hear any more disturbances until roughly half past six. At that point, a violent disagreement took place. Mrs. Graham also heard a curious banging, as if a chair or something similar had fallen down the stairs. Soon after, three rapid-fire shots rang out.[24]

Following a brief pause, two more reports issued from a revolver. Moments later, a smartly dressed Black man, who would later be identified as William Green, calmly exited the property, walking toward Tenth Street, his casual demeanor an oblique mask camouflaging the carnage he'd left behind.[25]

As neighbors and passersby rushed to the scene, they discovered Ivan Brooks, a Black man in his twenties, dead, with blood spurting from a bullet hole in his chest, pooling on the floor beneath him. The bullet pierced his lung and likely caused instantaneous death. Joseph Robinson, the other victim, had miraculously survived a gunshot wound to the back of his neck. The women present, Better Days, Bessie Minor, and Rose Simpson, survived, for the most part unscathed.[26]

As officers descended, Robinson headed to Hahnemann Hospital, Brooks to the morgue, and the surviving witnesses to the station to give statements. The shooter, William Green, however, next did something that virtually no Black man in the late nineteenth century who'd just shot two people would have willingly done: he walked straight to the police station and turned himself in.[27]

As it turns out, Green was some sort of undercover operative for the State Liquor League, a group that investigated and ferreted out speakeasies and other parlors that violated liquor laws. He claimed that he was investigating Better Days's house when the men present accused him of being a spy. Fearing for his safety (apparently, a timeless refrain), he drew his firearm and shot in self-defense.[28]

While confident of his own authority, if Green expected to merely file a report, he would be in for the rudest of awakenings. One wonders how much Green's stature worked against him in the face of the city's white police force. He wasn't impoverished and humbled before them. Rather, adorned in an all-black suit, crisp, white-collared shirt, and black necktie, and wearing shiny patent leather shoes, he carried a black hat and a light overcoat as he stood before Magistrate South in the central police station.[29]

THE SLAYER AND THE SCENE OF THE TRAGEDY.

William Green and the crime scene, *Philadelphia Inquirer*, October 15, 1895.

Facing murder charges for the death of Ivan Brooks and related felonies for the injuries Robinson sustained, Green was taken into custody and committed to the Philadelphia County Jail.[30]

Instrumental in these developments would be the statements taken from cooperating witnesses. Their accounts portray a terrifying scene where Hattie, a.k.a. Better Days, seems to have been one of the main targets. As Rose explained, "Green made two attempts to kill Hattie Stewart, and when he fired the shot that killed Brooks he aimed his revolver at her, too." Green then fired two shots at Robinson, "who was trying to run from the house." As the others fled, Rose turned to Green and said, "You've killed him." Green replied, "That's what I wanted to do," and after turning to face Rose, he threatened, "You make a fuss now and I'll fix you."[31]

That Green had been an otherwise upstanding citizen and acting as an agent of the State Liquor League did not carry the weight he imagined it would. Indicted a month later, Green would plead not guilty.[32] After lengthy legal wrangling, he went on trial the following year and was convicted of murder in the second degree. The defense counsel spoke eloquently on his behalf, but in the end, the judge handed down an unusually stiff sentence, saying: "Your position is a pitiable one, but it will serve as a lesson to all who go about armed ready to use their weapons upon all who assault them. In this large city, whose citizens are protected by an efficient system of police, we have brought into court every day prisoners charged with carrying concealed pistols, razors and such deadly weapons. Here is a lesson, and we trust that such persons may profit by it."[33] On May 26, 1896, William Green was received at Eastern State Penitentiary, where he was to serve a seventeen-year sentence for murder in the second degree. He was thirty-two years old at the time of his sentencing. He left behind a wife and a six-year-old child. Perhaps his case did serve as some kind of cautionary tale for those contemplating similar kinds of surveillance. Yet for Better Days and her companions, little seemed to change.[34]

She moved locations but continued plying her trade, running a disorderly house, which likely suborned the illegal sale of alcohol and probably prostitution too. The drinks flowed, boisterous carousing followed, and Mrs. Harriet "Better Days" Stewart remained at the center of it.

She had survived one death threat already, so when another foe came knocking on March 2, 1900, Better Days did not flinch.[35]

Early articles suggested that the two women were fighting over a man, presumably Better Days's husband, Charles Stewart. Other accounts implied that Better Days had separated from Charles and had taken up residence at the resort. However, the most consistent, and somewhat coherent, version is that another Black woman named Eva Dillon had left clothes in the house that she wanted returned. When she went to Better Days's spot, Eva's friend, Jennie Hooper, accompanied her—possibly as backup. Whatever their initial plan, it seems they ended up partying with Better Days and Charles instead. She was, after all, an experienced and successful host—a madam of some sort we might suppose. Eva seems to have worked for Better Days but clearly opted for a change, even as it didn't prevent them from having a good time together. At some point, though, as these things often do, the mood took a turn. Eva demanded her belongings.[36]

Better Days's alleged response was less than conciliatory: "You will have to fight me before you can get them."[37]

The dispute escalated, and the two fought. Clenching, biting, swinging, cursing. Then Eva grabbed a lighted lamp and hurled it at Better Days. The igneous liquid immediately drenched and ignited her skin, hair, and clothes. Those around her probably scrambled to try to extinguish the flames as they witnessed the horror of her morphing into a human torch. Though she clung to life despite the severity of her injuries, Better Days died at Hahnemann Hospital the next day.[38]

Eva was arrested, tried, and convicted of second-degree murder. She was sentenced to six years at the county prison.[39]

Better Days's life, foibles with the law, and death showcase a troubling mix of violence, surveillance, and criminalization. Alongside Eva Dillon's case, it brings the crazy and yet somehow quotidian brutality of their world into high relief. This story also helps distinguish vengeance feminism from routine arguments at the same time that it calls attention to the underside of female violence. The altercation between Better Days and Eva is akin to a *dueling furies* type of situation. By that, I mean we have two Black women, likely used to guarding their borders and having to be self-reliant, who end up turning to violence in situations that are not expressly racist or misogynistic. Theirs is not a case of vengeance feminism even though both women had their own sense of right and wrong and were willing to battle over it. It's hard to discern why Better Days was refusing to return Eva's belongings. Did Eva owe her money? Were the items a substitute for pay or some other form of collateral? Maybe Better Days was just a bully and decided she could keep the things left in her home. Even so, Eva and Better Days were two Black women on relatively comparable footing engaged in a property dispute gone terribly wrong.

THE DAY THAT LIZZIE WHITE ASSAULTED AN OFFICER, she was supposedly drunk on the train and acting in a way that endangered his life. If there was truth to his version of events, the fact that she was traveling with a knife and a blackjack tells us everything we need to know about her concern for her own safety. But what if she was telling the truth? Equally troubling is the thought that she could have been convicted of attempting to kill, armed only with a key, and based on a "disturbance on a train while she was returning from a picnic."[40] These scenarios frame the fraught nature of public space and mobility for Black women, and they gesture toward how white men could be complicit in those dynamics. Against this backdrop, Black badgers' actions take on additional meanings as they also possessed the ability to draw new kinds of urban maps, maps that demarcated spaces where white men could be imperiled and find state protection wanting. It may be bad or impolitic, but it is easy to see how wielding such power could be seductive.

But wielding and being seasoned by such attributes, particularly violence, was also inescapably corrosive. It could help beat back the gnawing powerlessness of being a Black woman in America, but often while incurring great costs in the process. In acting on fury, some women ran the risk of giving themselves over to it. Yet I don't just want to wallow in the tragic facets of female violence because, for me, those risks do not diminish its larger properties.

Vengeance feminism harnesses a searing power that evidences the consequences as well as the possibilities of Black women's fury. Black badgers were adept practitioners, but they weren't the only ones to exhibit it with terrifying aplomb. Far removed from sudden, explosive cries of vengeance, some proponents' acts exhibited a bleak calculation far more chilling.

FIVE

THEIR DEAD

The Three Marias and the Babies in the Privy

Then, too, a large number of these widows are simply unmarried mothers and thus represent the unchastity of a large number of women.

—W. E. B. Du Bois, 1899

I will be surprised if I don't unearth the bodies of several children, as I was informed that the yard of the house was converted into a burial ground.

—Detective Frank Paul, 1914

She did not want the baby.

City Marshal De Rochemont retrieved the newborn from Mr. Horton's privy on January 6, 1880. He pulled its naked body out of the icy waste in the structure's vault. The tiny frozen remains made the already vile tableau unbearable.[1]

Dried blood would have been everywhere—its source her own blood, which had run down her thighs along with a rush of water hours before when her lower parts erupted.[2]

She differed from many young women who found themselves pregnant and unwed: young women who knew nothing of coitus or conception; young women who sat doubled over in outhouses mistaking contractions for cramps; young women racked with pain and terror as a new life burst forth only to sink down the privy's hole. No. She was not like those girls.

Maria Waters understood the trouble that she was in. Eight months earlier, she had left her home in Philadelphia, Pennsylvania, to move in with an aunt in Newburyport, Massachusetts; a woman known in the community as Mrs. Gray.[3] She likely planned to return home alone—the fate of the infant was apparently to be a foregone conclusion.

A couple of families appear in census records that could have been hers. One lived in the kind of neighborhood where residents always wanted for money, but rarely lacked in spirit. She might have had an older sister who was the highest earner in the family, a seamstress. Her mother might have been a domestic servant, like she was, while her father could have been a day laborer—three occupations on the low end of already low-paying jobs. Under the circumstances, Maria's nine-month absence might not have raised any immediate alarms, as family members often relocated for better wages.[4] Yet if she belonged to the other family, she would have been a student along with two older sisters—the family whose father held a good job as a clerk and whose mother, too, labored as a domestic. Perhaps their aspirations for status might explain Maria's desire to conceal the shame of her pregnancy.[5]

Whatever her precise origins, leaving home could not have been easy. Maybe Maria's love for her family fueled her departure, as her swollen belly would have elicited collective condemnation. Maybe disappointment that she found herself in a bad way led her family to arrange for her exile.

Maybe she left for herself.

Growing up in the hazy jubilation of slavery's abolition, perhaps Maria dreamed of being more than a servant. The sixteen-year-old could probably read and write, as newly freed African Americans across every social stratum took pains to learn how during and after enslavement; and in Philadelphia, a variety of individuals and organizations offered literacy classes. She might have enjoyed the popular novel *Minnie's Sacrifice* penned by Frances Ellen Watkins Harper, a Black woman writer of the era. Perhaps the book and its author engendered bold aspirations in Maria. If she could only rid herself of the infant's body, those aims or future intentions could still be preserved.[6]

She may have intended to find a clandestine location to deliver the child, but uncontrollable wrenching pain compelled her to push the fetus out where she worked, in Mr. Horton's kitchen at 35 Market Street. Concealing the birth would have been moot at that point, but Maria was resolute. She carried the infant to the privy and flung it four feet down to its temporary resting place.[7]

The woman of the house was the first to discover evidence of the crime. The state of the kitchen and of Maria was enough for Mrs. Horton to know exactly what had transpired. A report was made at the station. Roughly two hours after the birth, Marshal De Rochemont arrived with Dr. Snow, the city's medical examiner, to collect the corpse.[8]

Yet even after hours in the elements, there were questions about whether there may be life in the body yet. They placed it in a warm bath, massaging it. The effort was a long shot, and yet after a half hour, the infant that had been presumed dead stirred and soon uttered full-throated cries. His wails left no room for doubt.[9]

Maria's baby boy was alive.

This revelation met her at a peculiar junction. Her failed effort to end his life likely caught the authorities off guard. So much so that they returned the baby to Maria and then returned both mother and child to the home of Mrs. Gray. The unusual outcome spared Maria a worse fate perhaps, but it is not clear whether it changed the steadfast resolve that had led her to enter the privy in the first place.[10]

She admitted to her pregnancy and the birth, though she claimed that the father intended to marry her. She said that she placed the baby (described as a mulatto in the news) "there just to keep him out of the way." She said she wanted him kept safe from the other children in the house. Authorities begged to differ.[11]

Summoned to appear before the superior court a month later, Maria was nowhere to be found. The record does not state whether she absconded with the baby.[12]

In 1880, the infant's resuscitation marked an extraordinary event. The fact that Maria had sought to conceal her pregnancy by killing the newborn did not. Her actions, and those of countless women and girls who found themselves in similar circumstances, reflect an interwoven, restrictive set of religious, social, financial, and legal realities—all of which solidified to form a near unfathomable, combustible mix of fear, desperation, and resentment.[13]

In this book, we have scrutinized the volatile and often violent tactics Black women used to defend their honor, to cleave out a space for themselves, and to uphold their bodily sanctity in a society that afforded them little regard. Sometimes Black women, in absence of formal birth control or legal abortions, used those methods when faced with unwanted pregnancies. It's probably more palatable to understand such conduct as another extension of their desperation and powerlessness—which in many ways it was. But I also want us to hold a space for their anger. I want us to consider the ways that the women's and girls' acts of infanticide might also operate as a form of reproductive retribution; that perhaps their deadly praxis constituted a vengeance feminist response to the inequalities that stigmatized them for having sex and for not wanting to be mothers, or for privileging themselves and their own desires. Exploring these possibilities might help us better understand what drove them to take violent control of their own wombs.[14]

MUCH OF REPRODUCTIVE RETRIBUTION IS GRIM. IT encompasses a variety of histories of loss for and of women and girls and of those newborns foisted upon them, whether the pregnancies resulted from sexual assault, passion, or seduction. Whereas the first would have been profoundly traumatic, the latter might have been especially stinging; as some women and girls were duped into trading their virginity for what they believed would be forthcoming marriage proposals. The subsequent betrayals broadcasted their naivete as much as it portended its own kind of communal death.[15]

"I knew that some girls had been seduced," wrote Jane Edna Hunter, an African American reformer and writer, when recalling her youth in South Carolina in the early twentieth century. "Their families had felt the disgrace keenly—the fallen ones had been wept and prayed over."[16]

Faced with having their private sins of fornication made public, alongside the shattering of their reputations and those of their families, there were still graver, long-lasting consequences to be considered. Losing one's virginity was bad enough—but having a child out of wedlock meant that their marriage prospects would cease to exist. Besides impacting their quality of life socially, this would be economically devastating too. Most Black families could barely get by on multiple salaries (mothers, fathers, and children all usually worked and pooled resources to survive), so trying to support oneself and a child on a single income would have been all but impossible. And financial support from the fathers could be wanting, if not altogether nonexistent.[17]

Discrimination barred Black women from the expanding manufacturing industries that had created new jobs for native-born whites and immigrant white ethnics; so, for example, even as German and Irish women worked in domestic service and as seamstresses, they also obtained jobs as weavers and mill workers in textile. Few Black women found work outside of extremely low-paying domestic service jobs and would have been lucky to earn twelve dollars a month at the turn of the twentieth century, when a single room could cost six to eight dollars monthly. Rooming houses could be especially exploitative, charging not just for the rooms but also tacking on additional charges for the use of things such as laundry or gas. As Hunter recalled of her own experience, "I remember one landlady in whose home there was an enamel tub; she permitted the use of a single tea kettle of hot water for a bath." Plus, domestics worked six to seven days a week for that money. Such schedules would leave little time for working unwed mothers to be present as mothers. Further, single motherhood would mark them as women of disrepute, which itself would make finding gainful employment more difficult; most better-paying servants' positions sought workers of good social standing. Alternatively, these women and girls might be forced to work in lower establishments—maybe cleaning brothels, maybe eventually being compelled to turn tricks in them.[18]

As Hunter noted, before moving to a large city, she had been "ignorant of the wholesale organized traffic in black flesh."[19]

Being unwed mothers would mean a life of incredible hardship—cruel and humiliating social isolation, hostile treatment in their own communities and wherever their circumstances might be known. Black women and girls who historically have been vulnerable to sexual violence would be that much more vulnerable because their offspring would essentially constitute proof that they were in fact "fallen women" of the worst sort. In this era especially, middle-class African Americans raised serious concerns about the "lack of respect for the marriage bond."[20]

It might be difficult to understand how a young woman's sex life could become so public as to limit job and marriage prospects, but even though large cities such as Philadelphia and New York afforded a substantial amount of anonymity, the world Black women and girls inhabited could still be incredibly small. Between poverty and racism, African Americans in Philadelphia could only live safely in a handful of sections in the city, such as the Seventh Ward, which housed major institutions of Black life. They attended the same churches, schools, shops, and social events. It was one thing for a young woman to hide a romantic tryst here and there, but an illegitimate child would have been another matter entirely.

It also did not matter whether the women had acted on lust or been seduced, or whether they had been raped, as they would be stigmatized either way; morally, people might view the victim of rape with sympathy, but it would not alter the fact that they had been "ruined."[21]

Both Black and white women confronted these pressures. But Black women carried the added burden of having their shame also reflect poorly on the entire race. To be an African American woman and an unwed mother would likely affirm long-standing myths of Black women as whores, as *unrapeable*.[22] African Americans also fretted over the sexual status of single Black women in the city. As W. E. B. Du Bois noted of the proliferation of widowed Black women, "Then, too, a large number of these widows are simply unmarried mothers and thus represent the unchastity of a large number of women." Reformers organized to meet young Black women migrating to cities at depots, to nab them as soon as they arrived, to prevent them from drifting to the city's vice corridors. Black women's sexuality was perilous terrain indeed.[23]

Pregnant under dubious circumstances, then, Black women found their backs up against a cold, hard, unyielding wall. If they intended to survive and retain some semblance of normal life, they would have to cleave out a new course. Through secrecy and flight, through blood and a lot of pain, Black pregnant women took deadly risks.

Separated by ten years, another young Black woman named Maria Waters was in trouble in Philadelphia. Like her predecessor, she, too, seemed aware of the gravity of her situation. At age seventeen, she had traveled from out of state to live with a relative in 1890—this time from Maryland, to stay with an uncle, a man named Edward Waters, who lived at 1501 Sansom Street, in the heart of the Seventh Ward.[24]

When she arrived in the city is a mystery. How she departed is not.

Maria bled out in the rear of a building at 1231 Bainbridge Street. She died of a hemorrhage after ingesting substantial doses of "noxious medicines" prescribed by a Black root doctor named Miles Nickoles. She could have been given pennyroyal, an herb grown in the region and known then to act as an abortifacient; an herb also known to be potentially toxic, fatally so.[25]

Officers believed the root doctor's treatment to be responsible for Maria's untimely demise, and they promptly placed him under arrest. But the coroner would release him and an alleged accomplice. After the postmortem, Dr. W. H. Brooks attributed Maria's death to natural causes. Even so, mainstream presses derided Nickoles, casting his knowledge into question by putting his credential in quotation marks. Existing evidence suggests that the papers' ridicule and cynicism were mislaid or, perhaps better put, not spread widely enough, as the coroner's actions could be credibly called into question as well.[26]

After having been freed by the coroner, Dr. Nickoles was arrested again.[27]

The gray-haired, eighty-one-year-old Virginia migrant and married father of two would pass through the security gates at Eastern State Penitentiary in 1899, on his way to serving five years and six months for abortion. The thirty-feet tall, foreboding, sandy-colored brick walls that framed the institution like a fortress might have rattled him on sight at his initial stay. But as it turns out, this was not Dr. Nickoles's first time doing time. He had served two years on an abortion charge in the Philadelphia County Prison, and he had done another three years at Eastern State Penitentiary in 1892. In that case, Virginia Johnson, a Black domestic, testified against Dr. Nickoles after her stillborn's corpse was discovered in an outhouse at 200 Chelten Avenue, where she worked. She had been lucky enough to survive.[28]

In 1887 when Dr. Nickoles was charged alongside another doctor, the case marked the death of yet another Black woman named Maria.[29]

Maria Harris, a twenty-five-year-old native of Baltimore, Maryland, died after days of suffering, racked with abdominal pain caused by peritonitis. She had paid thirty dollars for the procedure that ended her life and the pregnancy. Hers was a common end.[30]

Throughout the region, pregnant women and girls frequently died as a result of "criminal malpractice"—a sanitized way for presses to discuss illegal abortions. Deaths like that of Mrs. Lockwood, a mother of two, who died from criminal malpractice in 1896, and of Emma Jenkins in 1888. Her stillborn child had been thrown into a cesspool by Jenkins's sister, Sarah. Rachel Jackson, "a young colored girl of 622 Barclay Street," also met an untimely end by means of criminal malpractice. Margaret Simmons, "21 years old, colored," died on April 21, 1896, from criminal malpractice.[31]

There is a timelessness to the expendability of Black women's lives when it comes to reproduction. Whether in 1880 or 1930, press accounts of women's and girls' bloodstained losses bore a disturbing through line; the subtexts at once plainly visible and somehow externally and eternally shrouded.

Mrs. Ravena Haynes, already a mother to four, died at age twenty-four of "septic poisoning" after seeking an abortion in Harlem, New York, in 1928. Based on the *Philadelphia Tribune*'s reporting, we know the hard details about her death and that it took place at a hospital, which means she sought help and was fighting to survive. Was poverty the reason behind her decision to terminate the pregnancy? Did she simply not want any more children? The botched job reportedly took place in a room at 141 West 131st Street, performed by a sixty-two-year-old man named Adolphus Morgan, who would be arrested on criminal abortion charges.[32]

Between chancing life and death in their efforts to escape unwanted pregnancies, it is hard to imagine that the women's decisions were not also clouded, on some level, by rage. Whereas their lives could be reduced to tatters in the shadow of these unwanted fetuses and newborns and the obvious evidence of premarital sex, the men and boys who fathered such offspring often had far less to worry about. Not simply because it was easy for them to deny their progeny but also because men were more easily pardoned for lust and other sexual transgressions. They rarely had to answer questions about whether they caused the deaths of their newborns, as Henrietta Thompson did in 1887.[33]

When asked, she simply answered yes, adding to Special Officer Alexander, "But I couldn't help it."[34]

He arrested Henrietta for casting the baby into the cesspool across the street from her home on Gaskill. Its small corpse had been fished from the foul muck in early August—the city's dog days of summer.[35]

Henrietta had delivered at home, tidied as best she could, and then returned to work. Special Officer Alexander searched her home while she labored at a laundry on Twenty-Second and Pine Streets. He found evidence that she had given birth and arrested her at the job. According to the report, she went quietly, though her answers to the authorities belie a steely resolve.[36]

She said she could not keep the child, as she had "to go out and work for a living and could not afford to pay its board."[37] That she lived in abject poverty does not seem to be in dispute, as even the newspapers described her home as a "miserable hovel." Still, she would stand before a judge, facing the charge of "murder of a male child."[38]

Her life had been turned upside down. In the weeks following her arrest and indictment, she had pleaded not guilty.

During the trial, the press commented on Henrietta's "light skin" and noted that her "neatly dressed person and careworn look pleaded for sympathy."[39]

But her revised account in the hearing was vague. She said she passed out during the birth and did not end the infant's life. There was little use denying who threw it into the cesspool. Interestingly, without even leaving the bar to deliberate, the all-male jury acquitted the young woman.[40]

They must have been moved by her pitiable existence. Judge Arnold appears to have felt similarly, taking the opportunity to address the child's would-have-been father directly, a Black man named James Graves, who attended the hearing. Arnold advised him to act justly, to do right by Henrietta by "marrying her at once." Graves promised he would.[41]

How noble.

It's almost impossible to understand how Henrietta Thompson had spent the last nine months, before delivering and discarding the infant. Did she hang on in quiet desperation hoping the father would propose? Was she seething, gasping for breath between bouts of fear and desperation? She had spent August, September, and October in custody. Surviving in the even more miserable hovel that was the rat-infested cell at the Philadelphia County Prison, she awaited her trial in early November, the entire process itself serving as its own kind of punishment. The fear and dread of the trial, the public shame splashed across the headlines. She was acquitted, true, but by comparison, the father received a mild entreaty from the judge for his role in the lamentable affair.[42]

Often in history, we gloss over these kinds of wrongs and injustices as a part of the everyday realities of that era, which they certainly were. We typically don't spend a lot of time thinking about how the victims in these scenarios seriously felt. It isn't because we do not care as a discipline but rather that we tend to rely heavily on the written word—if we don't have documents that state clearly how the subjects felt, we usually don't attempt to state it for them. Scholars have written about and decried the failings of the archive in this regard, and in many respects, I concur.[43]

But these women's acts and endeavors speak volumes all their own. It's clear that they chafed against the social mores governing sex and reproduction. It's evident that they decided to take matters into their own hands. As much as these responses to unwanted pregnancies were an attempt to elude undue financial burden and public condemnation, there was also a different kind of political consciousness at work—one that viewed their own lives as more important than motherhood or the lives of the newborns. That in and of itself was a revolutionary concept, a vengeance feminist concept. This I think is especially so in the cases of women who waited until after they had given birth, because doing so meant that they had a greater chance to live. So many women died after botched abortions. But even their deaths during these procedures connotes a kind of martyrdom for their own causes, for the choice not to bear children or to be held responsible for children that they did not want.

By taking steps to end unwanted pregnancies and to cast off unwanted infants, these women and girls ultimately struck out at social and legal hypocrisy. The acts by themselves did not amount to vast structural changes, but their efforts and their plight did have a broader social impact. Many women who were brought before juries routinely received acquittals. Historians are not entirely clear on all the reasons why, partly the science couldn't prove exactly how the infants died, but it also seems that on some level, the men sympathized with many of the defendants, regardless of race and ethnicity. This is incredibly significant for Black women, who rarely benefited from such chivalry.[44]

The legal system is the last place we might have imagined Black women's womanhood being in some way on par with that of white women and girls, yet the lengths to which even Black women and girls would go to avoid becoming unwed mothers paradoxically signaled their belonging in the category of woman. These cases challenged old notions and prompted everyday white men to effectively, if unknowingly, sign off on the women's actions. This does not mean all stereotypes about Black women fell away; if anything, it points to the society's own willful dishonesty about them. Public narratives remained unchanged, but in courtrooms, the women were quietly acquitted, and especially if they claimed the infants were stillborn. The acquittals also suggest that the views held by the masses were largely at odds with the aims of lawmakers, law enforcement, and prosecutors.[45]

That chasm might explain how a network of what were then called *baby farms* reportedly took root in the city in the late nineteenth century, as the Philadelphia Society for Protecting Children from Cruelty claimed.[46]

The term *baby farm* operated as a sort of catch-all phrase for pens where women deposited infants they could not care for. At best, these sites functioned as early forms of infant care centers for working mothers or as adoption hubs; at worst, their lethality provided a shocking service, as described in a Philadelphia account in 1877:

> For the benefit of the uninitiated, it may be explained that the term "baby-farming" is applied to the abhorrent practice of placing infants that are not wanted where they will be likely to fade out of natural existence in a convenient time. In other words, babies whose birth entails shame on their mothers are placed in the custody of women who are known to be capable of ending their little lives as soon as possible, not by downright murder, which would be too easily discoverable, but by systematic neglect and ill-treatment, and particularly by continuous drugging.[47]

Drugging may have been the kindest form, as many other infants died of starvation, their remains hidden away in public toilets, burned in fireplaces, or buried in cellars and backyards.

"I'm going to do a little digging," said the coroner's detective on a balmy day in July in 1914. Detective Frank Paul would add, "I will be surprised if I don't unearth the bodies of several children, as I was informed that the yard of the house was converted to a burial ground."[48]

Suspected of concealing the deaths of unwanted babies beneath the backyard soil of a dilapidated two-story brick-fronted row home at 1524 South Lambert Street, Mattie Burke, a Black woman running an unlicensed baby farm, was accused of killing children.

Six infants were under her care at the time of her arrest. Three died after the authorities intervened.

Charles Turner.

Robert Washington.

Hope Dickerson.

Photos of their emaciated bodies were presented in court. A single can of condensed milk had been stretched between them and was apparently their only source of sustenance for seven days.[49]

"The infants slept most of the time on chairs," Dr. Wadsworth testified, and "virtually no attention had been paid to sanitary conditions."[50]

The mother of Charles Turner testified against Mattie, stating that her son had been in "good condition" when he was left in her care.

Mattie Burke was likened to a fiend in many ways. The comparison may well have had merit. Even so, "The mother of one of the other infants, however, gave testimony in favor of the accused woman."[51] The unimaginable truth of the thing is that women like Mattie performed a service for the community. They played necessary roles in a society where menstruation constituted a monthly sickness, and women and girls were easily and irreparably ruined by intercourse and reproduction. In late fall 1914, Mattie was indicted and tried for three counts of "voluntary manslaughter causing the death of Robert Washington" and Charles Turner and Hope Dickerson. She was found not guilty on two of the three charges and sentenced to eight months in the Philadelphia County Prison for causing Charles Turner's death.[52]

Some baby farmers operated in cramped rooms smelling of urine and feces, soured milk, sickness, and death. Some secreted away babies under beds in boxes to muffle their cries and hasten their ends. It could be a nightmarish trade, but it largely operated in the *gray*. The gray that allowed young women with resources to pay, to be freed of their living, breathing shame, and to be removed from the deaths of the infants. Delivering a baby only to surrender it to a slow death may seem exceedingly cruel, but it gave the women the best chance of survival, and they did not have to witness the devolution. They did not have to live across the street from the rotting, stinking remains as Henrietta Thompson might have. Plus, some baby farmers labored to provide the best care possible for children brought to them in bad shape, suggesting that some mothers hastened their infants' demise privately before dropping them off for the fees to finally have their offspring die under a stranger's care.[53]

Just how widespread such farms were is debatable. According to late-nineteenth- and early-twentieth-century accounts, the farms had their origins in Europe and had spread with white ethnic immigration, soon finding native-born white and African Americans operating such institutions as well. Philadelphia figured prominently in such stories.[54]

The *Baltimore Sun*'s February 26, 1904, special dispatch from Philadelphia, told of the city's battle with an organized ring of supposed baby murderers—those citizens engaged in helping women and girls terminate unwanted pregnancies and unwanted infants. Clearly, there is a measure of hysteria that casts doubt on the veracity, but the fact is: women and infants were dying in the City of Brotherly Love.[55]

According to the 1904 "Baby-Murder Syndicate" exposé, "Of the 16 bodies found upon dumps and in alleys in the northwestern section of the city since January 1 not one was old enough for insurance. Several were new-born."[56]

The infants met their deaths in one of three ways: starvation, exposure, or strangulation. Cruel, painful ends. Tragic ends. Ugly ends. Twenty-one women died, too, under "suspicious circumstances."[57]

Dying from sepsis and peritonitis, young women determined to end unwanted pregnancies sought out illegal procedures in soiled rooms in back-alley destinations. They spread their legs once more for women and men, most with little

medical training, to be scraped from the inside out. The punc-
tures bled, became infected, and rotted in ways that led to
their deaths.

I don't want to minimize the gravity of the losses—of wom-
en's and girls' lives and those of the unwanted newborns. I also
don't want to push past the other Black feminist actions surrounding these pregnancies. For me, it's also worth noting that
women and girls who had premarital sex, consensually, were
themselves gender rebels of a sort. Not only did they seek sen-
sual pleasure, but in acting on their desires, they subverted the
double standards of their time.

Imagine being a Black woman at this time deciding that
your sexual pleasure, gratification, and happiness were worth
the risks? Such were bold decisions in an unforgiving time.
Prosecuted for fornication in 1886, Ida Hitchens spent a
month in the county prison for her choice.[58]

For certain kinds of women, the carceral consequences of
taboo desires were truly severe. In 1881, Isaac "Lady Washington" Hall paid a hefty price. Lady Washington and a
lover, H. C. Campbell, knew each other. Intimately. Where
they met is a mystery, but the private details of their sexual
liaison were laid bare following their arrest. Lady Washington might have felt doubly aggrieved, first to be arrested and
facing sodomy and buggery charges, but then, too, because
Campbell cooperated with the authorities. According to the
indictment, Lady Washington did "permit the said H. C.
Campbell to wickedly and indecently and in a manner

against nature to penetrate the mouth of him the said Isaac R Hall alias Lady Washington with the private parts of him the said H. C. Campbell with and by carnal intercourse." Their "venereal affair and carnal intercourse and copulation" found Lady Washington convicted swiftly on all charges. Sentenced to pay a one-dollar fine and court costs, the eight-year sentence to Eastern State Penitentiary rivaled many homicide charges. Meanwhile, Campbell pleaded guilty, received a suspended sentence, and was discharged two days after Lady Washington was sentenced.[59]

Yet despite the risks, all types of Black women sought out and fulfilled illicit trysts. And they found ways to go hard when the affairs went sideways—even if it meant having to burn it all down. Mary Johnson, a young Black woman in 1893, seems to have found herself in just such a situation.

It's unclear what cast Mary Johnson and Ezekiel Scott in each other's paths, but their chemistry must have been undeniable. Perhaps they met while strolling the neighborhood. Ezekiel lived at 2028 Hampton, on a predominantly white side street that was also home to poor and working-class Black people. Mary lived about thirteen blocks away on another side street, at 1211 Brinton.[60] Scott was a married man with a family. Mary, a single woman, could have been deceived about his availability. Or she could have known about his marital status at the outset. Perhaps the adulterous nature of their affair heightened the thrill for both of them.

Sandwiched between the publicly, repressive sexual expectations of decent God-fearing women and men was a vibrant city teeming with activities, entertainment, excitement, and temptations. Theaters, parks, and dances found young women and men carousing outside the customary watchful eyes of relatives and neighbors. And depending on which alleyway one might turn down, there were even more illicit treats and parlors to be discovered. Unlicensed saloons, pubs, and brothels dotted the backstreets of the Seventh Ward and other sections in Philadelphia. In rented rooms, young people pressed up against each other in the throes of passion.

They wanted sex. Having a child together was a different matter—Ezekiel and Mary simply had too much to lose.

Sometime in November or December 1892, the two agreed that Mary should have an abortion. They went to a well-known abortionist. Dr. Amanda Pennington had been arrested many times for criminal malpractice. It cost them twenty dollars, and according to the *Times Philadelphia*, Mary forked over the lion's share—fifteen dollars—while Ezekiel only contributed the remainder. Although the *Times Philadelphia* never saw a lie or racist jibe it didn't like, I'm inclined to trust much of the notorious scandal rag's coverage in this instance because it might explain why events subsequently unfolded as they did.[61]

After paying more than the average servant made in monthly wages, Mary underwent the procedure, performed by Dr. Pennington. The operation was conducted in Ezekiel's presence, but both he and Mary alleged that it was "an unsuccessful operation." Roughly a month later, Mary returned to Dr. Pennington, at which time, a second attempt to abort the fetus was made, the result of which was the same "as the first." Mary wanted a refund and said as much. Said request was summarily denied. Two weeks after that and in bad condition, as Mary had been "suffering from the operation for the past month," and apparently still knocked up and out of her money, she went to the police.[62]

"[Ezekiel] was responsible for the trouble," she said. Mary also charged that he persuaded her to undergo the dangerous operation. She waited at the central station while the authorities swung into action.

Detectives Bond and Murray arrested Dr. Pennington and Ezekiel Scott. Pennington was held on $2,000 bail; Ezekiel's was $1,000.[63] Both would be freed. Dr. Pennington was indicted, but the verdict was not guilty. The abortion charges against Ezekiel were ultimately "ignored" by the court. Less is known about Mary's ultimate fate, as she drops from the record after the adjudication of the cases.[64]

Still, what glimpses we have lend much-needed detail to our view of reproductive vengeance. In the absence of reproductive justice, Black women took steps to be self-determining even if it undercut moral codes, appeared cruel, and was brutal—on their bodies, their families, and their newborns. Through these cases of young women like Mary, we get a window into the ways that Black women broke social rules and sought pleasure.

We also gain a view into the negotiations that occurred when they faced the costs of their erotic gratification; and we see how they lashed back even in those instances—including using the fraught legal system to discipline the fathers who impregnated them. Mary was not going to suffer the bad consequences of a botched abortion alone; she brought Ezekiel's house crashing down around him—arrested, his affair and her pregnancy all made public in the process. If his wife did not know about his adultery or the condition of his expecting lover, she would certainly have had no illusions after his arrest and subsequent press coverage of the case.

THE TANGLE OF SEX, LIES, BLOOD, BIRTH, AND DEATH revolving around the women's and girls' acts sketch a different kind of Black feminist archive. Their determination to terminate pregnancies and to be rid of unwanted infants doesn't just spotlight their desperation and poverty—though both are certainly evident; it also shows them acting decisively to take control of their own bodies. Those behaviors challenged worn-out notions of essentialist motherhood and marked spaces where women did not intend to be the only ones paying the price for illicit sex. They also cast a light onto the duplicitous cracks in the accepted social ideas and practices.

Black women's and girls' deadly efforts to evade motherhood then amounts to a kind of corporeal blow against the hypocrisy that would label them as fallen. Moreover, the irony that in ending unwanted pregnancies they should find a space in the court system where their womanhood was somehow acknowledged cannot be easily reconciled or dismissed. The carnage that resulted from their efforts to rid themselves of fetuses and newborns, then, leaves behind a *red record* that is all their own.[65]

CONCLUSION

Vengeance feminism wasn't clean. It wasn't neat. And it was usually illegal. And yet, it was a potent means for otherwise marginalized women to escape total victimization. There was a terrible and fantastic power to it. Its wrath cut through the noise and distilled circumstances, sometimes with a chilling efficiency, that evoked rare moments of truth from a society and juridical system that routinely effaced Black women. Through its extraordinary power, they compelled presses, officers, jurors, judges, and everyday people to grapple with Black femininity—in rare instances surfacing an acknowledgment of the women's ideals, honor, and angst. Vengeance feminists often found ways to leverage their dispossession to strike out at misogynoir and lawlessness. Whether violently or deceitfully, or both, its strength was in the way that it was unmoored from the frayed tethers of a hollowed-out morality—virtues lauded but only selectively practiced and applied in society and by the state.

I concentrated on the late nineteenth and early twentieth centuries, but there are vestiges of vengeance feminism that stretch further back. American history is punctuated by accounts of enslaved Black women who took deadly revenge on cruel enslavers and who fought back against enslaved men who sought to abuse them. But we don't only need to look to the past to see the legacies of vengeance feminism.[1]

In 2019, social media erupted, as is its wont, over a scandal involving a premier hip-hop star. The fracas was over revelations that the award-winning rapper and multimillion-dollar celebrity Cardi B had drugged and robbed men who wanted to have sex with her when she was an exotic dancer. The 2016 Instagram Live video resurfaced and featured her describing her tactics. The entire episode harkened back to the badger thieves of old, in the sense that because Cardi B was working as an exotic dancer at the time, men assumed she was sexually available, too, that she was some kind of whore. There was a vehemence in her commentary when she described her situation and her acts. In the video, she shouted: "The shit that I did to motherfucking survive . . . like I had to go strip; I had to go: 'oh yeah, you wanna fuck me? Yeah, yeah, yeah, let's go to this hotel.' And I drugged n—— up and I robbed them. That's what I used to do. Nothing was motherfucking handed to me, my n——, nothing!"[2] Some rushed to make false equivalencies, suggesting that her actions were no different from those of Bill Cosby, who was accused of multiple sexual assaults before being convicted in 2018, or R. Kelly, who preyed on and sexually-trafficked vulnerable Black girls.[3]

Most pushed back against such comparisons, and Maiysha Kai of The Root arguably summed it up best: "To compare drugging someone with the intent of stealing their money to drugging someone in order to sexually assault them is intellectually dishonest. It's also a distraction from the very real spectrum upon which sexual violence exists and ignores how gender dynamics are often and undeniably at play." Agreed. And yes, gender dynamics lie at the heart of this type of crime in the present and certainly in the past. Indeed, at the time, Cardi B was trying to flee an abusive relationship. She explained that at age nineteen, "I was poor as hell, I was living with my ex-boyfriend that was beating my ass, I had to drop out of school. I was like, um, living with his mama, two Pit Bulls in a bedroom. It was crazy." With no resources and little support, dancing was her way out, as she reasoned, "How was I gonna leave if I only made $200 every week? Ain't no way . . . that's why whenever I play the game, a lot of people be like 'Oh my gosh,' that they make it so negative but like it really saved me from a lot of things." She was poor but also steeled in her resolve, and she manipulated assumptions about her sexual proclivities in much the same way that Black badgers did in the past. Those dynamics are also inextricably linked to poverty and Black women's limited earning capacity. Beyond the common refrain about the sixty-seven cents that Black women make for every dollar a white man earns is an even starker reality: Black women have always been disproportionately poor, marginalized, and victims of sexual and physical assault in the United States.[4]

That history matters, and this history does, too, though I should confess now that I went back and forth with myself about whether it should be written in the first place. And if so, is this the right time? So much of our country is hotly divided—over race, gender, sexuality, class, religion, history itself, and rights (never mind the tensions between Black folks internally)—that this subject almost feels like throwing gasoline onto a bonfire that someone thought would be a good idea to start in a forest that hadn't seen rain for the last decade. Did I mention that the day's forecast called for high winds? *What could go wrong?*

Yet I decided to press on precisely because of this moment. Over the past two US presidencies, as the number and severity of violent bias crimes have skyrocketed, I have routinely heard, seen, and read platitudes emanating from lawmakers, pundits, and even everyday citizens—all calling for calm under the hollow mantra: *This is not who we are*—the "we" standing in for some imagined or fictive America. Our history proves otherwise. Racism, sexism, and all manner of violent discrimination has been codified by law. If white supremacy, misogynoir, and antiblack violence were seeds, America's legal system would be the farmers who harnessed and drove the cattle that carefully tilled the soil. It would be the cultivator who planted and fertilized those seeds. It would be the callused hands that meticulously pulled weeds and guarded against pests and other crop-damaging elements. It would be the growers who dutifully prayed for cooperation between the sun and the rain, and for abundance. If anything, this fraught moment has been the rule more than the exception.[5]

But a lot of today's theories and activism—those claimed by both Black and white feminism in the United States—are designed with a certain kind of government and society in mind—one that is largely democratic, even if corrupt and profoundly flawed, and one that, at a bare minimum, pays lip service to fairness and notions of equality. When traditional feminists engage in tactics such as civil disobedience, for example, those actions rest upon an anticipated reaction from the state (even adverse ones, such as arrest, police brutality, and criminalization) and pressure from the public. But it's becoming clearer and clearer that such responses and the basic pillars of democratic governance are by no means assured.

Such tactics are little help when you are in a situation like the one that Carlisha Hood found herself in at a Chicago restaurant in June 2023. She got into a verbal argument with a man inside, Jeremy Brown. He threatened that if she didn't stop talking, he was going to knock her out. She started texting her son, who came to the restaurant with a gun. Carlisha did not back down and continued talking. While others watched, Brown started beating her about the head and face. Her son witnessed the attack and opened fire on Brown, ultimately killing him. The two turned themselves in, and despite clear evidence of the violent assault—video footage including the audible crunch when she is struck—both Carlisha and her son initially faced murder charges. Those charges were eventually dropped, but not before the episode made the national news and not before the two were held in custody as her son was sent to a juvenile facility and Carlisha was held on a $3 million bail.[6]

Against the ongoing biases in the courts and policing and the routine accounts of Black women being killed or beaten by partners or for refusing men's sexual advances—and subsequently being blamed for their assault or penalized for defending themselves—it's easy to lose hope entirely.

I wrote this book because I believe we need something to help us push back against the persistent feeling of despair and peril as Black women in America. I know that most of us cannot beat up men trying to kill us. I understand that fighting back means we are as likely to find ourselves seriously harmed or killed as we are to find ourselves behind bars—unable to be served by the justice system, only to be punished by it. But this history shows us that we have been here before, many times, sadly. Mapping the primary attributes and strategies of vengeance feminism offers an opportunity to contemplate its key aspects with a clear-eyed look at potential advantages and deficits. Some Black women found ways to navigate such times without completely sacrificing themselves or their dignity. Some Black women stood at the precipice, leaped off, and somehow managed to walk away, with monsters slain in their wake. Admittedly, that's a slim glimmer of hope, but these days, I will take it.

And I want to be crystal clear here: I am not suggesting that vengeance feminism is a doctrine or practice for the long haul—we should continue organizing, educating, voting, creating, loving, living, petitioning, suing, praying, and marching. But we must find swift ways to save ourselves when our lives are in danger. We need real, fast ways to help poor and working-class women and girls who find themselves in need of an abortion in states where these rights have been stripped away. We especially need to go on the offense here, too, because even suffering a miscarriage now is likely to find Black women criminalized, as was the case of Brittany Watts in Ohio in 2023. Sick from a "potentially fatal miscarriage," Watts found herself arrested on charges of abusing a corpse. And we need to get ready to be loud, too, at the school board meetings about the need for accurate history books for students in states that seek to amplify heteronormative, white supremacist ideals while banning all other voices. In these kinds of moments, there is a need for a more urgent response (against a backdrop where it's clear that the legislatures have already failed us or will take an inordinate amount of time to effectively intervene) and it's here that I believe exploring these concepts and history can be most helpful.[7]

Vengeance feminists inhabited a world where the ground beneath their feet wasn't firm, a world where the only defense and an approximation of justice came from marking their own bloodred line in the sand. Black women's historic scorched-earth responses to misogynoir and lawlessness have the potential to create an alternative road map for Black feminist theories and activism in crucial ways. It can help remind us: sometimes, regardless of what we want, there is no running from the fight. It might even help us reclaim something else: sometimes the only sane recourse is to cross the line.

And it might leave us armed with this: even when our backs are up against the wall, losing is not a foregone conclusion.

AFTERWORD

IN 2017, MY MOTHER DIED.

She and I were extremely close.

For many years, it was mainly she and I, as my brother did not come along until much later in her life. She took pains to really talk to me about Black womanhood.

I remember her round face and serious eyes as she shared painful memories. She detailed her harrowing experience obtaining an illegal abortion as a teenager. She described her terror. She talked about the physical pain. She recalled the blood and her frenzy because even after the procedure, the fetus did not "come down" for two days. She was getting sick, and she thought she was going to die.

It was a male fetus, she told me, and every year, she thought about how old he would be had he lived.

She never wanted me to experience anything like that, so she spoke to me candidly about sex and protection and birth control.

My mother also talked to me about the abuse she suffered at the hands of her first husband. He was a large man, six feet, six inches. He was intelligent. She admired his mind, and they fell in love. But it became a nightmare soon after the wedding. He beat her, and she stopped loving him.

One day, she had reached her limit. He slapped her, and she hit back. The fight escalated, and she pulled a knife on him. She told him point-blank: "You hit me again, and I'll go to jail tonight." Something in her delivery convinced him to leave. She left too. She flew to Mexico and obtained a "quickie divorce."

She always warned, "Never let a man hit you, because believe me, the first hit is never the last."

Her stories and her frank understanding about her own vulnerability even as she was defending herself have never left me. Like the vengeance feminists of old, this was the choice before her: submit to abuse by her partner or resist and expect to be abused by the state. To go against this man meant accepting that she might have to go to prison. Her desperation and resolve were such that she had resigned to face that option.

I am proud to be June Maria Gross's daughter. My mother was a woman who survived and fought to control her own destiny, to make room for herself and her humanity during moments when it was literally illegal and disallowed. Against these wretched limitations, she also cultivated joy. She loved Black art, and Malcolm X, and Black women writers, and our family.

Most days, I remain awed by the fiery courage that has led Black women, past and present, women like my mother, to go to the extremes to avenge themselves.

On other days . . . *I am furious about it.*

ACKNOWLEDGMENTS

I HAVE BEEN THE BENEFICIARY OF EXTRAORDINARY scholarly support. I am eternally grateful to my manuscript workshop sister-scholars: Nicole Burrowes, Brittney Cooper, Aisha Finch, Rhonda Frederick, Cheryl Hicks, Talitha LeFlouria, Samantha Pinto, and Jennifer Nash, who, without harsh judgment or righteous condemnation, read and offered valuable feedback on the book at its raggediest phase. I am indebted for their vital feedback, wisdom, candor, and laughter. Later, I had the additional benefit of having Erica Armstrong Dunbar and Cheryl Hicks (for the second time) read the entire revised manuscript, and again, I am incredibly thankful for the astute observations and critiques. I owe a special debt to Rhonda Williams, upon whose mercy I threw myself. At the *twelfth* hour, I begged her to read the manuscript. Anyone who knows Rhonda Williams knows that she put it through the paces, and in record time over a weekend—pausing her own packing as she was moving—to help me. Thank you, my sister. Without question, all of this input made the book stronger.

A 2019 talk for the session on Global Black Feminisms at Columbia University's Institute for Research in

African-American Studies Twenty-Fifth Anniversary conference laid a significant portion of the book's foundation. Thanks
to my fellow panelists: Brittney Cooper, Adia Harvey Wing-
field, Mignon Moore, and Imaobong Umoren, and the chair,
Farah Jasmine Griffin. I need to thank Dr. Cymone Fourshey,
who kindly invited me to present at Bucknell University at
the Center for the Study of Race, Ethnicity & Gender in September 2019—the comments and valuable exchanges with the
students and scholars gave my ideas more sustenance to grow.
I must also thank the Coordinating Council for Women in
History, especially Nupur Chaudhuri, along with my fellow
panelists on the plenary session "Looking through the Glass
Window: Women without the Vote 100 Years Ago" at the
2020 American Historical Association conference: Natanya
Duncan, Crystal Feimster, Martha Jones, Febe D. Pamonag,
and Verónica Reyna, and the chair, Jesús Jesse Esparza. The
charge to think about and consider the political life of women
who were not suffragists further prompted questions about the
political ideologies of the women I study.

Tanya McKinnon is my intrepid literary agent, friend, and
doomsday sister—thank you for your tireless work on behalf
of this project and for your strong-arm tactics too. Kyle Gip-
son, my first editor, understood and enhanced the vision and
fought to get the book published; I am very grateful that
you saw a place for this project at Seal Press. Brandon Proia,
my current editor at Seal, inherited the project and made it
his own. Thank you for your precise readings of draft after

draft. I remain in awe of your editing skills and razor-sharp eye. My personal editor, Cynthia Gwynne Yaudes, remains invaluable—day or night, your phenomenal editorial talents have saved me from myself more times than I can remember. Senior Production Editor Annie Chatham, Copy Editor Sara Robb, and Proofreaders Laura Starrett and Lori Lewis ran every inch of the last mile with me—thank you.

My writing tutors at the University of Oxford were invaluable, and I would like to thank Dr. Rachel Bentham and Dr. Jane McVeigh—I learned a great deal from your classes and strive to implement all the knowledge of the craft that you imparted.

The archivists at the Philadelphia City Archives are always kind (and funny) and help me find the obscurest records. A special thanks to David Baugh, Raven Darkholme, Joshua Blay, and Kenneth Rice (who I hope is enjoying his retirement). Raven and David, your willingness to look up the citation details for one of the annual police reports minutes before I had to turn this book in was a lifesaver—thanks so much again!

I am grateful for the support I have received at Emory University, and my colleagues in the Department of African American Studies (AAS) set the bar high. A special thanks to Carol Anderson and Dianne M. Stewart: I would not have survived my first year as department chair without you. I must also thank Dr. Stephanie Evans for her sage advice about serving as chair. The AAS staff remains invaluable. Kudos go to:

Angelique Anderson, Olivia Chapes, Naomi Deimer, Charles Jackson, and Dr. Shamika Walls. I must also thank a few former Rutgers students: Kiamsha Bynes, Tracey Johnson, Adam McNeil, and Brooke Thomas. I would also like to thank Dr. Erica Bruchko, the African American Studies and US History Librarian at Emory, for her support and guidance on locating sources for this project.

My family and friends mean the world to me. Thanks and I love you goes out to: the Abrahams, the Lovells, the Ironses, the Hectors, the Hoskinses, the Ramoses, the Johnsons, the Kirbys, the Marshalls, and Nicole Childers, Rebecca Cohen, Rhonda Frederick, Jacob Gross, Cheryl Hicks, Nicole Burrowes, Lisa Bowleg, Rhonda Williams, and my home squad, Team Gross—you are my heart. Samanthi, I love you. Very much. I thank God for you.

June Maria Gross: I thank God that you were my Mother. Thank you for everything you did for me, Ma. I love you, and I miss you every day.

NOTES

Note on usage: I use *Black* and *African American* largely interchangeably. When it is historically relevant or appears in quoted material, I use historical terminology, such as *negro* or *colored*.

Preface

1. I am using the phrase "the savagery of the systems" to refer to broad structures and practices of inequality, such as racism, sexism, misogynoir, antiblackness, etc. Variations on the phrase, however, may be found in a variety of texts and disciplines such as Holloway Sparks, "Queens, Teens, and Model Mothers: Race, Gender, and the Discourse on Welfare Reform," in *Race and the Politics of Welfare Reform*, eds. Sanford Schram, Joe Soss, and Richard C. Fording (Ann Arbor: University of Michigan Press, 2003), 182; Ann E. Trapasso, "Returning to the Site of Violence: The Restructuring of Slavery's Legacy in Sherley Ann Williams' Dessa Rose," in *Violence, Silence, and Anger: Women's Writing as Transgression*, ed. Deirdre Lashgari (Charlottesville: University Press of Virginia, 1995), 224; Marc Stein, "Dessa Rose: Putting the 'Story' Back in History," in *Reclaiming Home, Remembering Motherhood, Rewriting History: African American and Afro-Caribbean Women's Literature in the Twentieth Century*, eds. Verena Theile and Marie Drews (Newcastle upon Tyne: Cambridge Scholars Publishing, 2009), 259.

Introduction

1. News articles listed her name as "Maggie Johnson," but in the Philadelphia County Prisoners for Trial Docket, she appears as Mary Johnson; see B, 189 Edw. Sydnor, October 27, 1886, "Charged on Oath of Mary Johnson." "The Weather," *Philadelphia Inquirer*, October 27, 1886; "The Local Justice Mill," *Philadelphia Inquirer*, October 28, 1886; "A Prisoner Turns the Tables," *Times Philadelphia*, October 28, 1886. The *Times Philadelphia* lists his name as Edward Snyder, but that is incorrect. See "Sydnor Edward, restaurant, 1204 Clover," in *Gopsill's Philadelphia City Directory for 1886* (Philadelphia: James Gopsill's Sons, 1886).

2. "The Local Justice Mill," *Philadelphia Inquirer*; "A Prisoner Turns the Tables," *Times Philadelphia*.

3. "A Prisoner Turns the Tables"; "Turning the Tables," *Philadelphia Evening Bulletin*, October 27, 1886.

4. "The Local Justice Mill"; "Turning the Tables."

5. According to the *Inquirer* and *Times* accounts, "Maggie Johnson" was initially charged with some form of assault and went before Magistrate Smith; however, only a "Mary Johnson" appears in connection to the case, and while accounts describe her arraignment, the docket only records what occurred with Edward. There is a Mary Johnson that shows up in the docket, but this Mary Johnson appears about two weeks earlier and went before Magistrate Lemmon, on the oath of an arresting officer who accused her of being a common scold—a kind of catch-all charge for disorderly or otherwise badly behaved and/or fractious women; see Prisoners for Trial Docket, B, Mary Johnson, September 30, 1886. The arresting officer on file is Officer Deaton. Ms. Johnson was released the next day. Then a Mary Johnson appears before Magistrate Smith on October 27, 1886, accusing Edward Sydnor of adultery and assault and battery. See Prisoners for Trial Docket, October 27, 1886. While it's possible that the Mary Johnson arrested in September is our Mary since papers made reference to the charges against her "finally" being dropped—suggesting that some time had elapsed—it seems unlikely given the inconsistencies with the arresting officers and the date associated with the assault. Also unclear is Edward's final fate. After his appearance in the Prisoners for Trial Docket, the trail runs cold, and no bills of indictment could be located for him or Mary. It may well have been that all charges were dropped. For Mary's version of events, see "Turning the Tables," *Philadelphia Evening Bulletin*, October 27, 1886.

6. "Mary Johnson Violent," *Philadelphia Evening Bulletin*, October 26, 1886.

7. Here I am referring to Darlene Clark Hine's pioneering article, in which she writes, "I suggest that rape and the threat of rape influenced the development of a

culture of dissemblance among Black women. By dissemblance, I mean the behavior and attitudes of Black women that created the appearance of openness and disclosure but actually shielded the truth of their inner lives and selves from their oppressors." See Darlene Clark Hine, "Rape in the Inner Lives of Black Women in the Middle West: Preliminary Thoughts on the Culture of Dissemblance," *Signs: Journal of Women in Culture and Society* 14, no. 4 (1989): quote on 912, 912–920. I am also engaging the groundbreaking work of Evelyn Brooks Higginbotham on Black women and the politics of respectability. See "The Politics of Respectability," chap. 7 in *Righteous Discontent: The Women's Movement in the Black Baptist Church, 1880–1920* (Cambridge, MA: Harvard University Press, 1994). My point in referencing these themes is not to discredit them; rather, it is to explore instances and examples of Black women who understood those tactics and expectations, but who nonetheless lived and acted in ways that countered the prevailing discourses.

8. I had the privilege of presenting at "Looking through the Glass Window: The Women without the Vote 100 Years Ago" as a part of the Coordinating Council for Women in History Plenary Session, 134th Annual Meeting of the American Historical Association, New York, New York, January 3–6, 2020; I explored notions of retributive and/or vengeance feminism in a talk titled, "Cardi, Bessie, and Black Badgers: A Meditation on Retributive Feminism," on the "Global Black Feminisms" session at the "Free to Be Anywhere in the Universe: An International Conference on New Directions in the Study of the African Diaspora," which was the IRAAS Twenty-Fifth Anniversary Conference, held at Columbia University, New York, New York, April 25–27, 2019. My thinking has also been influenced by Samantha Pinto's approach to celebrity and infamous Black women figures. In reading these women's words and bodies, Pinto brings us face-to-face with their political ideologies and offers new ways to ponder how Black women entered into male-dominated discourses on rights, citizenship, and humanity. See *Infamous Bodies: Early Black Women's Celebrity and the Afterlives of Rights* (Durham, NC: Duke University Press, 2020), introduction, 67. Sections of Lesel Dawson's discussion on gender and revenge have also been helpful; see introduction in Lesel Dawson and Fiona McHardy, eds., *Revenge and Gender in Classical, Medieval, and Renaissance Literature* (Edinburgh: Edinburgh University Press, 2021), 1–4. This approach is also in the vein of a number of feminist scholars who have helped reframe scholarship on marginalized Black populations by centering their stories—such as that of Deborah Gray White, *Ar'n't I a Woman?: Female Slaves in the Plantation South* (New York: W. W. Norton, 1987); Tera W. Hunter, *To 'Joy My Freedom: Southern*

Black Women's Lives and Labors After the Civil War (Cambridge, MA: Harvard University Press, 1997); Aisha Finch, *Rethinking Slave Rebellion in Cuba: La Escalera and the Insurgencies of 1841–1844* (Chapel Hill: University of North Carolina Press, 2015), 2–4, 141–144, chap. 5; Nicole A. Burrowes, "Building the World We Want to See: A Herstory of Sista II Sista and the Struggle Against State and Interpersonal Violence," *Souls* 20, no. 4 (October–December 2018): 376–377, 381–386. I am also trying to expand the ways we create and think about theory in accordance with Barbara Christian's "The Race for Theory," *Feminist Studies* 14, no. 1 (Spring 1988): 67–79.

9. The full quotation is as follows: "I use the term 'feminist' to capture the emancipatory vision and acts of resistance among a diverse group of African American women who attempt in their writings to articulate their understanding of the complex nature of black womanhood, the interlocking nature of the oppression black women suffer, and the necessity of sustained struggle in their quest for self-determination, the liberation of black people, and gender equality"; while much aligned with the first part of this definition, the women I study seem less concerned with the broader liberation of Black people or wider structural change. See Beverly Guy-Sheftall's field-shifting edited volume, *Words of Fire: An Anthology of African-American Feminist Thought* (New York: New Press, 1995), xiv; Marilyn Richardson, ed., *Maria W. Stewart: America's First Black Political Writer: Essays and Speeches* (Bloomington: Indiana University Press, 1987). While Nell Painter's work challenges the ways that white abolitionists deployed inaccurate images of Truth and her activism, Painter's work nonetheless shows that Truth was an avowed abolitionist and deeply concerned about the plight of Black women. As Painter explains, "As an abolitionist and feminist, she put her body and her mind to a unique task, that of physically representing women who had been enslaved. At a time when most Americans thought of slaves as male and women as white, Truth embodied a fact that still bears repeating: Among the blacks are women; among the women, there are blacks," see *Sojourner Truth: A Life, A Symbol* (New York: W. W. Norton Company, 1996), 3–4; Paula Giddings, *When and Where I Enter: The Impact of Black Women on Race and Sex in America* (New York: Bantam Books, 1984); Deborah Gray White, *Too Heavy a Load: Black Women in Defense of Themselves, 1894–1994* (New York: W. W. Norton Company, 1999); Erin D. Chapman, "A Historiography of Black Feminist Activism," *History Compass* 17, no. 7 (July 2019): e12576): 1–9; I also agree with Ula Taylor's observation when she writes, "It seems that far too many black people continue to link the feminist movement exclusively to the activism of bourgeois white women and not to the struggles initiated by African Americans

for freedom, justice, and equality." See her important essay, "Making Waves: The Theory and Practice of Black Feminism," *The Black Scholar* 28, no. 2, Black Social Issues (Summer 1998): 32. Treva B. Lindsey also notes this Black feminist genealogy, see *America, Goddam: Violence, Black Women, and the Struggle for Justice* (Oakland: University of California Press, 2022), 24, and discusses the multiple jeopardies that Black women face, 22–24.

10. The first iteration of the statement was circulated as a movement document in 1977. The final version was published in Zillah Eisenstein, ed., *Capitalist Patriarchy and the Case for Socialist Feminism* (New York: Monthly Review Press, 1979), and it was reprinted in *Monthly Review* on the fortieth anniversary of publication. See the Combahee River Collective, "A Black Feminist Statement," *Monthly Review*, January 2019, 29–36; Audre Lorde, *Sister Outsider: Essays and Speeches* (New York: Crossing Press, 1984), 106–109. Patricia Hill Collins's pioneering work also makes it clear that "maintaining the invisibility of Black women and our ideas is critical in structuring patterned relations of race, gender, and class inequality." See *Black Feminist Thought: Knowledge, Consciousness, and the Politics of Empowerment* (New York: Routledge Press, 1991), 5–6. Also, originally published in 1969, Frances Beals's powerful piece, "Double Jeopardy: To Be Black and Female" in *Meridians* 8, no. 2 (2008): 1–11, examined the multifaceted forms of oppression constricting Black women's lives. At the same time, Black feminism and intersectionality have been targeted and branded as dangerous ideologies that negatively police free speech and indoctrinate impressionable young minds—on the threats related to intersectionality; see Jennifer Nash, *Black Feminism Reimagined: After Intersectionality* (Durham, NC: Duke University Press, 2019), 1–2. On the term *misogynoir* see Moya Bailey and Trudy, "On Misogynoir: Citation, Erasure, and Plagiarism," *Feminist Media Studies* 18, no. 4 (2018): 762–768. My work also owes a debt to Brittney Cooper's work on Black feminism, for the concise yet layered ways that she defines and engages Black feminism and anger in her book *Eloquent Rage: A Black Feminist Discovers Her Superpower* (New York: St. Martin's Press, 2018), 3–6. To be clear, while I believe the overwhelming sentiment is anti-violence, there were segments of Black feminist theorists, activists, and writers who did embrace violence as a viable form of women's resistance. A recent discussion of this may be found in Stephen Dillon's work on the late poet June Jordan; see "'I Must Become a Menace to My Enemies': Black Feminism, Vengeance, and the Futures of Abolition," *GLQ: A Journal of Lesbian and Gay Studies* 28, no. 2 (April 2022): 195–201. In many ways, this research is also aligned with Bettina Judd's inquiry when she writes, "I'm interested in Black women's anger in order to sharpen a lens on the experience of racism, sexism, and

misogynoir and to examine how knowledge is produced through these experiences." My work explores how Black women have used the knowledge gleaned from those experiences to avenge themselves and to fight back against racism, sexism, and misogynoir. See Bettina Judd, "Sapphire as Praxis: Toward a Methodology of Anger," *Feminist Studies* 45, no. 1 (2019): 179.

11. I reference the Erinyes, the Furies, female deities who avenged and punished blood crimes. See the play *Eumenides* in Aeschylus, *Orestia: Agamemnon, Libation-Bearers, Eumenides*, ed. and trans. Alan H. Sommerstein (Cambridge, MA: Harvard University Press, 2009). On racism and misogynoir in the legal system: Mary Frances Berry, *Black Resistance/White Law: A History of Constitutional Racism in America* (New York: Penguin, 1994), chap. 9; A. Leon Higginbotham Jr., *In the Matter of Color: Race and the American Legal Process: The Colonial Period* (New York: Oxford University Press, 1980), chap. 7; "African American women experienced particular difficulty persuading law enforcers to protect them from abusive spouses"; Jeffrey S. Adler, "'I Loved Joe, but I Had to Shoot Him': Homicide by Women in the Turn-of-the-Century Chicago," *Journal of Criminal Law and Criminology* 92, no. 3 (Spring/Summer 2002): 892; Roth explains that Black women "could not rely on law enforcement and the courts, which were less likely to try to protect black women against domestic violence"; Randolph Roth, *American Homicide* (Cambridge, MA: Belknap Press, 2012), 272.

12. Most traditional forms of feminism (Black and white) are concerned with equality and using the legal system to ensure that women have equitable access and treatment; feminists also turn to the law and agitate for laws that are specific to the needs of women, and to address long-standing inequalities that have stemmed from patriarchal policies and practices. Dominance feminism asserts that women's subordination in society stems from a concerted effort on the part of men to oppress women, using violence and sexual assault, as well as the legal system, to continue to keep women down, vis-à-vis wage inequality and other laws and practices that keep women workers impoverished and powerless. Vengeance feminism doesn't wholly agree or disagree here; rather, its proponents placed little faith in the legal system—instead, many vengeance feminists exploited the racist and gendered failings of the law to lash back; and vengeance feminists themselves often turned to their own forms of violence to protect against abuse but also to punish men who had or aimed to hurt them or other Black women in misogynistic ways. For a succinct definition of some of the varied forms of feminism, see Andrea Mazingo, "The Intersection of Dominance Feminism and Stalking Laws," *Northwestern Journal of Law & Social Policy* 9, no. 2 (2014): 337–339;

Catharine MacKinnon, "Difference and Dominance: On Sex Discrimination," chap. 2 in *Feminism Unmodified: Discourses on Life and Law* (Cambridge: Harvard University Press, 1987). Vengeance feminism is distinct from most forms of radical feminism as well—here, I'm thinking of lesbian separatism, or the violent extermination of men as proposed in Valerie Solanas's *SCUM Manifesto*, rev. ed. (Chico, CA: AK Press, 2013).

13. Daphna Motro, Jonathan B. Evans, Aleksander P. J. Ellis, and Lehman Benson III, "The 'Angry Black Woman' Stereotype at Work," *Harvard Business Review*, January 31, 2022, accessed June 5, 2023, https://hbr.org/2022/01/the-angry-black-woman-stereotype-at-work; Janice Gassam Asare, "Overcoming the Angry Black Woman Stereotype," *Forbes*, May 31, 2019, https://www.forbes.com/sites/janicegassam/2019/05/31/overcoming-the-angry-black-woman-stereotype/?sh=4f0962721fce; Ritu Prasad, "Serena Williams and the Trope of the 'Angry Black Woman,'" BBC News, September 11, 2018, https://www.bbc.com/news/world-us-canada-45476500; Elizabeth Leiba, *I'm Not Yelling: A Black Woman's Guide to Navigating the Workplace* (Miami, FL: Mango, 2023). Historian Deborah Gray White helps chart the origins of these tropes in enslavement; see "Jezebel and Mammy: The Mythology of Female Slavery," chap. 1 in *Ar'n't I a Woman?* Also see J. Celeste Walley-Jean, "Debunking the Myth of the 'Angry Black Woman': An Exploration of Anger in Young African American Women," *Journal of Black Women, Gender + Families* 3, no. 2 (Fall 2009): 68–86. Trina Jones and Kimberly Jade Norwood show how the trope is also used to deflect attention away from racist aggression directed at Black women. See "Aggressive Encounters & White Fragility: Deconstructing the Trope of the Angry Black Woman," *Iowa Law Review* 102 (2017). Bettina Judd's essay on the Sapphire trope diagrams the ways that Black women are caricatured for anger; see "Sapphire as Praxis," 178–181.

14. I am using *vigilantism* here similarly to how Karlos Hill defines it in his work: "The criminal justice system's failure to prosecute crimes perpetrated against blacks is the primary context for understanding why black vigilantism occurred. This dynamic encouraged extralegal violence in the Deltas as well as in other regions of the South." See Karlos K. Hill, *Beyond the Rope: The Impact of Lynching on Black Culture and Memory* (New York, NY: Cambridge University Press, 2016), 16–17. However, vengeance feminism's violent responses are not only to address the void of legal protection and prosecutions; it's also about Black women exorcising rage. Nikki Taylor's work is instructive here, too, as she writes, "A Black feminist practice of justice insists that the proportionality of revenge is best determined by the victims of the unjust acts," in *Brooding Over Bloody*

Revenge: Enslaved Women's Lethal Resistance (Cambridge: Cambridge University Press, 2023), 12.

15. Tera Hunter explains, "Violence and crime were among the many challenges of urban life that required inventiveness for survival, in the absence of protection or support from governing authorities. Working-class women pieced together their livelihoods beyond the labor that they performed in exchange for wages, using the various consumption strategies described earlier that were critical both materially and socially. Scavenging, borrowing, and pan-toting helped to increase the provisions for subsistence of those with little cash. Domestic workers transformed raw products into consumable goods for their own families, the same labor that they performed in the homes of their employers, albeit with much more austerity"; see *To 'Joy My Freedom*, 60–61, quote on page 67. Also, Paula Giddings's foundational work documents the creation of the National Association of Colored Women (NACW) in 1896, as well as Black women's ongoing efforts to collectively organize for justice. See *When and Where I Enter* (New York: Bantam Books, 1984), for the founding of the NACW, see 93–95, chap. 6.

16. Notions of vengeance and revenge have long been discussed in feminist literature and theory, with discourses often falling into two categories: women defending and avenging themselves against gendered wrongs (e.g., battery or rape); or alternatively, the discussions resist characterizations of women's rage and anger as being derided as scorn. My work pairs vengeance and feminism specifically to give a name to the praxes I have observed in the historical cases of Black women in Philadelphia and the critical analysis evident in them. Examples of the range of feminist discussions of vengeance include Ruby Tapia's fascinating essay in which she examines Quentin Tarantino's film *Kill Bill* "to reveal its intertextual—indeed, comparative—racialization of feminist vengeance," in "Volumes of Transnational Vengeance Fixing Race and Feminism on the Way to Kill Bill"; see *Strange Affinities: The Gender and Sexual Politics of Comparative Racialization*, eds. Grace Kyungwon Hong and Roderick A. Ferguson (Durham, NC: Duke University Press, 2011), 133. Also see Laura B. Kellough-Pollock's honor's thesis, which considers whether the rape-revenge movie genre supports feminist aims, see "Feminist Vengeance?: Rape-Revenge and Women's Empowerment" (honor's thesis, University of Victoria, 2022). Agatha Ann Slupek's dissertation "explores how women and other feminized groups creatively negotiate the terms of their figuration as agents of vengeance to challenge our very understanding of what counts as a matter of public justice"; see the abstract in "Fury at the Limits of the Law: Toward a Political Theory of Vengeance" (Ph.D. diss., University of Chicago, 2022). When discussing June Jordan's poetry, author

Stephen Dillon writes, "In other words, vengeance, in Jordan's articulation, leads somewhere else, toward new forms of desire and becoming." See "'I Must Become a Menace,'" 201. I also found J. T. Roane's piece on the case of Donnetta Hill, a twenty-five-year-old Black sex worker convicted of murder in 1988 in Philadelphia, especially powerful. Roane analyzes Hill's courtroom conduct as a kind of feminist refusal and its own articulation of a political, feminist vengeance when he writes, "While Hill's spitting on jurors did not constitute a traditional feminist treatise, spitting, along with other embodied and visceral formulations of resistance and refusal on the part of the condemned, forms part of the arsenal of the dispossessed"; see "Spitting Back at Law and Order: Donnetta Hill's Rage in an Era of Vengeance," *Signs: Journal of Women in Culture and Society* 46, no. 4 (2021): 858. Elizabeth Flock's new book explores the cases of three women across the globe who mobilized deadly violence, and in her contemporary exploration, she, too, delves into how the women "handled matters on their own because the cops, courts, and state had failed to safeguard them." See *The Furies: Women, Vengeance, and Justice* (New York: HarperCollins, 2024), 3. The work of Damaris B. Hill captures the fury of Black women in the justice system, see *A Bound Woman Is A Dangerous Thing: The Incarceration of African American Women from Harriet Tubman to Sandra Bland* (New York: Bloomsbury Publishing, 2019).

17. I am building on the works of Frantz Fanon and Walter Rodney when they discuss violence as a means of empowerment on behalf of oppressed Black people. Fanon writes, "At the individual level, violence is a cleansing force. It rids the colonized of their inferiority complex, of their passive and despairing attitude." See Frantz Fanon, *The Wretched of the Earth*, tr. Richard Philcox (New York: Grove Press, 2004), 51. Walter Rodney explains, "We were told that violence in itself is evil, and that, whatever the cause, it is unjustified morally. By what standard of morality can the violence used by a slave to break his chains be considered the same as the violence of a slave master? By what standards can we equate the violence of blacks who have been oppressed, suppressed, depressed and repressed for four centuries with the violence of white fascists? Violence aimed at the recovery of human dignity and at equality cannot be judged by the same yardstick as violence aimed at maintenance of discrimination and oppression." See Walter Rodney, *The Groundings with My Brothers*, eds. Asha T. Rodney and Jesse Washington (London: Verso Books, 2019), 32. My thinking on these issues has also been influenced by Kellie Carter Jackson's important work on Black abolitionists' shift to the use of violence during enslavement. She writes that a "retreat from engaging in a complex understanding of the political purposes of violence limits both how we see and make use of the past. Within the field, there is a propensity to privilege

the performance of nonviolence and deny the possibility and utility of violence as the great accelerator in American emancipation." Kellie Carter Jackson, *Force and Freedom* (Philadelphia: University of Pennsylvania, 2019), 3–5, quote on 3.

18. Historically, vengeance feminism traces many of its roots to enslaved women who lashed back against their oppressors, whether physically resisting via assault, arson, and murder, or engaging in everyday acts of resistance, such as theft, breaking tools, or feigning illness to avoid work. For more on this, see Nikki M. Taylor, *Brooding Over Bloody Revenge*, 8–12. Michele Wallace, *Black Macho and the Myth of the Superwoman* (New York: Warner Books, 1980). Wilma King's essay also explores enslaved women's deadly resistance against attackers, but she also examines their crimes of infanticide; see "'Mad' Enough to Kill: Enslaved Women, Murder, and Southern Courts," *Journal of African American History* 92, no. 1 (Winter 2007); Lorde's heated treatise calls for and gives a potent sounding to Black female rage; at the same time, it cautions against the destructive aspects of that fire. In fact, she takes pains to delineate righteous rage, noting it is not bent on destruction but rather survival. She also states we are not fiery fingers of judgment. See Audre Lorde, "The Uses of Anger" (1981), reprinted in *Women's Studies Quarterly* 25, no. 1–2 (Spring/Summer 1997): 282–285. bell hooks, *Ain't I a Woman: Black Women and Feminism* (Boston, MA: South End Press, 1981) and *Killing Rage: Ending Racism* (New York: Henry Holt, 1995); Carla Kaplan, Sarah Haley, and Durba Mitra, "Introduction: Outraged/Enraged: The Rage Special Issue," *Signs: Journal of Women in Culture and Society* 46, no. 4 (2021): 785. Toni Cade Bambara's groundbreaking anthology also addresses the complexities of Black women's struggles in similar ways. Especially powerful is Cade's essay "The Pill: Genocide or Liberation?" and the aforementioned Frances Beale essay "Double Jeopardy: To Be Black and Female," which also appears in *The Black Woman*, ed. Toni Cade (New York: New American Library, 1970). Flo Kennedy discussed African Americans' use of violence as a response to mainstream racist and violent policies and practices, see Sherie M. Randolph, *Florynce "Flo" Kennedy: The Life of a Radical Black Feminist* (Chapel Hill: University of North Carolina Press, 2015), 82–83. For a history of Black feminist organizing, see Kimberly Springer, *Living for the Revolution: Black Feminist Organizations, 1968–1980* (Durham, NC: Duke University Press, 2005).

19. Mikki Kendall, *Hood Feminism: Notes from the Women That the Movement Forgot* (New York: Viking Press, 2020); Cooper, *Eloquent Rage*; Charlene Carruthers, *Unapologetic: A Black Queer, and Feminist Mandate for Radical Movements* (Boston: Beacon Press, 2018). Also see Angela Davis, *Abolition. Feminism. Now* (Chicago: Haymarket Books, 2022), and Barbara Ransby, *Making All Black*

Lives Matter: Reimagining Freedom in the Twenty-First Century (Oakland: University of California Press, 2018); Roxane Gay, *Bad Feminist: Essays* (New York: HarperCollins, 2014); Marquis Bey, *Black Trans Feminism* (Durham, NC: Duke University Press, 2022). Also, for work more expressly on patriarchy, see Imani Perry, *Vexy Thing: On Gender and Liberation* (Durham, NC: Duke University Press, 2018).

20. Barbara Christian's timeless essay on theory and Black life has been especially important here, not only for the ways she posits storytelling as central to Black theorizing but also for her critique of the ways Black women scholars have been pressured into "speaking a language and defining their discussion in terms alien to and opposed to our needs and orientation" (this is something I am trying to write against). See "The Race for Theory," 68.

21. I am not suggesting that they were anarchists like Lucy Parsons and her husband, who did not eschew violence, per se, but were focused on issues surrounding labor and capitalism. For more on Parsons, see Jacqueline Jones, *The Goddess of Anarchy: The Life and Times of Lucy Parsons, American Radical* (New York: Basic Books, 2017).

22. Christopher Collier and James Lincoln Collier, *Decision in Philadelphia: The Constitutional Convention of 1787* (New York: Random House, 1986). For works on slavery in Philadelphia, see Edward Bettle, *Notices of Negro Slavery, as Connected with Pennsylvania* (Philadelphia: M'Carty and Davis, 1826); the chapter on Pennsylvania in Higginbotham's *In The Matter of Color*; Erica Armstrong Dunbar, *A Fragile Freedom: African American Women and Emancipation in the Antebellum City* (New Haven, CT: Yale University Press, 2008); Beverly C. Tomek, *Slavery and Abolition in Pennsylvania* (Philadelphia: Temple University Press, 2021). On the early movement for women's rights, see Carol Faulkner, *Lucretia Mott's Heresy: Abolition and Women's Rights in Nineteenth-Century America* (Philadelphia: University of Pennsylvania Press, 2013); Christopher Densmore, Carol Faulkner, Nancy Hewitt, and Beverly Wilson Palmer, eds., *Lucretia Mott Speaks: The Essential Speeches and Sermons* (Chicago: University of Illinois Press, 2020).

23. For historical studies on Pennsylvania's legal system, see Negley K. Teeters, *They Were in Prison: A History of the Pennsylvania Prison Society, 1787–1937, Formerly the Philadelphia Society for Alleviating the Miseries of Public Prisons* (Philadelphia: John C. Winston, 1937) and *The Prison at Philadelphia, Cherry Hill: The Separate System of Penal Discipline, 1829–1913* (New York: Columbia University Press, 1957); Allen Steinberg, *The Transformation of Criminal Justice: Philadelphia, 1800–1880* (Chapel Hill: University of North Carolina Press,

1989); Jen Manion, *Liberty's Prisoners: Carceral Culture in Early America* (Philadelphia: University of Pennsylvania Press, 2015); Kali Nicole Gross, *Colored Amazons: Crime, Violence, and Black Women in the City of Brotherly Love, 1880–1910* (Durham, NC: Duke University Press, 2006); Jack Marietta and G. S. Rowe, *Troubled Experiment: Crime and Justice in Pennsylvania, 1682–1800* (Philadelphia: University of Pennsylvania Press, 2006); Leslie Patrick-Stamp, "The Prison Sentence Docket for 1795: Inmates at the Nation's First State Penitentiary," *Pennsylvania History: A Journal of Mid-Atlantic Studies* 60, no. 3 (July 1993): 353–382, and "Numbers That Are Not New: African Americans in the Country's First Prison, 1790–1835," *Pennsylvania Magazine of History and Biography* 119, no. 1–2 (1995): 95–128. There is a lot of emerging scholarship (and documentaries) on MOVE, but for this section, I specifically quoted from Mistinguette Smith's article, "The MOVE Bombing Was a Philadelphia Tragedy—and an American One," *Philadelphia Inquirer*, May 8, 2021. In 1989, Hallam Hurt, then chair of neonatology at Albert Einstein Medical Center on North Broad Street, initiated a study of "the effects of in-utero cocaine exposure on babies." The study centered on 224 near-term or full-term babies born at Einstein between 1989 and 1992, with half of the mothers having used cocaine during their pregnancies. Ultimately, the study (and similar ones around the country) reached the conclusion that "poverty is a more powerful influence on the outcome of inner-city children than gestational exposure to cocaine." See Susan Fitzgerald's piece, "'Crack Baby' Study Ends with Unexpected but Clear Result," *Philadelphia Inquirer*, July 21, 2013, accessed June 5, 2023, https://www.inquirer.com/philly/health/20130721__Crack_baby__study_ends_with_unexpected_but_clear_result.html.

24. The African Methodist Episcopal Church was founded in Philadelphia; see Richard S. Newman, *Freedom's Prophet: Bishop Richard Allen, the AME Church, and the Black Founding Fathers* (New York: New York University Press, 2008), 1–2. "African Methodism, even before it coalesced into a denomination, engaged survival issues that affected both enslaved and emancipated blacks in the Atlantic World"; see Dennis C. Dickerson, *The African Methodist Episcopal Church: A History* (Cambridge, England: Cambridge University Press, 2020), 30–38. The oldest "continuously circulating black newspaper" was founded in Philadelphia in 1884, though many of its earliest papers are lost, as it has only been archived since 1912. See V. P. Franklin, "'The Voice of the Black Community': The *Philadelphia Tribune*, 1912–1941," *Pennsylvania History* 51, no. 4 (1984): 261–264. W. E. B. Du Bois's *The Philadelphia Negro: A Social Study* (Philadelphia: Publications of the University of Pennsylvania, 1899); Greg Johnson, "The Times and Life of

"W. E. B. Du Bois at Penn," Penn Today, February 19, 2022, accessed February 15, 2024, https://penntoday.upenn.edu/news/times-and-life-web-du-bois-penn.

Chapter 1: Their Honor: Black Womanhood on Offense

1. "With Knife and Pistol," *Times Philadelphia*, September 17, 1893; articles such as "May Be a Murder," *Times Philadelphia*, January 13, 1894, detailing injuries and crimes committed on Lisbon Street, abound. In this instance, a woman's badly beaten body was discovered by police. Witnesses said she fell down the stairs, but her neighbors warned that the woman and the man she lived with quarreled daily.

2. In this instance, Blackston, then of 518 Lisbon Street, was the victim, having been struck in the head with a brick by another neighborhood tough; see "A Street Fight and Its Results," *Philadelphia Inquirer*, July 17, 1890, and "With Knife and Pistol"—this article lists his resort's address as 513 Lisbon Street.

3. Love reportedly stabbed Elliott in the neck; see "Frank Love's Knife," *Philadelphia Inquirer*, May 21, 1890; "Slight Pistol-Shot Wounds," *Times Philadelphia*, December 26, 1891; "Lisbon Street Revolvers," *Philadelphia Inquirer*, October 15, 1893; also see "Two Women Badly Kicked," *Philadelphia Inquirer*, September 25, 1893.

4. In various press accounts, Tenie's name appears as "Tennie," "Tinie," and "Tenny," and the *Times Philadelphia* initially reported the victim's name as "Antonio Farberis." Subsequent reports identified him as Dominico Farluiso or Farliesio; however, on the bill of indictment, his name appears as Domenico Fabrizio. See Comm. v. Mamie White, No. 360, November 26, 1890—White was sentenced to three years at Eastern State Penitentiary; also see Comm. v. William Price, George Cornish, Tenie Hogan, No. 363, November 26, 1890—Price and Cornish were sentenced to two years and six months each at Eastern, and Tenie was sentenced to two years and six months at the Philadelphia County Prison. See "'Tinie's' Thieving Way," *Times Philadelphia*, November 23, 1890; "Mamie Left the Town," *Times Philadelphia*, November 24, 1890; and "An Italian's Roll of Notes," *Philadelphia Inquirer*, November 24, 1890. "Probable Murder in the Slums," *Philadelphia Inquirer*, November 20, 1890, notes that a stabbing reportedly occurred in the house of "Tenie Cornish, on Lisbon street, above Hurst." This tactic of snatching hats was not unique to Philadelphia, it seems, as Emily Epstein Landau discusses a similar event in the Storyville section of New Orleans, when men who frequented vice districts were sometimes robbed "without even having 'the pleasure,'" as in the case of one man who said, "The woman ran up to him, 'snatched' his hat right off of his head, and retreated

to her crib with it. When August ran after her to get it, 'someone behind the door held [his] arms' down while the woman with his hat went through his pockets and took two and a half dollars from him." See *Spectacular Wickedness: Sex, Race, and Memory in Storyville, New Orleans* (Baton Rouge: Louisiana State Press, 2013), 22.

5. Cheryl Hicks's work examines extensively the ways that everyday and working-class Black women challenged restrictive notions of respectability, essentially defining it for themselves. See Cheryl D. Hicks, *Talk with You Like a Woman: African American Women, Justice, and Reform in New York, 1890–1935* (Chapel Hill: University of North Carolina Press, 2010), 9–10, 29, 31, 35; for discussion of some of the challenges and limitations of patriarchal protections, see 56–58. See also Farah Jasmine Griffin, "'Ironies of the Saint': Malcolm X, Black Women, and Price of Protection," in *Sisters in the Struggle: African American Women in the Civil Rights-Black Power Movement*, eds. V. P. Franklin and Bettye Collier-Thomas (New York: New York University Press, 2001), 215–219. However, I am also approaching this from a similar vantage that Rhonda Frederick employs in her book *Evidence of Things Not Seen* (New Brunswick, NJ: Rutgers University Press, 2022), when she discusses how logics of antiblackness exist and have persisted, yet that is not how Black women—or Black people, for that matter—have viewed themselves; see pages 4, 5, but especially page 15, when she explains that her book centers "fantastical blackness as an analytic that knows external and imposed logics but that does not accept an impossible black humanity as the only or primary defining truth."

6. For examples of Du Bois and other Black elites bemoaning the presence of poorer Black people, see Khalil Muhammad, *The Condemnation of Blackness: Race, Crime, and the Making of Modern Urban America* (Cambridge, MA: Harvard University Press, 2010), 207. For the Mary Church Terrell quotation, see "What Does the Future Hold for the Negro Woman in America? Mrs. Mary Church Terrell President of the National Association of Colored Women," *Philadelphia Times*, September 16, 1900; also see Mary Church Terrell, "Peonage in the United States: The Convict Lease System and the Chain Gangs," *Nineteenth Century and After* 62 (1907): 306–322. Sarah Haley references Terrell's activism in *No Mercy Here* (Chapel Hill: University of North Carolina Press, 2016), 14–15. On the practice of slumming, as Chad Heap notes, "despite its occasional egalitarian impulses, slumming proved to be largely complicit both in the efforts of previously nonwhite or 'in-between' racial groups to secure whiteness at the expense of black subjugation and in the refashioning of sexual normalcy and difference from a gendered system of marginalized fairies and mannish women to a

cultural dyad that privileged heterosexual object choice." See Chad Heap, *Slumming: Sexual and Racial Encounters in American Nightlife, 1885–1940* (Chicago: University of Chicago Press, 2009), 8–9, quote on 11.

7. Ida's alias notwithstanding, her last name Payton also appears as "Peyton" in the press accounts, but *Payton* is what consistently appears on court documents. "Ida Gibbs' Victim Dead," *Philadelphia Inquirer*, September 22, 1893; Ida was initially charged with assault and battery with intent to kill, though the docket noted that they would "await the result of injuries." See Philadelphia County Prisoners for Trial Docket, B, Ida Payton, September 16, 1893. The charge was upgraded upon Samuel Jackson's death; see Prisoners for Trial Docket, B, Ida Payton, September 22, 1893—it notes that she was convicted on November 1, 1893, and sentenced to twelve years; also see Philadelphia County Prison Commitment Docket, Female, Ida Payton, 1893.

8. "With Knife and Pistol."

9. In the *Times Philadelphia* account, there is some suggestion that Samuel Jackson was also involved in the altercation between John Blackston and his victim, William Brown. Subsequent accounts make no mention of this, though given that Samuel met his end in Blackston's resort, where Ida occupied a room, it is likely that Samuel Jackson, John Blackston, and William Brown knew one another; see "With Knife and Pistol." This account also suggests that Jackson hit Ida first. For the quote that she struck him in fun and her claim of self-defense, see "Ida Payton's Trial," *Philadelphia Public Ledger*, October 31, 1893.

10. "Ida Peyton on Trial," *Times Philadelphia*, October 31, 1893, reported that during the row, Jackson "threw her down and beat her head against the floor." Her possession of a firearm was itself a radical act; renowned historian Carol Anderson has shown the right to bear arms as defined by the Second Amendment was itself "designed and has consistently been constructed to keep African Americans powerless and vulnerable," as their ability to lawfully carry has always been flawed owing to racism and racist policing. See *The Second: Race and Guns in a Fatally Unequal America* (New York: Bloomsbury, 2021), 4–7, quote on 7; for examples of early statutes in Pennsylvania that limited Black people's access to firearms, see page 18, also see chap. 3.

11. "Ida Payton Trial," *Philadelphia Public Ledger*, October 31, 1893.

12. "Ida Peyton on Trial"; "Did She Shoot Him?," *Philadelphia Inquirer*, October 31, 1893. "Ida Payton Trial," *Philadelphia Public Ledger*, October 31, 1893.

13. "Ida Payton Trial"; Bill of Indictment, Comm. v. Ida Payton, No. 238, October 11, 1893. Payton was convicted and sentenced to twelve years; see Prisoners for Trial Docket, September 22, 1893.

14. Quarter Sessions Docket, Comm. v. Ida Payton, No. 238, October Sessions, 1893. "Two Violent Deaths Investigated," *Philadelphia Inquirer*, August 11, 1891. Howard was sentenced to twelve years for murder in the second degree, and with the state's commutation law, her sentence was to expire on January 29, 1901; see Eastern State Penitentiary, Convict Reception Registers, Ida Howard, A6066, October 29, 1891.

15. On Robert Adams Jr., see Pennsylvania Senate Library, accessed January 29, 2023, https://www.legis.state.pa.us/cfdocs/legis/BiosHistory/Mem Bio.cfm?ID=2474&body=S. "That Duel," *Daily Gazette* (Wilmington, DE), April 13, 1880—this account says the men were "placed at twenty-eight paces." Later articles appear to be doing damage control on the part of Dr. White, claiming that the dispute was over Dr. James William White's troop uniform with various explanations about its use. See also "A Bloodless Duel," *Boston Globe*, April 13, 1880, for details on duel pistols; "Why They Fought," *Times Philadelphia*, April 14, 1880; "That Affair of Honor," *Philadelphia Inquirer*, April 14, 1880. In discussing the role of duels in the Old South, Bertram Wyatt-Brown writes that the contests were about establishing leaders and dominance—implicit in these aims were dominance over women, but also, it gestured toward white elite supremacy as well. Even so, he acknowledges that: "Murder, or at least manslaughter, inspired the same public approval in some instances. Just as lesser folk spoke ungrammatically, so too they fought ungrammatically, but their actions were expressions of the same desire for prestige." In those instances, Wyatt-Brown is making the case here across whites of different classes, but my point is that I see Black women like Ida Payton deploying violence in a similar way—as an affirmation of standing on honor as she defined it. See Bertram Wyatt-Brown, *Southern Honor: Ethics & Behavior in the Old South* (New York: Oxford University Press, 1982), 353. Also, I see her actions functioning similarly to how historian Edward E. Baptist described violent retribution enacted by a white man in 1831: "Like a proper gentleman who shot someone in a duel to erase an insult, Potter believed that only an act of greater violation than what had been committed against him would erase the unmanning mark." See *The Half Has Never Been Told: Slavery and the Making of American Capitalism* (New York: Basic Books, 2016), 220.

16. Eastern State Penitentiary, Convict Reception Registers, Annie Cutler, A3013, sentenced October 16, 1885, received December 30, 1885; Kali Nicole Gross, *Colored Amazons: Crime, Violence, and Black Women in the City of Brotherly Love, 1880–1910* (Durham: Duke University Press, 2006), 90–92. For accounts that Knight wooed her and convinced her to follow him, see evidence of Knight's letters to her in "Her Life at Stake," *Philadelphia Inquirer*, May 19, 1885;

also, though prison records list her birthplace as Massachusetts, she seems to have spent much of her childhood in Newport, Rhode Island, as this is where she lived when she left to follow Knight and also where her mother resided at the time of the murder. See "Annie Cutler's Letter," *Times Philadelphia*, April 25, 1885, and "Her Life at Stake."

17. "Murdered in the Street," *New York Times*, April 23, 1885; "Annie Cutler to Be Hanged: The Colored Girl Who Killed Her Lover Sentenced Yesterday," *New York Times*, October 17, 1885; "Shot Her False Lover," *Scranton Republican* (Scranton, PA), June 8, 1885.

18. "Shot Her False Lover." During her hearing before the parole board, a statement read on Annie's behalf stated that she "had simply armed herself with a pistol to frighten him if he attempted a repetition of his attack made on her during the day of the crime"; see "For Annie Cutler's Life," *Times Philadelphia*, November 18, 1885; "A Woman to Hang," *Philadelphia Inquirer*, October 17, 1885; "Annie Cutler to Be Hanged"; Gross, *Colored Amazons*, 90–92. Tera Hunter writes powerfully and profoundly about the role of marriage in African American history during enslavement and afterward in the lives of Black people. For African Americans, marriage was a fundamental part of freedom and liberation, especially since historically it had been formally denied to enslaved people—that denial was pivotal to their oppression, see *Bound in Wedlock: Slave and Free Black Marriage in the Nineteenth Century* (New York: Belknap Press, 2019), 7–8. For a current examination of its importance, see Dianne M. Stewart, *Black Women, Black Love: America's War on African-American Marriage* (New York: Seal Press, 2020).

19. The *Scranton Republican* wrote, "It is alleged that under the promise of marriage Knight became unduly intimate with the girl, and afterwards, finding another girl who better pleased his fancy, he deserted Annie and married her, establishing his home partly with the money which Miss Cutler and her mother had given him"; see "Shot Her False Lover." Also see "Killed in the Street: A Discarded Mistress' Revenge," *Times Philadelphia*, April 23, 1885. She described being "enraged" and in a frenzy when she shot Knight; see "Annie Cutler to Be Hanged."

20. "Annie Cutler's Letter."

21. "Killed in the Street"; "The Story of the Murder," *Times Philadelphia*, April 25, 1885.

22. "The Story of the Murder"; Prisoners for Trial Docket, B, Annie Cutler, April 23, 1885, "Charged on Oath of John Hartshorn with Murder"; Prisoners for Trial Docket, B, Annie E. Cutler, April 24, 1885, "Charged on Oath of Wm.

H. Cook and Henry Apple with causing the death of Wm. H. Knight"; this entry notes that she was discharged from court on October 16 and was "Sentenced to be Hanged."

23. Purvis's mother was mixed race as well, having been born of Dido and a Jewish man named "Baron Judah"; see Margaret Hope Bacon, *But One Race: The Life of Robert Purvis* (New York: State University of New York Press, 2007), 1–2, 7–8, 24.

24. Bacon, *But One Race*, 30. Purvis's racial ancestry reflects one of the more unusual aspects of interracial relationships in the South. For more on Robert Purvis and examples of his extensive antiracist and social justice activism, see Julie Winch, *Philadelphia's Black Elite: Activism, Accommodation, and the Struggle for Autonomy, 1787–1848* (Philadelphia: Temple University Press, 1988), 43, 46, 69, 151.

25. Robert Purvis, *1870 United States Federal Census* (Year: 1870; Census Place: Philadelphia Ward 23 District 76, Philadelphia, Pennsylvania; Roll: M593_1410; Page: 250A), accessed via Ancestry.com. To calculate the value of Purvis's assets in our own time, I used the values for "wealth held" on the website www.measuringworth.com. For his address see *Gopsill's Philadelphia City Directory for 1885* (Gopsill's Sons Publishers, 1885). Purvis's home is still standing, though it is being renovated, see Michaela Winberg, "Historic Philly Underground Railroad House stop that freed 9,000 slaves is saved from brink of collapse," BillyPenn, September 20, 2019, accessed February 26, 2024, https:// billypenn.com/2019/09/20/historic-philly-underground-railroad-stop-that -freed-9000-slaves-is-saved-from-brink-of-collapse/.

26. Bacon, *But One Race*, 1–2. Harriet Jacobs, *Incidents in the Life of a Slave Girl. Written by Herself*, ed. L. Maria Child (Boston, 1861), 288–289. Thomas A. Foster also writes about the sexual exploitation of enslaved men; see *Rethinking Rufus: Sexual Violations of Enslaved Men* (Athens: University of Georgia Press, 2019).

27. Bacon, *But One Race*, 1–2, quote on 2 (an earlier version of the quote contains "should," see *History of Woman Suffrage: 1861–1878*, edited by Elizabeth Cady Stanton, Susan B. Anthony, and Matilda Joslyn Gage [New York: Fowler & Wells, Publishers, 1882], 265). This was an incredibly principled stance for him, as he was author of an appeal in the 1830s denouncing the proposed disenfranchisement of Black men in Philadelphia. In its concluding section, he wrote, "We take our stand upon that solemn declaration, that to protect inalienable rights 'governments are instituted among men, deriving their JUST POWERS from the CONSENT of the governed,' and proclaim that a government which tears away

from us and our posterity the very power of CONSENT, is a tyrannical usurpation which we will never cease to oppose." See *Appeal of Forty Thousand Citizens, Threatened with Disenfranchisement, to the People of Pennsylvania* (Philadelphia: Merrihew and Gunn, 1838), 18.

28. For example, in the 1840s, when the American Anti-Slavery Society splintered over whether a woman could serve on a committee, Robert Purvis voted in support of the woman. See Bacon, *But One Race*, 2.

29. The column does not have a title. However, the article appears under the "Weather" and a smaller heading "Indications"; see *Philadelphia Inquirer*, January 24, 1885, 4.

30. *Philadelphia Inquirer*, January 24, 1885, 4.

31. "The Wife-Beater Bill," *Times Philadelphia*, January 30, 1885.

32. "Talk on Wife-Beating," *Times Philadelphia*, February 20, 1885; "The Defeat of the Wife-Beater's Bill," *Altoona Times*, February 28, 1885.

33. Reva B. Siegel, "'The Rule of Love': Wife Beating and Prerogative and Privacy," *Yale Law Journal* 105, no. 8 (1996): 2117–2207; on page 2137, Siegel notes that beginning in the 1880s, "prominent members of the American Bar Association" campaigned for the return of the whipping post as a punishment for wife beaters and that twelve states considered the measures while such bills were actually enacted "in Maryland (1882), Delaware (1901), and Oregon (1906)." The authority to beat one's wife was, in certain states, even ironically granted to enslaved Black men. For example, in Missouri in the 1830s, a group of petitioners appealed to the governor on behalf of an enslaved man who had violently attacked an enslaved woman he considered his wife; they felt he was operating in the exercise of his "connubial rights" to silence her with a slap. As David Peterson del Mar explained, "Even a slave enjoyed the right to use a certain amount of violence to 'enforce his authority' over his spouse"; see *What Trouble I Have Seen: A History of Violence Against Wives* (Cambridge, MA: Harvard University Press, 1996), 12.

34. "The Ballot," *Philadelphia Inquirer*, February 4, 1885.

35. "The Ballot."

36. Bacon, *But One Race*, 132.

37. Edward M. Davis was a Quaker, born in Philadelphia, 1811–1887; see his birth record in "U.S. Quaker Meeting Records, 1681–1935," https://www.ancestry.com/search/collections/2189/. At a Women's Suffrage Convention in Washington, Davis confronted Elizabeth Cady Stanton and Susan B. Anthony, arguing that the women had a "duty to defer to black suffrage"; Faye E. Dudden, *Fighting Chance: The Struggle over Woman Suffrage and Black Suffrage in*

Reconstruction America (New York: Oxford University Press, 2011), 171; also see "Edward Morris Davis," Historic Fair Hill, accessed October 10, 2023, https://historicfairhill.com/edward-morris-davis/#:~:text=Edward%20M.,to%20raise%20and%20support%20troops. "A Rationalist's Room," *Times Philadelphia*, April 21, 1875.

38. Despite falling short of votes in February, the issue and legislation relating to it clearly had not died, as "Chairman Purvis proceeded to discuss and advocate the bill before the State Legislature authorizing the use of the whipping post in the punishment of wife beaters"; "Women After Office," *Philadelphia Inquirer*, May 6, 1885. Further, Pennsylvania's *Altoona Tribune* published an impassioned piece reading in part: "We have steadfastly believed that the whipping post for wife-beaters would be a good thing. It is a degrading punishment, it is true, but can anything further degrade the man who brutally degrades the woman he has promised to cherish and protect?"; *Altoona Tribune*, May 7, 1885. The group's name varied in accounts but was mainly listed as the Citizen's Suffrage Association, although the *Times Philadelphia* referred to it as the Women's Suffrage Association; see "Believers in Women's Suffrage," *Times Philadelphia*, May 6, 1885. The account also mentioned, "A committee was appointed to visit Annie Cutler, the young colored woman who shot and killed her betrayer on Arch street two weeks ago, to assist her in arranging for her defense."

39. "Women After Office."

40. "Women After Office." On pay disparities, see Isabel Eaton's "Special Report on Domestic Service" in the appendices in W. E .B. Du Bois's *The Philadelphia Negro: A Social Study* (Philadelphia: Publications of the University of Pennsylvania, 1899). On Black women and the pay gap today, see "Black Women & the Pay Gap," AAUW, accessed February 15, 2024, https://www.aauw.org/resources/article/black-women-and-the-pay-gap/. "In addition, Black women experience a gender wage gap compared to Black men: among full-time, year-round workers, Black women typically make just 93 cents for every dollar paid to Black men"; see "It's Time to Pay Black Women What They're Owed," National Women's Law Center, accessed February 15, 2024, https://nwlc.org/resource/black-womens-equal-pay-day-factsheet/. Also see Robin Bleiweis, Jocelyn Frye, and Rose Khattar, "Women of Color and the Wage Gap," Center for American Progress, accessed February 15, 2024, https://www.americanprogress.org/article/women-of-color-and-the-wage-gap/.

41. The article also mentions that "the lady's spirited remarks had a visible effect on the meeting"; see "Women After Office."

42. "Women After Office."

43. "Women After Office."

44. "Humanitarians," *Philadelphia Inquirer*, June 3, 1885; "Robert Purvis, the first speaker, thought the case an appealing one and he approved of the girl's action," in "Sympathy for Annie Cutler," *Times Philadelphia*, June 3, 1885; "For Annie Cutler's Life," *Times Philadelphia*, November 18, 1885; reportedly Cutler's mother pleaded, "Oh, gentlemen, let me take my child home! Don't let her go to the state prison! She will be disgraced for life. Oh, let me take my child home and I will take care of her," see "Board of Pardons," *Harrisburg Telegraph*, December 16, 1885; "Annie Cutler," *Philadelphia Inquirer*, December 8, 1885. For more on the cause célèbre aspects of the case, see "Annie Cutler's Case: A Letter of Explanation from One Who Has Espoused Her Cause," *Times Philadelphia*, October 25, 1885; "Case of Annie Cutler," *Philadelphia Inquirer*, November 17, 1885. The *Evening Bulletin* piece does not have a title, however, the article appears next to a story titled, "Judge Yerkes' Successor," see *Evening Bulletin*, October 17, 1885, 4.

45. "False Sympathy for a Murderess," *Times Philadelphia*, October 18, 1885; also see "Death Defeats Justice: Ex-Dive Keeper Mettler's Life Taken by Violence," *Times Philadelphia*, March 10, 1892. The article discussed Mettler's saloon and alleged that it was a disorderly house that permitted "minors to remain in a concert salon and place of amusement." However, the allegations and charges Mettler faced stemmed from raids that occurred in 1886, after Annie's crime and subsequent incarceration.

46. "Woman's Rights: A Member of the Citizens' Suffrage Association Resigns on Account of a Discussion," *Philadelphia Inquirer*, June 3, 1885; "Sympathy for Annie Cutler."

47. Eastern State Penitentiary, Convict Reception Registers, A3013; Gross, *Colored Amazons*, 92.

48. The article initially lists her name as "Mamie"; see "She Was Bent on Murder," *Philadelphia Inquirer*, June 3, 1890.

49. See "Jackson, William J., 248 Duponceau St, Machinist," *Gopsill's Philadelphia, Pennsylvania, City Directory, 1890* (Philadelphia: James Gopsill's Sons, 1890). Court records indicate that she was a married woman, so it may have been an adulterous affair as well, see Bill of Indictment, Comm. v. Mary Crawford, No. 122, No. 123, No. 124, June 6, 1890.

50. "Jackson, William J., 248 Duponceau St, Machinist." A William Jackson also lived on Duponceau St. in 1889, however, by 1891, William Jackson is no longer listed as living on Duponceau St., see *Gopsill's Philadelphia, Pennsylvania, City Directory, 1889* (Philadelphia: James Gopsill's Sons, 1889) and *Gopsill's*

Philadelphia, Pennsylvania, City Directory, 1891 (Philadelphia: James Gopsill's Sons, 1891).

51. Prisoners for Trial Docket, June 3, 1890; Quarter Sessions Docket, Comm. v. Mary Crawford, No. 122; also see No. 123 and No. 124.

52. Quarter Sessions Docket, Comm. v. Mary Crawford, No. 122; also see No. 123 and No. 124. *Playfully* here means "reckless," as the statute forbids anyone in the commonwealth from "playfully or wantonly" pointing or discharging a firearm. See S. B. Boyer, *A Digest and Index: Together with a Table of Cases: To all Criminal Cases adjudged by the Supreme Court of Pennsylvania from First Binney, 1799, to the One Hundred and Fortieth Pennsylvania State Report, 1891, Inclusive. ALPHABETICALLY ARRANGED. WITH AN APPENDIX CONTAINING THE REPORT OF THE COMMISSIONERS APPOINTED TO REVISE THE PENAL CODE OF PENNSYLVANIA, THE REVISED PENAL CODE; And all Criminal Statutes from 1860 to 1891* (Sunbury, PA: Austin WILVert, 1891), 444.

53. This case is similar to one cited in Talitha LeFlouria's book about a Black woman who had been beaten up and cut at a party: "Ruby quietly nursed her stinging wound while plotting her revenge. She even pretended to make good with Gus and consented to another dance. Around 11:30 p.m., as the couple slow dragged, 'apparently having settled their differences,' Ruby made her move on Gus and pierced him in the heart. . . . The policeman, Ruby, and Gus conversed for approximately ten minutes; then the wounded man 'slipped from the officer's grasp and fell to the ground. He evidently realized that he was dying, for he stated that Ruby Jones had stabbed him. Those were his last words.'" See *Chained in Silence: Black Women and Convict Labor in the New South* (Chapel Hill: University of North Carolina Press, 2015), 38.

Chapter 2: Their History: Lawlessness and Black Womanhood

1. "Lost Both Lover and Liberty," *Times Philadelphia*, September 7, 1895. The article also refers to Sarah as a "dusky maid," which I have taken to have a double meaning, referring to her as both a youth Black woman and also as a young servant, though it may also reference the term "maiden."

2. "Lost Both Lover and Liberty."

3. "Lost Both Lover and Liberty." The two bills of indictment in the case describe Sarah Ward as a "married woman" who fired a revolver at Laura Anderson on the "fifth day of September in the year of our Lord one thousand eight hundred and ninety-five." See Bill of Indictment, Quarter Sessions Docket, Comm. v. Sarah Ward, No. 481 and No. 482, September Sessions, 1895, True Bill.

4. These details appear in the press accounts; see "Lost Both Lover and Liberty." Also, the papers spelled it "Radcliffe," but it's actually "Ratcliffe," and it was a tiny street that ran south from 726 Minster Street to Lombard Street in the Seventh Ward; see "Street Index," in *Gopsill's Philadelphia, Pennsylvania, City Directory, 1890* (Philadelphia: James Gopsill's Sons, 1890). Court documents list Laura's roommate as "Mamie Brooks," see Bill of Indictment, Comm. v. Sarah Ward (482) No. 477, September Sessions, 1895, True Bill.

5. "Lost Both Lover and Liberty."

6. "Lost Both Lover and Liberty."

7. "Lost Both Lover and Liberty." Philadelphia County Prisoners for Trial Docket, September 6, 1895. The paper and bills of indictment list his name as Zintl; however, in the Trial Docket, it reads as "Bentel." W. E. B. Du Bois described Ratcliffe Street and the surrounding environs, including Barclay Street, as "haunts of noted criminals, male and female, of gamblers and prostitutes, and at the same time, of many poverty-stricken people, decent but not energetic"; *The Philadelphia Negro: A Social Study* (Philadelphia: Publications of the University of Pennsylvania, 1899), 60.

8. "Lost Both Lover and Liberty."

9. "Lost Both Lover and Liberty."

10. Comm. v. Ward, No. 481, 215; Comm. v. Ward, No. 482, 215. Also see notations on the bills of indictment, Comm. v. Ward, No. 481 and (482) No. 477, True Bill. For Samuel G. Maloney, see "Maloney, Samuel G., constable, 121 S. 7th, h 811 Lombard," in *Gopsill's Philadelphia City Directory for 1896* (Philadelphia: James Gopsill's Sons, 1896). Also, the Philadelphia County Prison received Sarah Ward on September 6, 1895, and she was discharged the same day; see Philadelphia County Prison Commitment Docket, Female, Sarah Ward, 1895.

11. Winthrop Jordan, *White over Black: American Attitudes Toward the Negro, 1550–1812*, 2nd ed. (Chapel Hill: University of North Carolina Press, 2012); quote is on page 7. Those notions would be amplified and used to excuse and justify racial enslavement. English men also cast themselves as victims of African women's seductions to excuse their sexual assault of the women. They claimed "so great is their inclination to white men" that "temper hot and lascivious," African women would "prostitute themselves to the *Europeans* for a very slender profit." Others charged that African women would "come to the Place the Man sleeps in, they lay themselves softly down by him, soon wake him, and use all their little Arts to move the darling Passion"; *White over Black*, 35. Jordan also explains that while whiteness like that of Queen Elizabeth (set against red hair and rosy cheeks) was the ideal of feminine beauty, "by contrast, the Negro

was ugly, by reason of his color and also his 'horrid Curles' and 'disfigured' lips and nose." Eighteenth-century quotations from Jordan, page 8. See also Ibram X. Kendi, *Stamped from the Beginning: The Definitive History of Racist Ideas in America* (New York: Nation Books, 2016), 17–19, 22. Also see Deborah Gray White, "Jezebel and Mammy: The Mythology of Female Slavery," chap. 1 in *Ar'n't I a Woman?: Female Slaves in the Plantation South* (New York: W. W. Norton, 1987).

12. Jennifer L. Morgan, *Laboring Women: Reproduction and Gender in New World Slavery* (Philadelphia: University of Pennsylvania Press, 2011), 72; This law followed earlier statutes that decreed all Black women tithable. The statutes constructed Black womanhood as indelibly tied to work, but also, they disallowed for Black women to occupy the category of woman in ways that conferred protection, or humanity, or femininity; see Kathleen M. Brown, "Engendering Racial Difference: 1640–1670," chap. 4 in *Good Wives, Nasty Wenches, and Anxious Patriarchs: Gender, Race, and Power in Colonial Virginia* (Chapel Hill: University of North Carolina Press, 1996). Or put another way: "All adult men were tithable and, in addition, Negro women"; Jordan, *White over Black*, 77; Rachel Feinstein, *When Rape Was Legal: The Untold History of Sexual Violence During Slavery* (New York: Routledge, 2019), 3. For more on such laws as well as the sexual economy of forced breeding, see Adrienne Davis, "'Don't Let Nobody Bother Yo' Principle': The Sexual Economy of American Slavery," *Black Sexual Economies: Race and Sex in a Culture of Capital*, eds. Adrienne Davis and the BSE Collective (Chicago: University of Illinois Press, 2019), 17, 20–21.

13. Quoted in White, *Ar'n't I a Woman*, 28–30, quotes on 30.

14. Henry Bibb's account is quoted in White: *Ar'n't I a Woman*, 33; also see Harriet Jacobs, "Trials of Girlhood" and "The Jealous Mistress," in *Incidents in the Life of a Slave Girl. Written by Herself*, ed. L. Maria Child (Boston, 1861). For the second Bibb quote and details about "Big Jim," see Feinstein, *When Rape Was Legal*, 4, 16–17, Bibb and "Big Jim" quote on 20. Tera Hunter's work on the violations, as well as the ways that enslaved Black people fought to preserve their unions, is evocative and profoundly important; see *Bound in Wedlock: Slave and Free Black Marriage in the Nineteenth Century* (New York: Belknap Press, 2019), chap. 2.

15. Feinstein, *When Rape Was Legal*, 4. The second quote is from the attorney representing George and may be found in Davis, "'Don't Let Nobody Bother Yo' Principle,'" 25.

16. A. Leon Higginbotham Jr., *In the Matter of Color: Race and the American Legal Process: The Colonial Period* (New York: Oxford University Press, 1980), 269, 272.

17. Higginbotham, *In the Matter of Color*, 281–282; Henry Flanders and James T. Mitchell, *Statutes at Large of Pennsylvania: From 1682 to 1801*, 18 vols. (Harrisburg: 1896–1915); for distinct punishments for Black men's rape or attempted rape of white women and white girls, see "An Act for the Trial of Negroes" (1700), in *Statutes at Large*, 2:77–79. Also see "An Act for the Trial of Negroes" (1705), in *Statutes at Large* 2:233–236. See "An Act Against Rape of Ravishment" (1700) for white men's punishment for sex crimes against white women in *Statues at Large*, 2:7; Du Bois, *Philadelphia Negro*, 13; Leslie Patrick-Stamp, "Numbers That Are Not New: African Americans in the Country's First Prison, 1790–1835," *Pennsylvania Magazine of History and Biography* 119, no. 1–2 (1995): 95–128; Kali Nicole Gross, *Colored Amazons: Crime, Violence, and Black Women in the City of Brotherly Love, 1880–1910* (Durham: Duke University Press, 2006), 24–25.

18. For a discussion of enslaved women's varied forms of resistance, see Stephanie M. H. Camp, *Closer to Freedom: Enslaved Women and Everyday Resistance in the Plantation South* (Chapel Hill: University of North Carolina, 2004), 3–9, 61–68; Tamika Y. Nunley, *The Demands of Justice: Enslaved Women, Capital Crime, and Clemency in Early Virginia* (Chapel Hill: University of North Carolina, 2023), chap. 2; Vanessa Holden, *Surviving Southampton: African American Women and Resistance in Nat Turner's Community* (Chicago: University of Illinois Press, 2021). For the quote, see Nikki M. Taylor, *Brooding Over Bloody Revenge: Enslaved Women's Lethal Resistance* (Cambridge: Cambridge University Press, 2023), 17. Even so, African American jury participation was uneven and short-lived in many parts of the country; see Alexis Hoag, "An Unbroken Thread: African American Exclusion from Jury Service, Past and Present," *Louisiana Law Review* 81, no. 1 (2020): 57–62.

19. Flanders and Mitchell, *Statutes at Large*; Higginbotham, *In the Matter of Color*, 282. Davis is speaking specifically about *George v. State*, but the larger point remains true for such statutes in Pennsylvania and similar ones across the nation. These practices show how the law "created and legitimized black women's sexual vulnerability," see Davis, "'Don't Let Nobody Bother Yo' Principle,'" 25.

20. Taylor, *Brooding Over Bloody Revenge*, chap. 3, especially 67, 77–78.

21. Gerda Lerner, ed., *Black Women in White America: A Documentary History* (New York: Random House, 1972), 34–40, quote on page 35; the source credited is Ophelia Settle Egypt, J. Masuoka, and Charles S. Johnson, *Unwritten History of Slavery, Autobiographical Accounts of Negro Ex-Slaves*, Social Science Documents no. 1 (Nashville, TN: Fisk University Social Science Institute, 1945), bound transcript, 284–291.

22. Quoted in Feinstein, *When Rape Was Legal*, 25; Melton McLaurin, *Celia: A Slave* (Athens: University of Georgia Press, 1991), 117, 134–135, for her

execution; Melton A. McLaurin, "Celia," in *Encyclopedia of African-American Culture and History*, 2nd ed., vol. 2, ed. Colin A. Palmer (Detroit: Macmillan Reference USA, 2006), 432–433, Gale eBooks, accessed February 7, 2024, https://link-gale-com.proxy.library.emory.edu/apps/doc/CX3444700256/GVRL?u=emory&sid=bookmark-GVRL&xid=501a78b1.

23. I mention myths about Black women being unrapeable in Gross, *Colored Amazons*, 82. I am specifically referring to the poem by Isaac Teale, *The Sable Venus. An Ode. Inscribed to Bryan Edwards, Esq.* (Kingston, Jamaica: Bennett and Woolhead, 1765) and the etching by Thomas Stothard, *The Voyage of the Sable Venus, from Angola to the West Indies* (1794); see a copy at the NYPL Digital Collections, https://digitalcollections.nypl.org/items/510d47e4-603b-a3d9-e040-e00a18064a99; it is a sanitized image of the Middle Passage. See Marcus Wood, ed., *The Poetry of Slavery: An Anglo-American Anthology, 1764–1865* (New York: Oxford University Press, 2003), 30; also see Regulus Allen, "'The Sable Venus' and the Desire for the Undesirable," *Studies in English Literature, 1500–1900* 51, no. 3 (Summer 2011): 667–668.

24. Quote from Lerner, *Black Women in White America*, 51–52. Mary Boykin Chesnut, *A Diary from Dixie: As Written by Mary Boykin Chesnut, Wife of James Chesnut, Jr., United States Senator from South Carolina, 1859–1861, and Afterward an Aide to Jefferson Davis and a Brigadier-General in the Confederate Army* (New York: Peter Smith, 1929).

25. On Betty Jean Owens, see Danielle McGuire, *At the Dark End of the Street* (New York: Vintage, 2011), 130–154.

26. On Holtzclaw, see Patty Santos, "Former OKC Police Officer Daniel Holtzclaw Sentenced to 263 Years in Prison," KOCO, January 21, 2016, accessed February 24, 2024, https://www.koco.com/article/former-okc-police-officer-daniel-holtzclaw-sentenced-to-263-years-in-prison/4307909. On lynching of Black women and men, see Crystal Feimster, *Southern Horrors: Women and the Politics of Rape and Lynching* (Cambridge, MA: Harvard University Press, 2009), 159–160, 172. For images of lynching culture, see James Allen, *Without Sanctuary: Lynching Photography in America* (Los Angeles: Twin Palms Publishing, 1999).

27. Michael Philip Jagger and Keith Richards, "Some Girls," on Rolling Stones, *Some Girls*, June 1978. Rev. Jesse Jackson's Operation PUSH raised objections as the song "is morally offensive and degrading to black women," see "Ertegun Wants 'Some Girls' Lyric Cut," *Variety* (Archive: 1905–2000); October 11, 1978, 292, 10; Entertainment Industry Magazine Archive, page 167.

28. "Gaily Attired," *Philadelphia Inquirer*, September 27, 1886. Press accounts name the family as "Colridge," but court records list the family as Eldridge; the

article also claimed that she stole gold jewelry, but the charging documents listed only the dress and the coat. See Bill of Indictment, Quarter Sessions Docket, Comm. v. Mary Ann Jackson, No. 657, September 30, 1886.

29. *Annual Report of the Chief of Police of the City of Philadelphia, for the Year 1885* (Philadelphia: Dunlap & Clarke Printers, 1886), on the number of patrolmen, 6; on page 8, it references two known thieves who "were arrested by Detective Miller, and committed for ninety days, under the Professional Thieves Act, but were afterward released on Habeas Corpus"; *Annual Report of the Bureau of Police of the City of Philadelphia for the Year Ending December 31, 1915* (Issued by the City of Philadelphia, c. 1916); for the quote on panhandlers, 6; on scope of the force in early twentieth century, 25–28; on extra surveillance or "quarantine" on bawdy houses, 10. For more on the scope of the force in late nineteenth century, see Howard O. Sprogle, *The Philadelphia Police, Past and Present* (Philadelphia, 1887); the state legislature passed the Act for the Identification of Habitual Criminals, which instructed wardens to provide detailed descriptions of repeat offenders, and it stipulated that the district attorney furnish arrest histories to the wardens. See No. 109 in *Laws of the General Assembly of the State of Pennsylvania* (Harrisburg: Edwin K. Meyers, State Printer, 1889).

30. The chief of police reported on officers' surveillance of those deemed to be professional criminals and using preemptive arrests to terrorize them: "By a number of judicious arrests, even before they had committed any specific offense," Philadelphia police had "inspired the criminal classes with such a wholesome dread of the vigilance of our officers"; see *Annual Report of the Chief of Police of the City of Philadelphia, for the Year 1885*, 13; *Annual Report of the Director of the Department of Public Safety and of the Superintendent of the Bureau of Police for the Year Ending in December 31, 1910* (Philadelphia: Dunlap Printing, 1911), 8. On racial profiling, see Code No. 207, Beggars, Vagrants and Tramps, *Patrolman's Manual: Bureau of Police in the City of Philadelphia* (Philadelphia: Department of Public Safety, 1913), reprinted in *Metropolitan Police Manuals, 1871, 1913*, ed. Richard C. Wade (New York: Arno Press, 1974), 62; Roger Lane writes of racist policing and profiling, including examples of a Black man being detained because of his size and that he had a prior. See *Roots of Violence in Black Philadelphia, 1860–1900* (Cambridge, MA: Harvard University Press, 1986), 87; Kali Nicole Gross, *Hannah Mary Tabbs and the Disembodied Torso: A Tale of Race, Sex, and Violence in America* (Oxford: Oxford University Press, 2016), 29–30; for examples of racism, corruption, and brutality, see Khalil Muhammad, *The Condemnation of Blackness: Race, Crime, and the Making of Modern Urban America* (Cambridge, MA: Harvard University Press,

2010), 49, 201, 232–233. On violence in policing, see David R. Johnson, *Policing the Urban Underworld: The Impact of Crime on the Development of American Police, 1800–1887* (Philadelphia: Temple University Press, 1979), 103. On racialized and biological notions of criminality, see "The Born Criminal," chap. 12 in *Female Offender*, eds. Cesare Lombroso and William Ferrero (New York: D. Appleton, 1895), 147–172; R. L. Dugdale, *"The Jukes": A Study in Crime, Pauperism, Disease and Heredity, also Further Studies of Criminals* (New York: G. P. Putnam's Sons, 1877); Nicole Hahn Rafter, *Creating Born Criminals* (Urbana: University of Illinois, 1997), 86–89. "New patrolman's manual compiled and printed to replace the old manual issued in 1897, which had become obsolete"; *Annual Report of the Bureau of Police of the City of Philadelphia for the Year Ending December 31, 1915*, 4.

31. "Gaily Attired," *Philadelphia Inquirer*, September 27, 1886. Comm. v. Mary Ann Jackson; Mary was released on January 4, 1887; see Philadelphia County Entry Docket, Female, Mary Ann Jackson, 1887. Kali Nicole Gross, "Policing Black Women's and Girls' Bodies in the Carceral United States," *Souls* 20, no. 1 (2018): 1–6. For Henrietta Cook, see Kali N. Gross, "Exploring Crime and Violence in Early-Twentieth-Century Black Women's History," in *Contesting Archives: Historians Develop Methodologies for Finding Women in the Sources*, eds. Nupur Chaudhuri, Sherry Katz, and Mary Elizabeth Perry (Chicago: University of Illinois Press, 2010), 59. In court, Banks testified, "they taken [*sic*] me in this big room there and stood me up in front of those men that had those masks on. That frightened me too, because I had never seen anything like that before"; see Comm. v. Banks, No. 307, 147, 74–79.

32. Nicole Hahn Rafter, *Partial Justice: Women in State Prisons, 1800–1935* (Boston: Northeastern University Press, 1985), 155. Du Bois noted that for many, the crime problem and the Negro problem were one and the same. In 1893, a Philadelphia criminal court judge implored Black people who claimed to care about the future of their race to investigate "what is radically wrong that produces this state of affairs and correct it, if possible." In the full quote, the judge endeavors to appear balanced by adding, "There is nothing in history that indicates that the colored race has a propensity to acts of violent crime; on the contrary, their tendencies are most gentle, and they submit with grace to subordination." See Du Bois, *Philadelphia Negro*, 241, fn14.

33. Rafter, *Partial Justice*, 142–144.

34. Gross, *Colored Amazons*, 136. Although he references an earlier period, the case of Mary Ann Costill, "a black girl, was committed, indicted, tried, convicted, and imprisoned for larceny within two hours," is a useful example of the

history of railroading that I am engaging. See Allen Steinberg, *Transformation of Justice, Philadelphia, 1800–1880* (Chapel Hill: University of North Carolina Press, 1989), 108.

35. "Magistrate Smith Blushed," *Times Philadelphia*, August 13, 1890; Gross, *Colored Amazons*, 115.

36. Prisoners for Trial Docket, B, Mary Harris, "Charged on oath of Annie Davis with assault and battery," August 12, 1890.

37. Quote is from an anonymous article in *The Independent*, September 18, 1902, 2221–2224, in Lerner, *Black Women in White America*, 167, for accounts of assaults on Black women 172–186. Feimster, *Southern Horrors*, 159–160, 172.

38. On Black women seeking to leave the South to escape sexual violence, see Fannie Barrier Williams, "A Northern Negro's Autobiography," *Independent*, July 4, 1904, in Lerner, *Black Women in White America*, 165; Addie Hunton, "Negro Womanhood Defended," *Voice of the Negro* 1, no. 7 (July 1904): 280–282, in *"We Must Be Up and Doing": A Reader in Early African American Feminisms*, ed. Teresa C. Zackodnik (Peterborough, Ontario: Broadview Press, 2010), 251; bell hooks, *Ain't I a Woman: Black Women and Feminism* (Boston, MA: South End Press, 1981), 55–57.

39. Warden William Cassidy misspelled "hight" and "superfulers" in the original text. See *Eastern State Penitentiary Warden's Journal*, vol. 4, March 3, 1885; also see Eastern State Penitentiary Convict Description Register, Sarah Scott, A2565, March 3, 1885. Scott's arrest appears in the chief of police's annual report: "Sarah Scott, a noted badger thief, was arrested by officer McGarrity, of Nineteenth District, charged with badgering a man; sentenced February 12, to three years in Penitentiary"; see *Annual Report of the Chief of Police of the City of Philadelphia, for the Year 1885*, 55; Gross, *Colored Amazons*, 143. Sarah Haley discusses the prevalence of carceral sexual assault as well as the difficulties in documenting it, see *No Mercy Here* (Chapel Hill: University of North Carolina Press, 2016), 104–105, also for an example of a woman who was impregnated in custody, 106. For additional works on Black women's historical carceral experiences, see Theresa R. Jach, "'I thought if I got a chance I would do it': Sexual Negotiation by Black Women Convicts in Texas, 1875–1915," specifically page 59 for an example of a Black woman impregnated while in custody, and T. Dionne Bailey, "'I Beg for Your Mercy': The Business of Black Women's Bodies in the Carceral State, 1880s–1960s," which also mentions Black women's deaths while in custody on page 81, in Erica Rhodes Hayden and Theresa R. Jach, eds., *Incarcerated Women: A History of Struggles, Oppression, and Resistance in American Prisons* (Lanham: Lexington Books, 2017).

40. The article notes that "the only persons in the family who were not taken sick were Martha Davis and a daughter of Mr. and Mrs. Ervin"; "Martha Davis' Crime," *Philadelphia Inquirer*, November 21, 1890; Quarter Sessions Docket, Comm. v. Martha Davis, No. 36, No. 37, No. 38, and No. 39, November Sessions, 1890, "Administering poison with intent to kill"; Bills of Indictment, Comm. v. Davis, No. 36, No. 37, No. 38, and No. 39, True Bill, "Administering poison with intent to kill" (listed victims: Anthony Ervin, Ida E. Ervin, Edwin H. Ervin, William Ervin). Blanche was four years old on the 1880 census, so she would have been roughly fourteen years old at the time of the crime; see *1880 US Federal Census* (Year: 1880; Census Place: Philadelphia, Philadelphia, Pennsylvania; Roll: 1188; Page: 204A; Enumeration District: 625), Anthony F. Ervin, "Blanche S. Ervin, 4."

Chapter 3: Their Weapons: Danger and Survival, on Multiple Fronts

1. "Man Stabbed to Death by Woman," *Times Philadelphia*, Tuesday, September 25, 1900; "Lillie Fisher Held for Court," *Times Philadelphia*, September 26, 1900; Philadelphia County Prisoners for Trial Docket, B, Lillie Fisher, "Charged on Oath of Lt. O'Brien with Murder of Wm. Campbell held to await action of Coroner," September 25, 1900.

2. "Man Stabbed to Death by Woman"; "Lillie Fisher Held for Court."

3. "Man Stabbed to Death by Woman"; "Lillie Fisher Held for Court"; and "Woman Stabs a Man," *Lancaster Examiner*, September 26, 1900.

4. "Man Stabbed to Death by Woman." On Pennsylvania Hospital, see "A History of the Pennsylvania Hospital," *Boston Medical and Surgical Journal* 132, no. 19 (1895): 470–471; Russell Weigley, Nicholas B. Wainwright, and Edwin Wolf, eds., *Philadelphia: A 300-Year History* (New York: W. W. Norton, 1982), 82–83; David May, "2017 Health Care Hall of Fame," *Modern Healthcare* 47, no. 13 (March 27, 2017): pH011–H011.

5. Quote about her apprehension is from "Stabbed Her Lover to Death," *Harrisburg Daily Independent*, Tuesday, September 25, 1900. Quote about awaiting trial in "Lillie Fisher Held for Court"; also see "Man Stabbed to Death by Woman"; "Woman Stabs a Man"; Philadelphia County Prisoners for Trial Docket, B, Lillie Fisher, September 25, 1900, and Prisoners for Trial Docket, B, Lillie Fisher, September 26, 1900, "Charged on oath of Jas. A. Richardson et al. with causing the death of William Campbell."

6. "Says She Stabbed in Self-Defense," *Philadelphia Inquirer*, September 26, 1900; "Stabbed Her Lover to Death." One account noted that "Martha Reese, who claims to have been a sweetheart of Campbell's and who took laudanum with

the intention of ending her life when she was told of his death, is still in the Pennsylvania Hospital"; "Lillie Fisher Held for Court." For more on Black men and intimate partner violence, see Douglas Flowe, "To Let Her Know She Did Me Wrong," chap 4. in *Uncontrollable Blackness* (Chapel Hill: University of North Carolina Press, 2020).

7. Quote in "Says She Stabbed in Self-Defense"; "Lillie Fisher Acquitted," *Times Philadelphia*, December 29, 1900.

8. "Campbell Buried," *Times Philadelphia*, October 2, 1900; Philadelphia County Prison Commitment Docket, Female, 1900, notes that Lillie Fisher was received on September 25, and notes that she was recommitted, and then a few lines down, she is relisted as having been discharged at court on December 28.

9. "Campbell Buried."

10. W. E. B. Du Bois, "On Negro Suffrage," in *The Philadelphia Negro: A Social Study* (Philadelphia: Publications of the University of Pennsylvania, 1899), 378–379.

11. Du Bois, *Philadelphia Negro*, 379.

12. Du Bois wrote, "Their organization, tacit or recognized, is very effective, and no one can long watch their actions without seeing that they keep in close touch with the authorities in some way," in *Philadelphia Negro*, 312; he also speaks of some variation in the clubs and notes that "the Citizens' Club on Broad street, which has the best Negroes of the city in its membership, allows no gambling and pays its own expenses," 379. Also see "Former Policeman Faced Magistrate: William Mayo, Once Hero of Race Riot, Held on Charge of Running a Speak-Easy," *Philadelphia Inquirer*, July 17, 1905; "Suspend Bluecoats in Robbery Case: Two City Policeman Charged with Conspiracy with Negress to Steal from Man," *Philadelphia Inquirer*, December 18, 1919. In his study of Philadelphia's political machine and ward bosses, Peter McCaffery noted that "it effectively prevented political parties and government from responding to the real needs of the city's poor inhabitants, and also thwarted the emergence of alternative structures that could have met those needs"; *When Bosses Ruled Philadelphia: The Emergence of the Republican Machine, 1867–1933* (University Park: Pennsylvania State University Press, 1993), 178, quote on 190.

13. Khalil Muhammad, *The Condemnation of Blackness: Race, Crime, and the Making of Modern Urban America* (Cambridge, MA: Harvard University Press, 2010), 193–194, quote on 194.

14. Muhammad, *The Condemnation of Blackness*, on evidence of police failing to intervene when white people attacked African Americans, 9, 11–13, 115; even reformer Sarah Wharton references ineffectual police raids, 148. Roger Lane

noted racism among the city's police; see *Roots of Violence in Black Philadelphia, 1860–1900* (Cambridge, MA: Harvard University Press, 1986), 87; Lane also details the differences in prison sentences for Black and white men, and Black women and white women—Black women serving on average 14.1 months in prison as compared to 8.5 months served by white women, 88. Philadelphia Prisoner's for Trial Docket, September 26, 1900.

15. "Says She Stabbed in Self-Defense"; Prisoners for Trial Docket, B, Lillie Fisher, "Discharged December 28, 1900"; Quarter Sessions Docket, Comm. v. Lillie Fisher, No. 46, October Sessions, 1900; also see "Lillie Fisher Acquitted."

16. Carol Anderson, *The Second: Race and Guns in a Fatally Unequal America* (New York: Bloomsbury, 2021), 17–18; Kellie Carter Jackson writes, "Few good things can be acquired from those in power except by force, often violent force." See *Force and Freedom: Black Abolitionists and the Politics of Violence* (Philadelphia: University of Pennsylvania, 2019), for the quote, 3; for examples of Black women's armed resistance, 61, 92. Wells wrote, "The lesson this teaches and which every Afro-American should ponder well, is that a Winchester rifle should have a place of honor in every black home, and it should be used for that protection which the law refuses to give." See "Southern Horrors" in Ida B. Wells-Barnett, *The Collected Works of Ida B. Wells-Barnett* (PergamonMedia, 2015). Also, Adella Bonds, a Philadelphian who shot at racist whites attempting to attack her home in the 1920s; see Muhammad, *Condemnation of Blackness*, 212–216.

17. "Husband Found Shot," *Evening Public Ledger*, April 5, 1920; "Woman Charged with Murder," *Philadelphia Inquirer*, July 25, 1920; "Woman Freed of Murder Charge," *Philadelphia Inquirer*, April 1, 1921. Prisoners for Trial Docket, B, Anna May Hubbard, "Charged on Oath of Officer Comdico with Manslaughter await the action of the Coroner," April 6, 1920. On April 16, her charges were upgraded; see Prisoners for Trial Docket, B, Anna May Hubbard, "Charged . . . with Homicide in Causing the Death of Clifford Hubbard"; Prison Commitment Docket, 33, Hubbard, Ann May, B, April 16, 1920.

18. "Husband Found Shot: Police Catch Wife Running from House—Charge Her with It," *Evening Public Ledger*, April 5, 1920; "Woman Charged with Murder," *Philadelphia Inquirer*, July 25, 1920; "Woman Freed of Murder Charge," *Philadelphia Inquirer*, April 1, 1921; Annie Hubbard, *1920 United States Federal Census*; Clifford Hubbard, *Pennsylvania, US, Death Certificates, 1906–1968*. Clifford Hubbard was described as "Tall" and "Stout" on his draft card; see Clifford Hubbard, *US, World War I Draft Registration Cards, 1917–1918*.

19. "Police Intelligence," *Philadelphia Inquirer*, May 14, 1884; "Criminal Court Notes," *Philadelphia Inquirer*, May 29, 1884; Prisoners for Trial Docket,

B, Jos. W. Barrett, "Charged on oath of Mary Barrett with Assault + Battery to Kill == Also With Carrying Concealed Deadly Weapon." The record notes that he was convicted.

20. "Stabbing Affray," *Philadelphia Inquirer*, May 28, 1885. "Stabbed in St. Mary Street," *Times Philadelphia*, May 28, 1885; this account alleges that Sarah Williams entered Helen's room and refused to leave, and this is how the fight started (both had rooms at 622 St. Mary Street—this is a rough slum, so this may have been some kind of brothel beef). Still, it, too, notes that "Nellie was not seriously injured"; see Bills of Indictment, Quarter Sessions Docket, Comm. v. Sarah Williams, No. 9, June Sessions, 1885.

21. For example, in 1909, Helen Thomas and Mamie Brown, two African American women sex workers, were both convicted for the death of a white man named Anthony Madden after he refused to leave their parlor and threatened them with violence; see Comm. v. Helen Thomas and Mame Brown, Trial Transcript in the Court of Quarter Sessions and Oyer and Terminer of Philadelphia County, No. 375, October Sessions, 1908, January 4, 1909, and "Negress Guilty of Murder," *Philadelphia Inquirer*, January 9, 1909. Amid a love triangle and violent confrontation with her husband, Elmer Freeney, Mary Freeney "did not deny the shooting, but her defense was that she shot to save her own life"; see "Verdict in the Freeney Case," *Chester Times*, October 17, 1914; "Woman on Trial for Murder," *Philadelphia Evening Ledger*, October 12, 1914; "Manslaughter in Killing of Husband," *Philadelphia Inquirer*, October 18, 1914.

22. For Bertha Richardsin (records list it as *Richardson*, but in her handwritten note included with the Bill of Indictment, she spells it this way), see Bills of Indictment, Quarter Sessions Docket, Comm. v. Bertha Richardson, No. 138, September Sessions, 1910, "Sentence reconsidered: Defendant sentenced to Two (2) years C.P."

23. Bills of Indictment, Quarter Sessions Docket, Comm. v. Mary Wright, No. 391, June Sessions, 1901, "Murder"; notes of testimony in the Court of Oyer and Terminer for the County of Philadelphia, Comm. v. Mary Wright, No. 391, "Murder," Judge Ralston, Philadelphia, December 2, 1901.

24. She was twenty-one years old; see Comm. v. Wright, 279.

25. "Mystery in Dying Woman's Strange Wounds," *Philadelphia Inquirer*, June 5, 1901; "Servant Baffles Police in Haggenbotham Mystery," *Philadelphia Inquirer*, June 6, 1901; "Charged with Mother's Death," *Philadelphia Inquirer*, June 13, 1901.

26. "Mystery in Dying Woman's Strange Wounds"; "Charged with Mother's Death"; "Hagginbotham [*sic*] May Establish Alibi," *Times Philadelphia*, June 14,

1901; "Haggenbotham in a Hospital; Offers an Alibi," *Philadelphia Inquirer*, June 14, 1901. "Mr. John Haggenbotham the lessee of the Hotel Anchorage (formerly the St. Charles) has purchased the property and will as soon as possible alter the same into 'an all the year house'"; "Somers Point," *Pleasantville Weekly*, December 1, 1897. "Proprietor Haggenbotham is making improvements to the 'Anchorage' and building a fine new wharf for the hotels [*sic*] use"; "Somers Point," *Pleasantville Weekly Press*, May 18, 1898. Basing their ages off census data for "Sarah Higginbotham, 46," which lists her children William, twelve, and John, eight, in 1870, US Census 1870 (Year: 1870; Census Place: Philadelphia Ward 15 District 43, Philadelphia, Pennsylvania; Roll: M593_1399; Page: 391B), via Ancestry.com, and "Sarah A. Haggenboth [User Correction: Sarah Higginbotham]" of 3216 Chestnut Street, which lists her children, "May Haggenbotham, 50," and "John Haggenbotham, 36," US Census 1900 (Year: 1900; Census Place: Philadelphia Ward 27, Philadelphia, Pennsylvania; Roll: 1469; Page: 2; Enumeration District: 0665), via Ancestry.com.

27. The region had English settlers as early as the seventeenth century, but it seems that it wasn't actually called "Somers Point" until some years later. William E. Kelley and Laura Musmanno Albert, *300 Years at the Point: A History of Somers Point, New Jersey* (New Jersey: Somers Point City Clerk, 1994), 38–39, 71; also their sources indicate that the Anchorage was formerly the Trenton Hotel, 71.

28. "Servant Baffles Police in Haggenbotham Mystery"; "Mystery in Dying Woman's Strange Wounds."

29. Henry Gardner testified that Mary had had a white man caller. See Henry Gardner testimony in Comm. v. Wright, No. 391, 86–87, and Mary Wright's statement on 265, when she explains, "Monday night a friend named Robert Caldwell called about 8 o'clock P.M. and remained until 9:55 P.M. when he left."

30. Mary Wright testimony, Comm. v. Wright, No. 391, 280–281. "Mystery in Dying Woman's Strange Wounds"; "Servant Baffles Police in Haggenbotham Mystery." The brick incident is the subject of much testimony as well. See Henry Gardner testimony in Comm. v. Wright, No. 391, in which he discusses Mary's fear about returning to the house and being alone in the house after the brick incident, 82–83; also, Samuel Moore's testimony, 95–96.

31. Comm. v. Wright, No. 391, 83—it says *Mr. Jim*, rather than *Mr. John*, but I believe this is either a nickname or that Henry misspoke during his testimony. Mary's account is similar (see 282), though in her testimony, she asks if John was going for an officer, and it is Sarah who says, "The man has gone and I don't see any use now." "Charged with Mother's Death." For descriptions of Mrs.

Haggenbotham being excited, see "Servant's Tales Were Conflicting," *Philadelphia Inquirer*, December 5, 1901; in this account, Mrs. Haggenbotham said her back was turned when the brick was thrown, though it maintains that she raised concerns about her safety and that "the son tried to calm her by saying it was only an effort to scare her."

32. "Near her were several pieces of a broken ginger ale bottle, which were splattered with blood"; "Mystery in Dying Woman's Strange Wounds"—also in the early accounts, presses referred to Mary Wright as "Mary Rider." "Found in Her Home with Broken Skull," *Times Philadelphia*, June 5, 1901; "Servant Baffles Police in Haggenbotham Mystery"; "Haggenbotham Servant Held," *Times Philadelphia*, June 7, 1901. "Several other witnesses told of having seen the body and the pieces of glass lying about. They were all positive that at no time was the defendant near Mrs. Haggenbotham during their presence. The witnesses also noticed blood stains upon the clothing of the defendant"; "Strong Evidence Against Servant," *Philadelphia Inquirer*, December 4, 1901.

33. "Son Accused of Mother's Murder," *Times Philadelphia*, June 13, 1901; "Haggenbotham to Face Grand Jury," *Times Philadelphia*, June 19, 1901. Comm. v. Mary Wright, No. 391, 269; but during her actual testimony, she tells of her horror, 286–287.

34. "Haggenbotham to Face Grand Jury."

35. The coroner is quoted as having said, "Yes, and I think that the man whom you implicate in your statement has been also anxious to see you"; "Charged with Mother's Death." "No Bail for Mary Wright," *Philadelphia Inquirer*, June 7, 1901; "Haggenbotham Servant Held," *Times Philadelphia*, June 7, 1901.

36. "Servant Baffles Police in Haggenbotham Mystery"; "Charged with Mother's Death."

37. In 1946, a young Black housekeeper named Corrine Sykes, twenty-two, was the last woman to be electrocuted in the state. Found guilty of fatally stabbing Freda Wodlinger and stealing jewelry and other valuables, Sykes met "Old Sparky" for the first and last time; over and above protests and calls for a commutation of her sentence, as it was well known that she had the mental capacity of an eight-year-old. See John H. Maurer, No. 1020, *In the Supreme Court of the United States: Corrine Sykes alias Heloise T. Parker (Petitioner) v. The Commonwealth of Pennsylvania, October Term, 1945* (Washington, DC: US Supreme Court Records, 2011); "Corrine Sykes Pays with Life for Knife Slaying," *Chicago Defender*, October 26, 1946; "Corrine Sykes Dies in Chair," *New York Amsterdam News*, October 19, 1946.

38. Comm. v. Wright, No. 391, 74–75.

39. "The cause of death was exhaustion following these injuries, complicated, of course, with the hemorrhage, that being the part of the injuries"; Comm. v. Wright, No. 391, 75.

40. For examples and discussions of Black women's resistance during enslavement, see Stephanie M. H. Camp, *Closer to Freedom: Enslaved Women and Everyday Resistance in the Plantation South* (Chapel Hill: University of North Carolina, 2004), 3–9, 61–68; Thavolia Glymph, *Out of the House of Bondage: The Transformation of the Plantation Household* (Cambridge, England: Cambridge University Press, 2012), 66–72; Deborah Gray White, *Ar'n't I a Woman?: Female Slaves in the Plantation South* (New York: W. W. Norton, 1987), 77–79; Virginia Christian was tried for killing her white employer in Virginia in 1912. See LaShawn Harris, "The 'Commonwealth of Virginia vs. Virginia Christian': Southern Black Women, Crime, and Punishment in Progressive Era Virginia," *Journal of Social History* 47, no. 4 (Summer 2014): 922–942; "Fire Followed Upon Robbery: Colored Servant Girl Charged with Arson as Means of Hiding Alleged Theft," *Philadelphia Inquirer*, February 25, 1903; "Sets Employer's Home Afire: Negress Starts Blaze in the Dwelling of Dr. F. C. Van Gasken," *Evening Public Ledger*, October 28, 1915; Bill of Indictment, Quarter Sessions Docket, Comm. v. Lizzie Robinson, No. 746, March Sessions, 1913, "Arson," True Bill. Robinson was initially sentenced to five years in the county prison; however, the prison doctors believed Robinson to be insane and believed that she needed to be placed in "a hospital or other establishment where insane are detained for care and treatment." In Lizzie's case, she set fire to her landlord's rooming house, allegedly in the "spirit of revenge"; see "Woman Sentenced for Arson," *Harrisburg Daily Independent*, April 10, 1913, and "Woman Is Accused of Firing Home," *Philadelphia Inquirer*, March 31, 1913. See also Nikki M. Taylor, *Brooding Over Bloody Revenge: Enslaved Women's Lethal Resistance* (Cambridge: Cambridge University Press, 2023), 168–169. Also, after initial speculation that Mary's motive was her impending firing for staying out and drinking, reports then made much of Mary having been chastised by Sarah for allowing a cat to steal some fish Sarah planned for a meal, but nothing ultimately came of this; see "Mystery in Dying Woman's Strange Wounds."

41. Comm. v. Wright, 272–273.

42. "John picked up a brick that was in the room and struck his mother about three times on the back and then he threw the brick down on her head, and the blood spurted all over me and the hallway"; Comm. v. Wright, 274.

43. "Charged with Mother's Death"; Comm. v. Wright, 286.

44. "Charged with Mother's Death"; "Maniac Accused of Mother's Murder," *Buffalo Review*, June 15, 1901.

45. "His actions could either be judged as that of an insane man or a person who was under the influence of a drug"; "Charged with Mother's Death."

46. For examples of various drinking establishments, see Peter Thompson, *Rum Punch & Revolution: Taverngoing & Public Life in Eighteenth-Century Philadelphia* (Philadelphia: University of Pennsylvania Press, 1999), 51; Thompson also notes that women running tippling houses were sometimes associated/accused of other forms of vice, 44–45. *A Guide to the Stranger, or Pocket Companion for the Fancy, Containing a List of the Gay Houses and Ladies of Pleasure in the City of Brotherly Love and Sisterly Affection* (Philadelphia, 1849); *A Report on Existing Conditions with Recommendations to the Honorable Rudolph Blankenburg, Mayor of Philadelphia* (Philadelphia: Vice Commission of Philadelphia, 1913). Timothy Guilfoyle's study of George Appo helps give a sense of how opium and illicit drug use operated in the urban north; see *A Pickpocket's Tale: The Underworld of Nineteenth-Century New York* (New York: W. W. Norton, 2006).

47. "Charged with Mother's Death"; William Haggenbotham denied allegations about his brother's alleged opium use. See "Son Accused of Mother's Murder." For Dr. Andrews's quote, see "Haggenbotham in a Hospital; Offers an Alibi."

48. "Charged with Mother's Death"; "Haggenbotham in a Hospital; Offers an Alibi." Quote in "This Murder Puzzles Police," *Brooklyn Citizen*, June 13, 1901; Comm. v. Wright, 284. Also notes that a witness corroborated Mary's account of the quarrel over dinner meat; see "Reward Offered for Unknown," *Philadelphia Inquirer*, June 25, 1901.

49. "Sensation in Murder Case," *Brooklyn Times Union*, June 12, 1901—in addition to describing his dazed odd conduct, this article also writes that John called to Mary, saying: "'Mary, Mary,' he cried, 'come to me.'" "Police Puzzled by Murder Case," *Standard Union*, June 11, 1901; "This Murder Puzzles Police."

50. "Charged with Mother's Death"; quote in "Haggenbotham in a Hospital; Offers an Alibi."

51. "Haggenbotham in a Hospital; Offers an Alibi."

52. "Haggenbotham in a Hospital; Offers an Alibi."

53. "'She Will Tell Who Did This': John Haggenbotham Wants to Be Confronted by His Accuser, Mary Wright: TALKS RATIONALLY AT LAST," *Philadelphia Inquirer*, June 16, 1901.

54. "Witnesses Found May Prove Alibi," *Times Philadelphia*, June 15, 1901.

55. The article noted, "This marks a turning point, the police practically admitting that they have abandoned the case against John Haggenbotham"; "Mary Wright's Trunk Seized by the Police," *Philadelphia Inquirer*, June 19, 1901; "Aid Comes to Mary Wright," *Philadelphia Inquirer*, June 21, 1901; "Haggenbotham

to Face Grand Jury," *Times Philadelphia*, June 19, 1901; "Haggenbotham Case All Ready," *Times Philadelphia*, June 22, 1901. LaShawn Harris writes about a similar practice used against Black women in New York; see "'Women and Girls in Jeopardy by His False Testimony': Charles Dancy, Urban Policing, and Black Women in New York during the 1920s," *Journal of Urban History* 44, no. 3 (2018): 457–475.

56. "Aid Comes to Mary Wright"; "Mary Wright's Trunk Seized by the Police"; "Haggenbotham Case All Ready." "So far the police have not examined the clothing worn by Haggenbotham from the day his mother was assaulted"; see "'She Will Tell Who Did This,'" *Philadelphia Inquirer*, June 16, 1901. Also, Mary told authorities the intruder left her a threatening note about talking to authorities, and such a note was recovered; however, investigators believed Mary had written it in a "false hand," and they tried to use two letters she sent to Robert Caldwell as proof because the paper seemed to match; ultimately, nothing came of this. See "Letter May Give Haggenbotham His Freedom," *Philadelphia Inquirer*, June 15, 1901.

57. Mary was received at the county prison on June 25 and discharged at court on December 7; see Philadelphia County Prison Commitment Docket, Female, Mary Wright, 1901. Also, the *Times Philadelphia* noted that a conversation with detectives revealed that there were likely to be two points of contention during the hearing—one was John's insistence on speaking with Mary and the other was that "the defense will not allow the detectives to have possession of John's clothes, worn on the day of the assault. The detectives say that the first point shows complicity, and intimate that the clothes will probably show blood stains." See "Haggenbotham to Face Grand Jury."

58. "Haggenbotham Indictments: Mary Wright Said to Have Been Active in Church Work," *Times Philadelphia*, June 22, 1901—her attorney had "a letter from Rev. Alexander Wilbanks, the pastor, to the effect that she was an active church worker and a member in good standing in a Baptist church." On Black Baptist women's organizing and their representation in the Black Baptist church and its convention movement, see Evelyn Brooks Higginbotham, *Righteous Discontent: The Women's Movement in the Black Baptist Church, 1880–1920* (Cambridge, MA: Harvard University Press, 1994), 7–9.

59. Bills of Indictment, Quarter Sessions Docket, Comm. v. John Haggenbotham, No. 422, "Murder—'Ignored,'" June 25, 1901; "Haggenbotham Is Free and Wedded," *Times Philadelphia*, June 26, 1901. He did a repeat performance of this during Mary's trial; see "Son Denies He Knows of Crime: John Haggenbotham's Mind a Blank as to Events After His Mother's Murder," *Times Philadelphia*,

December 6, 1901. Once indicted, enough grand jurors have to vote affirmatively for a *true bill* finding, which means the case is headed to trial; if the votes fall short of the required count, then the charges are "ignored." See *Handbook for Jurors: Serving in Superior Court in Delaware* (Court Administrator, 2013), 12.

60. "Editor of The Philadelphia Inquirer: 'Dear Sir—I want to thank you most deeply for my brothers and myself for the very kind and impartial manner in which you have dealt with our trouble in stating it to the public. We shall always remember that you detail gentlemen to do work for The Inquirer. Yours most sincerely, MAY HAGGENBOTHAM'"; see "Haggenbotham Free, Weds Miss Ferner," *Philadelphia Inquirer*, June 26, 1901; "Haggenbotham Is Free and Wedded."

61. "Mary Wright Despondent Over Her Indictment," *Philadelphia Inquirer*, June 27, 1901. I write about something similar happening in the Hannah Mary Tabbs case in 1887. In that instance, I argue that Tabbs deployed tears and performed domesticity purposefully in ways that made the jury see her in a different light; see, Kali Nicole Gross, *Hannah Mary Tabbs and the Disembodied Torso: A Tale of Race, Sex, and Violence in America* (Oxford: Oxford University Press, 2016), chap. 6. Also, some Black women in custody became suicidal. For an example of a Black woman who took her own life in the county prison, see "Death in Her Cell," *Philadelphia Inquirer*, May 20, 1894; "Accused Servant Pleads Not Guilty," *Philadelphia Inquirer*, July 9, 1901; "Negress Tries to End Life," *Evening Public Ledger*, September 29, 1914. Even as race and misogynoir mark deep fault lines in the city's history, Philadelphians across myriad social strata cried foul. The most surprising contingent, in fact, was to be found among the detectives investigating the case. The differences of opinion that strained relationships during the investigation exploded as brothers in blue leveled serious charges. See "Detective War to be Probed," *Philadelphia Inquirer*, December 11, 1901, and "Detective Crawford Has Secret Hearing," *Philadelphia Times*, December 12, 1901. The congregation and her attorney even offered a reward for the suspect Mary described. See the "Reward Offered for Unknown." Wright's case was deferred, and her attorney received a continuance; see "Mary Wright's Trial Postponed," *Philadelphia Inquirer*, October 19, 1901; "Haggenbotham Case Deferred," *Times Philadelphia*, October 19, 1901.

62. "The Weather," *Philadelphia Inquirer*, December 2, 1901. The nature of race and gender, at least publicly, led to a broad collective blindness about the third option in the scenario—that Mary and John were in it together.

63. On Durham's credentials, see "Aid Comes to Mary Wright." For quote, see "Son Denies He Knows of Crime."

64. "Wright Case in Hands of Jury," *Philadelphia Inquirer*, December 7, 1901; "Mary Wright Not Guilty of Murder," *Times Philadelphia*, December 8, 1901.

Chapter 4: Their Games: Black Badgers, Better Days, and the Limits of Fury

1. "A Resort for Rowdies," *Times Philadelphia*, June 16, 1890; "Ulrich Held for Trial," *Times Philadelphia*, June 19, 1890; "Free Fights at Pastime Park," *Philadelphia Inquirer*, June 17, 1890.

2. "A Resort for Rowdies"; "Free Fights at Pastime Park."

3. "The Criminal Courts," *Philadelphia Public Ledger*, September 5, 1890; "Some of the Punishments Inflicted on Offenders," *Times Philadelphia*, September 5, 1890; Lizzie White, "Charged on oath of Jos. H. Shuck with Assault with a knife & carrying a Black Jack." See Philadelphia County Prisoners for Trial Docket, August 26, 1890; "Coming Home from a Picnic," *Philadelphia Inquirer*, September 5, 1890; Quarter Sessions Docket, Comm. v. Lizzie White, No. 55, "Assault with Intent to Kill," True Bill. Several witnesses were listed at the hearing, but I have not been able to discern the nature of the testimony. Bill of Indictment, Quarter Sessions Docket, Comm. v. Lizzie White, No. 55, September Sessions, September 4, 1890. Quarter Sessions Docket, Comm. v. Lizzie White, No. 68, September Sessions, September 4, 1890.

4. Black women being in public itself was not a new phenomenon, but their numbers in the city doubled in the decades after the Civil War and continued to climb, and so, too, did the risks. "These middle-class workers discovered what poor and working-class women had known all along: when women intruded into streets considered men's territory, they compromised their safety and respectability," see Sharon E. Wood, *The Freedom of the Streets: Work, Citizenship, and Sexuality in the Gilded Age* (Chapel Hill: University of North Carolina Press, 2005), 6–7, quote on 7. One of the best discussions about the climate for Black women appears in a 1904 article: see "A Southern Colored Woman" [pseud.], "The Race Problem—An Autobiography," *Independent* March 17, 1904, 587–589, in Gerda Lerner, ed., *Black Women in White America: A Documentary History* (New York: Random House, 1972), 158–159. As Anne Gray Fischer explains, "Women's right to the city has been historically fragile and contested. Across the twentieth century, as Black and white women made distinct claims to public space—to more workplaces, downtown commercial districts, and other formerly white male spaces—police officers adjudicated the deep legacies of the 'public woman' and her associations with commercial sex." See *The Streets Belong to Us: Sex, Race, and Police Power from Segregation to Gentrification* (Chapel Hill: University of North Carolina Press, 2022), 4.

5. "Police Court Chronicle," *Evening Public Ledger*, December 4, 1916. The article says Magistrate Imber released her upon hearing the full details. This story is a curious one, as I could not locate Lukens in the Prisoners for Trial Docket or in other corresponding criminal dockets; still, I am loath to dismiss it because other aspects check out—for example, there was indeed a Magistrate Imber working in 1916, and he adjudicated assault cases involving Black women, but none exactly lined up. I suspect that "Nancy Lukens" was an alias not just because it doesn't appear in the dockets but also because the story says the woman "who gave her name as Nancy Lukens" was glad the charges were dropped. Sharon E. Wood also discusses challenges women faced entering the public sphere, see *Freedom of the Streets*, 6–7.

6. See "The Race Problem—An Autobiography." Wood, *Freedom of the Streets*, chap. 1. .

7. On Anna Julia Cooper, see Brittney Cooper, *Beyond Respectability: The Intellectual Thought of Race Women* (Urbana: University of Illinois Press, 2017), 8. Quarter Sessions Docket, Comm. v. Bessie Elizabeth Minor Banks, No. 307, January 6, 1911, August Sessions, RG 21.5: Notes of Testimony (1877–1915), 132–135; "Held on Murder Charge," *Philadelphia Inquirer*, July 13, 1910; Kali Nicole Gross, "Policing Black Women's and Girls' Bodies in the Carceral United States," *Souls* 20, no. 1 (2018): 1–6.

8. "Quarter Sessions," *Philadelphia Public Ledger*, August 22, 1860. A variation of this quote appears in Roger Lane, *Roots of Violence in Black Philadelphia, 1860–1900* (Cambridge, MA: Harvard University Press, 1986), 107–108.

9. Benjamin Franklin, *Poor Richard's Almanac* (1733; repr. Renaissance Classics, 2012), 17.

10. Lane, *Roots of Violence*, 108.

11. I corrected the spelling in the title; it originally appears as "The Badger Game Once More: A Soap Fat Alley Syren Beguiles Verdant Man," *Times Philadelphia*, November 7, 1892; Robert Carter, who ended up being arrested for the theft, see Quarter Sessions Docket, Comm. v. Robert Carter alias Cuff, No. 318, November Sessions, 1892, "Larceny"; "Sentences Reconsidered: Judge Beitler's Action in the Cases of the Badger Thieves," *Philadelphia Inquirer*, April 3, 1896.

12. Kali Nicole Gross, *Colored Amazons: Crime, Violence, and Black Women in the City of Brotherly Love, 1880–1910* (Durham, NC: Duke University Press, 2006), 77–81; Emily Epstein Landau's work on vice in Storyville notes similar practices, though often sex workers engaged in intercourse and robbed tricks; see *Spectacular Wickedness: Sex, Race, and Memory in Storyville, New Orleans* (Baton Rouge: Louisiana State University Press, 2013), 7, 21–23.

13. Gross, *Colored Amazons*; "Criminal Court Notes," *Times Philadelphia*, June 12, 1901.

14. "Criminal Court Notes"; see Eastern State Penitentiary, Convict Reception Registers, B986, Julia Mason, June 11, 1901.

15. "Eliza Slipped Out," *Philadelphia Inquirer*, October 30, 1899; "Colored Women Worked Badger Game," *Times Philadelphia*, August 12, 1900; "Negress Accused of a Hold Up," *Philadelphia Inquirer*, October 17, 1904; Gross, *Colored Amazons*, 78–79.

16. Eastern State Penitentiary, Convict Reception Registers, A4445, Sarah E. Palmer, August 9, 1888. Gross, *Colored Amazons*, 80. After an earlier failed attempt, Palmer succeeded in taking her own life in 1894; see "Ended Their Lives While Despondent," *Philadelphia Inquirer*, May 20, 1894; "Suicide in Her Cell," *Times Philadelphia*, May 20, 1894.

17. Gross, *Colored Amazons*, 79.

18. Anna Julia Cooper, *A Voice from the South: By a Black Woman of the South*. (Xenia, OH: Aldine Printing House, 1892), 28–29. Brittney Cooper's work explains that among Anna Julia Cooper's key tenets were "1) a commitment to seeing the Black female body as a form of possibility and not a burden, and 2) a commitment to centering the Black female body as a means to cathect Black social thought." See Cooper, *Beyond Respectability*, 3; also see 1–10.

19. Cooper, *A Voice from the South*, 31.

20. Cooper, *Beyond Respectability*, 1–10.

21. "Woman to Answer for Murder," *Times Philadelphia*, March 5, 1900; "Eva Dillon Indicted," *Philadelphia Inquirer*, March 13, 1900; "Eva Dillon Indicted for Murder," *Times Philadelphia*, March 13, 1900.

22. "Woman to Answer for Murder"; "Shot Through the Heart," *Philadelphia Inquirer*, October 15, 1895.

23. Lane, *Roots of Violence*, 111, 113–114.

24. "Shot Through the Heart."

25. "Shot Through the Heart." One account suggests that Green rushed past someone on the sidewalk with the smoking revolver in hand and also says he was arrested before he reached the station; see "Killed One and Wounded Another," *Times Philadelphia*, October 15, 1895.

26. "Fight in a Disorderly House," *Buffalo Enquirer*, October 15, 1895; "Murder in a 'Speak-Easy,'" *Evening Republican*, October 16, 1895. There may have been another man inside the home, too, as the primary witnesses listed in the Prisoners for Trial Docket included a man named William Davis and Bessie Minor; see Prisoners for Trial Docket, October 16, 1895.

27. "Detective and His Gun," *Scranton Tribune*, October 15, 1895; Hahnemann Hospital mentioned in "Will Be Tried for Murder," *Times Philadelphia*, October 17, 1895; "A Colored Sleuth," *Times-Tribune* (Scanton), October 19, 1895.

28. "Green was an agent of the Liquor League and it was supposed that this fact might have had some significance in regard to the murder"; "Shot Through the Heart." Also, "it was learned that Green was a stool-pigeon, in the employ of the State Liquor League" acting as a "spy"; see "Killed One and Wounded Another." Another account described Green as a "colored detective for the State Liquor League," see "Philadelphia Tragedy," *The Wilkes-Barre News*, October 15, 1895.

29. "Green Committed to Prison," *Times Philadelphia*, October 16, 1895.

30. "Green Committed to Prison."

31. After failing to secure a continuance some months later, he went on trial in May 1896. "Will Be Tried for Murder," *Times Philadelphia*, October 17, 1895. In another article, Rose (whose name sometimes appears as *Rosa*) alleges that Better Days and William had an argument; "Green Held to Answer," *Philadelphia Inquirer*, October 16, 1895—"Rosa Simpson testified that Green had quarreled with Mrs. Stewart prior to the tragedy, and that he fired two shots at her."

32. "Green Indicted for Murder," *Times Philadelphia*, November 28, 1895; "To Stand Trial Now," *Times Philadelphia*, May 16, 1896.

33. "Verdicts of Guilt," *Philadelphia Inquirer*, May 27, 1895.

34. Eastern State Penitentiary, Convict Reception Registers, William Green, A8757, May 26, 1896.

35. "Held Responsible," *Philadelphia Inquirer*, March 7, 1900; "Didn't Murder 'Better Days' She Says," *Times Philadelphia*, March 16, 1900; "Both Pleaded Guiltless," *Philadelphia Inquirer*, March 16, 1900.

36. "Guilty of Murder," *Philadelphia Inquirer*, March 27, 1900; "Convicted of Murder in Second Degree," *Times Philadelphia*, March 27, 1900.

37. "Held Responsible," *Philadelphia Inquirer*, March 7, 1900.

38. "Charged with Throwing a Lamp," *Philadelphia Inquirer*, March 3, 1900.

39. Prisoners for Trial Docket, Eva Dillon, March 2, 1900, and March 6, 1900; Quarter Sessions Docket, Comm. v. Eva Dillon, No. 210, March Sessions, 1900, "Murder of Harriet Stewart."

40. "The Criminal Courts."

Chapter 5: Their Dead: The Three Marias and the Babies in the Privy

1. Two papers covered this case—the *Newburyport Daily Herald* and the *Boston Daily Globe*. The *Herald*'s coverage is more extensive and may have served

as the basis for the *Globe*'s smaller article. In both papers, the first name of the young mother is Maria, but the *Herald* lists her last name as "Waters" while the *Globe* lists it as "Walters." I searched census data using both surnames and using the first name "Mary"—a common iteration of Maria for the period. I also combined information from both stories to piece together the narrative. See "Crime's Record.: A Newburyport Man Accused of Causing a Girl's Death; A Domestic Attempts to Destroy her Child—Attempted Infanticide: A Newly Born Child Thrown Into a Vault, and Resuscitated After Two Hours' Exposure—A Strange Case," *Newburyport Daily Herald*, January 13, 1880, and "A Sensation in Newburyport: A Colored Woman Gives Birth to a Child in a Kitchen and Then Tries to Destroy It," *Boston Daily Globe*, January 13, 1880.

2. "Crime's Record"; "A Sensation in Newburyport."

3. "Crime's Record"; "A Sensation in Newburyport."

4. *1880 US Federal Census*, Mary Waters (Year: 1880; Census Place: Philadelphia, Philadelphia, Pennsylvania; Roll: 1169; Page: 106A; Enumeration District: 078), accessed August 8, 2022, via Ancestry.com. On grades of service, see Isabel Eaton, "Special Report on Negro Domestic Service in the Seventh Ward Philadelphia," in W. E. B. Du Bois, *The Philadelphia Negro: A Social Study* (Philadelphia: Publications of the University of Pennsylvania, 1899), 444–455.

5. *1870 US Federal Census*, Mary Waters (Year: 1870; Census Place: Philadelphia Ward 23 District 75, Philadelphia, Pennsylvania; Roll: M593_1410; Page: 155B), accessed August 21, 2022, via Ancestry.com.

6. For early education and literacy of Black people in Philadelphia during and after enslavement, see Du Bois, "Education and Illiteracy," chap. 8 in *Philadelphia Negro*; Gary Nash and Jean R. Soderlund, *Freedom by Degrees: Emancipation in Pennsylvania and Its Aftermath* (New York: Oxford University Press, 1991), 52; Jean Lee Cole, "Information Wanted: 'The Curse of Caste, Minnie's Sacrifice,' and the 'Christian Recorder,'" *African American Review* 40, no. 4 (Winter 2006): 731–733.

7. "Crimes Record"; "A Sensation in Newburyport"; *1880 US Federal Census*, Lewis A. Horton (Year: 1880; Census Place: Newburyport, Essex, Massachusetts; Roll: 532; Page: 476A; Enumeration District: 226), accessed February 22, 2024, via Ancestry.com.

8. "Crimes Record"; "Attempted Infanticide," *Daily Evening Item*, January 13, 1880.

9. "A Sensation in Newburyport." One account says it was a half hour; see "Attempted Infanticide."

10. "A Sensation in Newburyport."

11. "Crimes Record."

12. "The Grand Jury found a bill against Maria Waters, a negress, who attempted to murder her new born [*sic*] babe. It is reported that Maria has skipped"; "Newburyport and Vicinity," *Newburyport Daily Herald*, February 3, 1880.

13. On the tangle of hardships and circumstances driving infanticide, see Sherri Broder, *Tramps, Unfit Mothers, and Neglected Children: Negotiating the Family in Late Nineteenth-Century Philadelphia* (Philadelphia: University of Pennsylvania Press, 2002), chap. 5, especially pages 168–169; Katie M. Hemphill, "'Driven to the Commission of This Crime': Women and Infanticide in Baltimore, 1835–1860," *Journal of the Early Republic* 32, no. 3 (Fall 2012): 437–461; Elna C. Green, "Infanticide and Infant Abandonment in the New South: Richmond, Virginia, 1865–1915," *Journal of Family History* 24, no. 2 (April 1999): 189–199, 201–203; G. S. Rowe, "Infanticide, Its Judicial Resolution, and Criminal Code Revision in Early Pennsylvania," *Proceedings of the American Philosophical Society* 135, no. 2 (June 1991): 200–232; Kali Nicole Gross, "Exploring Crime and Violence in Early-Twentieth-Century Black Women's History," in *Contesting Archives: Finding Women in the Sources*, eds. Nupur Chaudhuri, Sherry J. Katz, and Mary Elizabeth Perry (Chicago: University of Illinois Press, 2010).

14. For a discussion of the history, see Alesha Doan, *Opposition and Intimidation: The Abortion Wars and Strategies of Political Harassment* (Ann Arbor: University of Michigan Press, 2007), chap. 2, especially pages 42–51. I see the woman as resisting the overarching narratives of the time to cleave out their paths. For work on the stigmas surrounding Black mothers see Dorothy Roberts, *Killing the Black Body: Race, Reproduction, and the Meaning of Liberty*, 2nd ed. (New York: Vintage Books, 2017), 8–15.

15. I am making a kind of relational argument to the ways that Orlando Patterson describes how enslavement marked Black people—the idea that it was so dehumanizing that it effectively rendered enslaved people as nonhuman; similarly, for women of this era, the loss of their virginity and subsequent debasement stemming from out-of-wedlock births contributed to a kind of irrevocable scarlet letter on their femininity; this is especially the case for Black women whose womanhood was already largely disallowed and much maligned, that this further fall would effectively place them outside of society and humanity, even among other African Americans. See *Slavery and Social Death: A Comparative Study* (Cambridge, MA: Harvard University Press, 1982), 38–44. Also, seduction had criminal implications in the late nineteenth and early twentieth centuries, as it was described by Cornell's Legal Information Institute: "Seduction, in law, refers to

an act by which a person entices another to have unlawful sexual intercourse with them by means of persuasions, promises, flattery or bribes without using any physical force or violence." "Seduction," Cornell Law School, accessed February 17, 2024, https://www.law.cornell.edu/wex/seduction#:~:text=Seduction%20 was%20a%20crime%20in,or%20otherwise%20unable%20to%20consent. On the perils of being ruined see Sharon E. Wood, *The Freedom of the Streets: Work, Citizenship, and Sexuality in the Gilded Age* (Chapel Hill: University of North Carolina Press, 2005), 7.

16. Jane Edna Hunter, *A Nickel and a Prayer: The Autobiography of Jane Edna Hunter*, ed. Rhondda Robinson Thomas (Morgantown: West Virginia University Press, 2011), 69. She also discusses the dangers and how she was saved when one young man at a party informed her: "'Little girl,' he said, looking seriously at me and speaking somewhat severely, 'you're in the wrong church and the wrong pew. This is not the place for nice girls like you. I want you to meet my mother and sister.'" See page 70.

17. Just as an exemplar, recall the 1886 dustup between Mary Johnson and the father of her child, Edward Sydnor, over money for the child's nurse, which was discussed in the introduction. Also see "A Prisoner Turns the Tables," *Times Philadelphia*, October 28, 1886. Broder, *Tramps, Unfit Mothers*, 174–176.

18. On increased work for white women, see Broder, *Tramps, Unfit Mothers*, 175. On Black women's wages, see Isabel Eaton, "Special Report on Negro Domestic Service in the Seventh Ward Philadelphia," in *Philadelphia Negro*, and see page 289; Kali Nicole Gross, *Colored Amazons: Crime, Violence, and Black Women in the City of Brotherly Love, 1880–1910* (Durham, NC: Duke University Press, 2006), 46–52. Wood, *Freedom of the Streets*, 6–7, 16–17. For Jane Edna Hunter's quote, see Hunter, *Nickel and a Prayer*, 71.

19. Hunter, *Nickel and a Prayer*, 69.

20. Du Bois's discussion and concern about the conjugal condition among African Americans in the Seventh Ward gives us some sense of the surveillance and shame associated with single women and those women who might be single mothers; see "Conjugal Condition," chap. 6 in *Philadelphia Negro*. Jane Edna Hunter's narrative also gives us an insight into the ways these issues impacted Black women and girls in the South, as well as their families; see Hunter, "Early Days in Cleveland," chap. 6 in *Nickel and a Prayer*, but these concerns for women had national implications. Also see Hazel V. Carby, "Policing the Black Woman's Body in an Urban Context," *Critical Inquiry* 18, no. 4 (1992): 738–755. Regina Kunzel's important work documents the rhetoric as well as the ways that white evangelical reformers aimed to push back against it. She includes a vital

discussion about the melodramatic scripts associated with white women who had been seduced and then abandoned. At the same time, though, Kunzel shows how reformers sometimes transformed the narratives into "a politicized discourse to express anger at male sexual license and to denounce the injustices of the sexual double standard, evangelical women railed against the convention that labeled women 'fallen,' while absolving men of all guilt." See Regina Kunzel, *Fallen Women, Problem Girls: Unmarried Mothers and the Professionalization of Social Work, 1890–1945* (New Haven, CT: Yale University Press, 1995), 21–22, especially 23. The metaphors reformers used related to the plight of unmarried mothers (e.g., women basically standing on "cliff edges," "floods," and "slippery slopes") did contribute to the divide between notions of good and bad women, but at the same time, I agree that they also underscored the precarity of respectability and sexual virtue for women. See Kunzel, *Fallen Women*, 19.

21. Black women such as Annie Cutler described themselves as "ruined" after their loss of virginity to men who did not marry them—"She told [Magistrate Pole] she had shot Knight because he had ruined her and then got married"; see "Annie Cutler in Court," *Times Philadelphia*, May 19, 1885. But also important is that this notion of women being ruined by premarital sex is long rooted in American history and religious traditions; beliefs can be spied beginning in the colonial era (and arguably right up until now)—for historical examples of this, see John D'Emilio and Estelle B. Freedman, *Intimate Matters: A History of Sexuality in America* (New York: Harper & Row Publishers, 1988), 22; for white slavery scares and notions of sexual ruin, see 208–209. Sharon Wood explained that for women and men, respectability was a kind of capital, "the greater the investment, the richer the social and employment opportunities." Although primarily focused on white Americans, many African Americans also held such ideals. She notes that "a 'ruined' woman had no recourse but the brothel. Reputation was something no woman risked lightly." Wood, *Freedom of the Streets*, 7.

22. Deborah Gray White, "Jezebel and Mammy: The Mythology of Female Slavery," chap. 1 in *Ar'n't I a Woman?: Female Slaves in the Plantation South* (New York: W. W. Norton, 1987); Rachel Feinstein, *When Rape Was Legal: The Untold History of Sexual Violence During Slavery* (New York: Routledge, 2019), 74–77.

23. Carby, "Policing the Black Woman's Body in an Urban Context"; Gross, *Colored Amazons*, 64–65; Du Bois, *Philadelphia Negro*, chap. 6, quote on 67–68; Cheryl D. Hicks, *Talk with You Like a Woman: African American Women, Justice, and Reform in New York, 1890–1935* (Chapel Hill: University of North Carolina Press, 2010), 7–13, 54, and chap. 3, "I Want to Save These Girls: Single Black Women and Their Protectors, 1895–1911."

24. "City Notes," *Times Philadelphia*, July 3, 1890; "Her Body Identified," *Philadelphia Inquirer*, July 3, 1890. Newspapers list him, and there is an Edward F. Waters in the 1900 census who was born in Maryland, but it's hard to know whether it is the same uncle, as many Black folks migrated from Maryland to Philadelphia especially. Still, see *US Federal Census* (Year: 1900; Census Place: Philadelphia Ward 26, Philadelphia, Pennsylvania; Roll: 1468; Page: 7; Enumeration District: 0636; FHL microfilm: 1241468), accessed via Ancestry.com.

25. "Died from Natural Causes," *Times Philadelphia*, July 4, 1890; "Maria Waters' Death," *Philadelphia Inquirer*, July 4, 1890. W. B. Vallance wrote, "PENNYROYAL has long had a reputation as an abortifacient, although its action is known to be unpredictable and even dangerous. In the following case it produced abortion, vaginal bleeding, haemolytic anaemia, and acute tubular necrosis of the kidney, with death from uraemia"; see "Pennyroyal Poisoning: A Fatal Case," *Lancet* 269, no. 6895 (1955): 850. Even though the authors dismiss the herb's ability to induce abortion as "folklore medicine," they nonetheless report on the dangerous side effects of its usage; see John B. Sullivan, Barry Rumack, and Harold Thomas, "Pennyroyal Oil Poisoning and Hepatotoxicity," *Journal of the American Medical Association* 242, no. 26 (1979): 2873–2874.

26. "Died from Natural Causes"; "Maria Waters' Death."

27. "Died from Natural Causes"; "Maria Waters' Death."

28. The papers list his name in a variety of ways; however, the city directory lists a Miles W. Nickoles, a physician at 1409 Gulielma Street, in Philadelphia, Pennsylvania, where he resided in 1887. See *Gopsill's Philadelphia City Directory for 1887* (Philadelphia, PA: James Gopsill's Sons, 1887); Eastern State Penitentiary, Convict Reception Registers, 1842–1929, Miles W. Nickoles, B36, January 20, 1899—this record also mentions his prior at the Philadelphia County Prison; Eastern State Penitentiary, Convict Reception Registers, 1842–1929, Miles W. Nickoles, A6324, May 31, 1892. For Virginia Johnson details, see "A Doctor Seriously Charged," *Philadelphia Inquirer*, May 15, 1892, and "A Warrant for a Colored Doctor," *Times Philadelphia*, May 15, 1892. I rounded the wall height up; technically, it is twenty-seven feet high. See *Description of the Eastern State Penitentiary of Pennsylvania* (Philadelphia: C. G. Childs, Engraver, 1829), 4.

29. For the death of Maria Harris (or "Hains" as the *Times* reported), see "Held by the Coroner," *Philadelphia Inquirer*, April 28, 1887, and "Doctors in Trouble," *Times Philadelphia*, April 28, 1887.

30. "Held by the Coroner"; "Doctors in Trouble."

31. "Died from Malpractice," *Times Philadelphia*, January 2, 1896; "Miss Jenkins died from criminal malpractice on Sunday night. It was testified that a still-born

child was thrown into a cesspool of the house by her sister Sarah, who admitted that it was her sister's child." See "Dr. Reed Committed: The Coroner's Jury Find Him Guilty of Causing Emma Jenkins' Death," *Times Philadelphia*, May 2, 1888. Rachel Jackson's death is mentioned at the end of an article titled "Miss Scholl's Sad Death," *Times Philadelphia*, January 18, 1884. "Dr. Fisher Again Accused," *Times Philadelphia*, May 8, 1896. "Homicide: The Bloody Deaths of a Decade," *Philadelphia Inquirer*, June 1, 1882—notes that thirty-six women died as a result of malpractice between 1871 and 1881; a man and woman were charged in the "abortion case of Annie Dean," in "The Dean Malpractice Case," *Times Philadelphia*, October 12, 1880. Also, the following listing isn't meant to be exhaustive, but I did want to provide some additional examples across the period of study of women sentenced for crimes such as infanticide, concealing infant deaths, and abortion that appear in the Female Discharge Docket, Philadelphia County Prison Register: Elizbeth McCresson, No. 284, "Concealing Death of Bastard," November 3, 1893, two years (white); Emma Spencer, No. 387, "Abortion," December 14, 1894, two years (Black); Sentenced (Sent.)., Emma Dicks, "Abortion," December 24, 1897, two years (white); Anna Simmons, No. 777, "Abortion," October 4, 1900, one year (white); Sent., Gertrude Regan, "Abandoning an Infant," May 4, 1905, three months (white); Minnie Fillburn, No. 1208, "Abortion," September 28, 1905, two years (white); Carrie Blanchard, No. 1347, "Abortion," June 15, 1907, two years (Black); Annie Schoenborn, No. 1480, "Abortion," January 15, 1909, twenty months (white); Marion Lovey, No. 1713, "Abortion," June 26, 1912, one year (white); Sent., Octavia Winbush, "Concealing Death of Bastard," September 24, 1913, six months (Black); Mary Satch, No. 1874, "Abortion," April 13, 1915, six months (white).

32. "Alleged Abortion Causes Mother's Death," *Philadelphia Tribune*, November 15, 1928.

33. In the colonial era, men and women would be punished harshly for bastardy and fornication; however, by the late nineteenth century, policing of such crimes shifted, and women primarily bore the brunt of stigmas and reproach; see D'Emilio and Freedman, *Intimate Matters*, 8–13, 32–35. Lawrence M. Friedman's work also helps map shifts in the punishment of moral crimes, see *Crime and Punishment in American History* (New York: Basic Books, 1993), 125–132. On page 139, he writes, "Laws against adultery and fornication were certainly not rigorously enforced. Arrests were, at most, sporadic."

34. "Charged with Infanticide. A Young Colored Woman Arrested for Killing Her Newly-Born Child," *Times Philadelphia*, August 4, 1887.

35. "Charged with Infanticide"; "Many Homicide Cases," *Times Philadelphia*, October 7, 1887. Philadelphia County Prisoners for Trial Docket, B, Henrietta

Thompson, August 2, 1887, "Charged on Oath of Special Officer Thos. Alexander with causing the death of her child."

36. "Charged with Infanticide."

37. "Charged with Infanticide."

38. See Quarter Sessions Docket, Comm. v. Henrietta Thompson, No. 76, October Sessions, 1887.

39. "Acquitted of Infanticide," *Times Philadelphia*, November 3, 1887.

40. "Acquitted of Infanticide."

41. "Acquitted of Infanticide."

42. Thompson was received at the Philadelphia Country Prison on August 6 and discharged at court on November 2; see Philadelphia County Prison Commitment Docket, Female, August 1886.

43. Michel-Rolph Trouillot, *Silencing the Past: Power and the Production of History* (Boston: Beacon Press, 1995); see the entire first chapter, "The Power in the Story," but especially page 26, where he explains, "Silences enter the process of historical production at four crucial moments: the moment of fact creation (the making of *sources*); the moment of fact assembly (the making of *archives*); the moment of fact retrieval (the making of *narratives*); and the moment of retrospective significance (the making of *history* in the final instance)." Saidiya Hartman discusses the frustrating limitations of the archive in "Venus in Two Acts," *Small Axe: A Caribbean Journal of Criticism* 12, no. 2 (2008): 1–14. She also writes, "Every historian of the multitude, the dispossessed, the subaltern, and the enslaved is forced to grapple with the power and authority of the archive and the limits it sets on what can be known, whose perspective matters, and who is endowed with the gravity and authority of historical actor." See Saidiya Hartman, "A Note on Method" in *Wayward Lives: Beautiful Experiments: Intimate Histories of Social Upheaval* (New York: W. W. Norton, 2019); Gross, *Colored Amazons*, 4–6; Talitha L. LeFlouria, *Chained in Silence: Black Women and Convict Labor in the New South* (Chapel Hill: University of North Carolina Press, 2015), 17; Sarah Haley, *No Mercy Here* (Chapel Hill: University of North Carolina Press, 2016); LaShawn Harris, *Sex Workers, Psychics, and Numbers Runners* (Urbana: University of Illinois Press, 2016). See also Marisa Fuentes, *Dispossessed Lives: Enslaved Women, Violence, and the Archive* (Philadelphia: University of Pennsylvania Press, 2016), 1–6; Aisha Finch, *Rethinking Slave Rebellions in Cuba* (Chapel Hill: University of North Carolina, 2015), chap. 5.

44. Although her work examines these issues in an earlier period, G. S. Rowe's conclusions are helpful for understanding some of the attitudes and outcomes in the late nineteenth and early twentieth centuries; see "Infanticide, Its Juridical Resolution, and Criminal Code Revision in Early Pennsylvania"; also see Gross, "Exploring

Crime and Violence." At the same time, even as these acquittals occurred, there are plenty of examples of women who were convicted and sentenced, see fn31. Further, Black women not benefiting from chivalry in the legal system is well documented, but some of the most helpful texts for me have been Nicole Hahn Rafter's discussion in *Partial Justice: Women in State Prisons, 1800–1935* (Boston: Northeastern University Press, 1985), 134, 155; Hicks, "A Rather Bright and Good-Looking Colored Girl: Black Women's Sexuality, 'Harmful Intimacy,' and Attempts to Regulate Desire, 1917–1928," chap. 7 in *Talk with You Like a Woman*; Haley, "Carceral Constructions of Black Female Deviance," chap. 1 in *No Mercy Here*, especially the varied, sickening violations of Eliza Cobb and the comparison of her case with that of a white woman named Martha Gault, 17–26.

45. "'Driven to the Commission of This Crime,'" 449; Green, "Infanticide and Infant Abandonment in the New South," 202–203; Rowe discusses fluctuations in conviction rates but notes that sympathy and compassion factored into verdicts as well, "Infanticide in Early Pennsylvania," 218, 220–221. I also note how juries seemed to seize on any indication of accidental suffocation or stillbirth to ignore charges or acquit women, see "Exploring Crime and Violence," 66–67. Broder, *Tramps, Unfit Mothers*, 161.

46. Sherri Broder's work offers an important, nuanced discussion about baby farms and the ways that race played a central role in the discourse surrounding them; but also, her work shows how the higher rates of Black infant mortality reflected Black women's poverty as well as the fact that greater numbers of Black women worked outside the home and were more reliant on such institutions. See Broder, *Tramps, Unfit Mothers*, 159—really the entirety of Chapter 5, "Murderous Mothers or Mercenary Baby Farmers?" I also agree with Broder when she writes on page 166, "Infanticide and abandonment can be viewed as reproductive strategies to avoid motherhood used chiefly by women lacking social and/or economic resources who believed they had no viable alternative" and also that "even more than other reproductive strategies, they were practiced in secret, not only because discovery could lead to criminal prosecution and popular opprobrium, but because when the motive was to preserve a single mother's reputation and her family's honor, secrecy was itself the crime's intent." However, we cannot ignore/disallow for the reality that those strategies also included women's own eruptions of rage and frustration at their situations and the unwanted fetuses/infants, particularly as there were places such as Haven (page 181), adoption arrangements, and so on.

47. The definition of the baby farms appears in a special Philadelphia dispatch to the *Tribune*. See "Baby-Farming," *Chicago Tribune*, June 24, 1877.

48. "To Dig Up Yard of Alleged Baby Farm," *Philadelphia Inquirer*, July 21, 1914. For his first name, see Frank A. Paul, "Detective," in 1909, *U.S., City Directories, 1822–1995* [database online]. Lehi, UT: Ancestry.com Operations, Inc., 2011.

49. "Negress Conducted 'Baby-Farm,' Charge," *Philadelphia Inquirer*, July 29, 1914. The account initially reported six infants were found, one dead, and four died later; however Burke was only charged with the three deaths.

50. "Negress Conducted 'Baby-Farm,' Charge."

51. "Negress Conducted 'Baby-Farm,' Charge."

52. Quarter Sessions Docket, Comm. v. Mattie Burke, No. 293, September Sessions, 1914, "Voluntary manslaughter causing death of Robert Washington," November 18, 1914, "Not guilty"; Quarter Sessions Docket, Comm. v. Mattie Burke, No. 294, September Sessions, 1914, "Voluntary manslaughter causing death of Charles Turner," October 28, 1914, the court mandated that she "undergo imprisonment at the Philadelphia County Prison for the term of eight months," plus the costs of court; Quarter Sessions Docket, Comm. v. Mattie Burke, No. 293 (295), September Sessions, 1914, "Voluntary manslaughter causing death of Hope Dickerson," November 18, 1914, "Not guilty."

53. Broder's work discusses how Black women were denied licenses to run legal baby farms, as well as how the press sensationalized narratives that also fed into and reflected cultural anxieties about the establishments; she also discusses how in some cases desperate mothers abandoned infants at baby farms, putting proprietresses in an awkward position. See *Tramps, Unfit Mothers*: on the women who deserted babies in farms, 181–182; on licensing, see 186–188; on narratives and media tropes, see 191–194.

54. "Baby-Farming."

55. "Baby-Murder Syndicate: Many Cases Are Being Investigated in Philadelphia," *Baltimore Sun*, February 26, 1904.

56. "Baby-Murder Syndicate."

57. "Baby-Murder Syndicate."

58. Prisoners for Trial Docket, B, Ida Hitchens, October 16, 1886. Ida was committed on October 16 and discharged November 16, 1886; see Prison Commitment Docket, Female, Ida Hitchens.

59. The language on the indictment is confusing and difficult to interpret, as parts are a standard form and other details were written by hand. See Bills of Indictment, Comm. v. Isaac R. Hall alias Lady Washington, 1309 Germantown Avenue, No. 328, "Sodomy and Buggery"; Quarter Sessions Court Docket, Comm. v. Isaac R. Hall alias Lady Washington, No. 328, May Sessions, 1881, May 25, 1881, "Sodomy and Buggery," True Bill; Quarter Sessions

Court Docket, Comm. v. H. C. Campbell, No. 329, May 25, 1881, "Sodomy and Buggery," True Bill, 377, "May 27th, 1881 Sentence suspended and defendant discharged"; "Criminal Court Notes," *Philadelphia Inquirer*, May 26, 1881. Lady Washington's case went before the Board of Pardons in 1884, to no avail; see "Board of Pardons," *Philadelphia Inquirer*, June 18, 1884; "The Board of Pardons," *Times Philadelphia*, December 17, 1884: "Pardon recommendations were refused in the cases of Isaac R. Hall, alias Lady Washington, of Philadelphia; Thomas Barrett, murder in the second degree, Lackawanna."

60. For details about Hampton, see Du Bois, *Philadelphia Negro*, map of the Seventh Ward after page 60. For Brinton Street, see "Map of Philadelphia [horse car routes], 1875," Free Library of Philadelphia, https://libwww.freelibrary.org /digital/item/zoom/65449.

61. "Dr. Pennington Again Arrested," *Times Philadelphia*, January 3, 1893. Press coverage listed his name as "Ezetule Scott," but he appears in the Quarter Sessions Docket, Comm. v. Ezekiel Scott, No. 374, February Sessions, 1893, "Abortion—Ignored." Prisoners for Trial Docket, Amanda Pennington, January 3, 1893, "Charged on Oath of Mary Johnson with Attempt to procure an abortion."

62. "Dr. Pennington Again Arrested." Quote about suffering for the past month from "Again Under Arrest: Mrs. Amanda Pennington Charged with Another Serious Crime and Sent to Jail," *Philadelphia Inquirer*, January 3, 1983. Dr. Pennington was indicted but was found not guilty; see Quarter Sessions Docket, Comm. v. Amanda Pennington, No. 625, January Sessions, 1893.

63. For not affording the bail, see "Again Under Arrest." Although one account reported that neither had posted bail, the commitment docket shows that she was received and discharged on January 3, 1893; see Philadelphia County Prison Commitment Docket, Female, Amanda Pennington, 1893.

64. Dr. Pennington was indicted but was found not guilty, see Comm. v. Pennington, No. 625; Comm. v. Scott, No. 374.

65. This refers to the study about lynching conducted by legendary activist Ida B. Wells-Barnett. Her work exposed racist mob violence, a violence predominantly enacted against Black men, even though Black women were also victims of lynching. Still, her publications and the campaign against lynching gave us language and a critical framework to analyze ongoing instances of racist violence against Black people—for example, people routinely refer to the murders of Emmett Till and George Floyd as modern-day lynchings. Conversely, the kinds of brutality and bloody violences encapsulated in the lives of Black women and girls tends to happen in ways that are more shrouded in secrecy—often because of where the things happen and also because the women carry undue shame; being

raped and/or in trouble are violences visited upon Black womanhood indiscriminately, yet we don't quite have a "red record" culturally to really document or refer to it in quite the same ways. See Ida B. Wells-Barnett, *A Red Record: Tabulated Statistics and Alleged Causes of Lynchings in the United States, 1892–1893–1894* (Chicago: Donohue & Henneberry, 1895). For work on Black women and lynching, see Crystal Feimster, *Southern Horrors: Women and the Politics of Rape and Lynching* (Cambridge, MA: Harvard University Press, 2009), chap. 6.

Conclusion

1. Nikki M. Taylor, *Brooding Over Bloody Revenge: Enslaved Women's Lethal Resistance* (Cambridge: Cambridge University Press, 2023)—the entire book is dedicated to this subject. Wilma King, "'Mad' Enough to Kill: Enslaved Women, Murder, and Southern Courts," *Journal of African American History* 92, no. 1 (Winter 2007).

2. Mesfin Fekadu, "Will Cardi B, Under Fire for Foul Past, Get Past the Moment?," Associated Press, March 28, 2019, https://apnews.com/article /music-ap-top-news-hip-hop-and-rap-crime-entertainment-da3e3b8911634 823975257a5df4fc11c; "Cardi B Explains Why She 'Drugged and Robbed' Men," *BBC News*, March 27, 2019, https://www.bbc.com/news/entertainment-arts -47718477; Alyssa Bailey, "Cardi B Admits to Drugging and Robbing Men: 'I Have a Past That I Can't Change. We All Do,'" *Elle*, March 26, 2019, https:// www.elle.com/culture/celebrities/a26950832/cardi-b-drugging-robbing -men-response/; Monica Barton, "Cardi B Confesses She Used to Drug and Rob Men When She Was a Stripper, Stands by It," Newshub, March 26, 2019, https:// www.newshub.co.nz/home/entertainment/2019/03/cardi-b-confesses-she -used-to-drug-and-rob-men-when-she-was-a-stripper-stands-by-it.html.

3. Charlie Savage, "Bill Cosby's Release from Prison, Explained," *New York Times*, July 1, 2021, updated October 14, 2021, accessed February 19, 2024, https://www.nytimes.com/2021/07/01/arts/television/bill-cosby -conviction-overturned-why.html; "He was convicted in September on three counts of producing child pornography and three counts of enticing a minor to engage in sexual activity"; see Diane Pathieu and Leah Hope, "R. Kelly Sentenced to 20 Years in Prison in Chicago Federal Sex Crimes Case," ABC7 Eye Witness News, accessed February 19, 2024, https://abc7chicago .com/r-kelly-news-charges-chicago-sentence/12864908/. Also see "R. Kelly will serve a total of 31 years in prison for child pornography, racketeering and sex trafficking convictions, a judge in Illinois decided Thursday," see *Forbes*, February 23, 2024, accessed February 23, 2024, https://www.forbes.com/sites/conor

murray/2023/02/23/r-kelly-sentenced-again-heres-an-overview-of-the-charges
-and-allegations-against-him/?sh=7b98f27c181d.

4. Maiysha Kai, "#SurvivingCardiB? Predation Is a Genderless Crime, but
Cardi B Drugging and Robbing Men Is Not Rape," *The Root*, March 26, 2019,
https://www.theroot.com/survivingcardib-predation-is-a-genderless-crime
-but-1833583404. In this clip, she talks about how "playing the game" saved
her: see "Cardi B: I Became a Stripper to Escape Domestic Violence," YouTube
video, 6:26, posted by "djvlad," January 12, 2016, https://www.youtube.com
/watch?v=vzfcNl-o9bI; also see "It's Time to Pay Black Women What They're
Owed," National Women's Law Center, accessed February 15, 2024, https://nwlc
.org/resource/black-womens-equal-pay-day-factsheet/.

5. For data on bias crimes in the United States, see "2021 Hate Crime
Statistics," United States Department of Justice, https://www.justice.gov
/hatecrimes/hate-crime-statistics, and for concerns that the data might be
masking even more instances of bias crimes, see "Analysts Say Hate Crimes
Are Increasing but That's Not Reflected in FBI Data," NPR, https://www.npr
.org/2022/12/26/1145509230/analysts-say-hate-crimes-are-increasing-but-thats
-not-reflected-in-fbi-data. Joshua Zeitz makes reference to the pundits' refrain and
shows examples in our history that relate to the current times: see "History Dept.:
Where Will This Political Violence Lead? Look to the 1850s," *Politico*, October 29, 2022, accessed February 16, 2023, https://www.politico.com/news/mag
azine/2022/10/29/political-violence-1850s-paul-pelosi-00064107. In response
to assault on the Capitol, see "Editorial: A sad day for this nation. This is not who
we are," *Post and Courier*, January 2, 2021, updated January 3, 2021, https://www
.postandcourier.com/opinion/editorials/editorial-a-sad-day-for-this-nation-this
-is-not-who-we-are/article_05941878-5061-11eb-b387-bf15b6fa8ee0.html. In
advance of midterm elections, President Biden appealed to voters, stating that
too many things going on in our country related to the division and extremism
were "not normal"; see Kevin Liptak, Phil Mattingly, and Kaitlan Collins, "Biden
Warns Trump and His Closest Followers Are Trying to Undermine American Democracy in Combative Speech," CNN, September 1, 2022, accessed
February 16, 2023, https://www.cnn.com/2022/09/01/politics/joe-biden
-democracy-speech/index.html. In his remarks during the January 6 hear-
ings, US representative from California Adam Schiff said, "In city councils and town councils, on school boards and election boards, from the
Congress to the courts, dedicated public servants are leaving their posts
because of death threats to them and to their families. This is not who we are";
see "Here's Every Word from the Fourth Jan. 6th Committee Hearing on Its

Investigation," NPR, June 21, 2022, accessed February 16, 2023, https://www.npr .org/2022/06/21/1105848096/jan-6-committee-hearing-transcript. For works related to racist violence in American history, Carol Anderson's powerful scholarship is a must-read: see *White Rage: The Unspoken Truth of Our Racial Divide* (New York: Bloomsbury, 2016) and *The Second: Race and Guns in a Fatally Unequal America* (New York: Bloomsbury, 2021); Kidada E. Williams's important work covers the violence visited upon African Americans during Reconstruction: see *I Saw Death Coming: A History of Terror and Survival in the War Against Reconstruction* (New York: Bloomsbury, 2023) and *They Left Great Marks on Me: African American Testimonies of Racial Violence from Emancipation to World War I* (New York: New York University Press, 2012). Also see Hannah Rosen's evocative book, *Terror in the Heart of Freedom: Citizenship, Sexual Violence, the Meaning of Race in the Postemancipation South* (Chapel Hill: University of North Carolina Press, 2009).

6. Todd Feurer and Charlie De Mar, "Charges Dropped Against Mother and Son in Deadly West Pullman Shooting; Video Shows Man Punching Woman," 2 CBS News Chicago, June 27, 2023, accessed October 20, 2023, https://www.cbsnews .com/chicago/news/charges-dropped-carlishia-hood-son-murder-jeremy-brown/.

7. Maham Javaid and Kim Bellware, "She Miscarried in Her Bathroom. Now She's Charged with Abuse of a Corpse," *Washington Post*, December 15, 2023, https://www.washingtonpost.com/nation/2023/12/15/ohio-woman -miscarriage-abuse-of-corpse-grand-jury/. Almost equally disturbing is the notion that the state's wishes take precedence over that of women. As an example, on May 24, 2023, shortly after his state voted to restrict abortion at six weeks, South Carolina state senator Tom Davis said: "At some point, the right of the state to see the unborn child born does take precedence over the woman's right to her body." Madelon Bloom, "In South Carolina, Women Are Subjugated to the State," *Washington Post*, May 29, 2023, https://www.washingtonpost.com /opinions/2023/05/29/south-carolina-women-subjugation/. Also see Kylie Cheung, "Alabama Jailed Pregnant Woman for Months, Made Her Sleep on Floor Over Alleged Marijuana Use," Jezebel, September 7, 2022, accessed February 17, 2023, https://jezebel.com/alabama-jailed-pregnant-woman-for-months -made-her-slee-1849507595; Decca Muldowney, "Alabama Officials Back Down on Jailing Pregnant Women to 'Protect' Fetuses," Daily Beast, September 26, 2022, accessed February 17, 2023, https://www.thedailybeast.com/five-pregnant -woman-who-were-jailed-in-etowah-county-alabama-to-protect-their-fetuses -are-released; Marisa Iati, "Pregnant Women Were Jailed over Drug Use to Protect Fetuses, County Says," *Washington Post*, September 8, 2022, accessed February 17, 2023, https://www.washingtonpost.com/nation/2022/09/08 /pregnant-women-drugs-jail/.

INDEX

Abolition, 8, 14
abolitionists, 8, 34, 36, 40
the hazy days of, 135
legacy in Pennsylvania, 56
abortion, 20
as an act of agency and control,
157–158
criminalization of, 165
lack of justice for failed abortions,
155–156
women's deaths resulting from,
142–144, 147–148, 152–153
See also infanticide
acquittals
for abortion charges after a failed
procedure, 156–157
Black badger thieves targeting
white men, 115–117
Black women's fight against
racism and white people's
perceptions, 82
factors in Lillie Fisher's, 84–85
for infanticide, 146–149
in the murder of Sarah
Haggenbotham, 102–105, 107
state negligence with Black
women's safety, 52–54
Adams, Robert, Jr.
dueling, 30–31
wife-beating laws, 36–40, 47

adultery
Annie Cutler's murder of her lover,
32–34
charging Mary Johnson's
abuser, 3–6
the lack of retributive justice for
women involved in, 154–157
shooting at a lover's other woman,
49–52
African Methodist Episcopal Church,
18–19
agency
abortion as an act of agency and
control, 157–158
the agency and liberation of Black
women, 121–122
alcohol
addictions and mental state of John
Haggenbotham, 97–98
debauchery at political clubs, 80
increasing domestic violence,
78–79
leading to domestic violence and
murder, 27–28
murder by a State Liquor League
operative, 123–128
vice and mayhem in Pastime Park,
109–111
Allen, Regulus, 61
Anderson, Laura, 50–53

Index

Andrews, Thomas, 98
anger: defining and characterizing vengeance feminism, 12–14. *See also* fury
angry Black woman trope, 10–11
assault and battery, 46
  beating and murder of Sarah Haggenbotham, 89–94, 96
  beatings by Black badger thieves, 120
  men accosting Black women in the streets, 113
  rape of enslaved Black women, 56
  sentencing Black men for assaulting Black women, 84–85
  vengeance on a lover's other woman, 51–53
  wife beating and, 40

baby farms, 149–152
Badaracka, Dido, 34–35
badger thieves
  Cardi B's acts against men, 160
  escaping punishment for, 116–117
  expressions of power, 130–131
  feminist perspective of, 122–123
  history of, 114–115
  life journeys of, 119–120
  profits from, 117–118
  as response to racialized sexual harassment, 112
  serial offenses, 115–116, 118–119
Banks, Bessie, 114
Barrett, Joseph R., 84–85
Barrett, Margaret, 84–85
beatings. *See* partner abuse and violence
betrayal. *See* infidelity

Better Days (Harriet Stewart), 109(quote), 112, 123–130
bias crimes, 162–163
Bibb, Henry, 55–56
Black Bess, 119
Black Macho and the Myth of the Superwoman (Wallace), 13
Black men and women
  abolitionists, 35
  disproportionate representation in prison, 67–68
  employment discrimination, 139
  housing costs, 139–140
  inequities in the rape laws, 58
  justice system's devaluing of Black men's lives, 82, 85
  low wages, wage disparities, 117, 161
  neighborhoods, the Seventh Ward, 45, 51, 76, 109, 140, 142, 155
  political actors, 7, 8, 80–82, 147
  racial profiling, 65–67
  separate Negro Courts, 57
  sexual stereotypes, 54–56
  sexual stereotypes about Black women, 60, 141
  suffrage, 35–36, 40–41
  as *unrapeable*, 60, 141
  as victims of white violence, 54–56, 58, 60–62, 113–114
blackjacks, 27–28, 111–112, 130–131
Blackston, John, 24–25
Blankenburg, Rudolph, 81
Bond, Thomas, 76–77
Bregy, Frank, 49(quote), 71–72
brick: the beating and murder of Sarah Haggenbotham, 89–93, 96

Brooding Over Bloody Revenge (Taylor), 13

Brooklyn Citizen newspaper, 98

Brooks, Ivan, 125, 127

Brooks, Mamie, 50–53

Brooks, W. H., 142

Brown, Jeremy, 163–164

Brown, William, 24

Burke, Mattie, 150–151

Caldwell, Robert, 89, 101

Campbell, H. C., 153–154

Campbell, William
death by stabbing, 75–77
Lillie Fisher's acquittal for the murder of, 84–85
political connections, 79–82
various accounts of the stabbing of, 78–79

Cardi B, 160–161

Carothers, Mary, 58–59

celebrity crimes, 160–161

Chesnut, Mary Boykin, 61

child support motivating partner abuse, 4–6

children
baby farms, 149–152
Black feminism addressing children's needs, 14
murder of white children by enslaved Black women, 58–59
resulting from the rape of enslaved Black women, 54–56
violence over child support payments, 4–5
white women's views of enslaved Black women and, 61–62
See also infanticide; reproduction

churches. *See* religious organizations and orders

Citizens' Suffrage Association, 36, 44, 47

civil rights movement and era: gang rape of a Black woman, 62

class stratification
the murder of Sarah Haggenbotham, 87–105
violence intersecting race and, 47

Clay, Edward, 18

Cloe (enslaved teenager), 58–59

collective fury of Black women, 120–122

colonial era
origins of vengeance feminism, 53–54
the rape of enslaved Black women, 54–58

confessions, extorting, 66–67

Cooper, Anna Julia, 113–114, 120–122

Cooper, Brittney, 14

corruption
blaming white men's moral turpitude on Black women, 61–62
in political clubs, 80–82

Cosby, Bill, 160

Crawford, Mary, 45–48

"crime class," Philadelphia's, 65–66

criminal malpractice, abortion as, 143–144

culture: enslavement and the maligning of Black women, 54

Cutler, Annie, 26, 32–34, 41–47

Index

Davis, Annie, 69

Davis, Edward M., 40–41

Davis, Martha, 71–72

death penalty

    calls for hanging immoral women, 43–44

    enslaved Black women fighting back, 60

    the murder of Sarah Haggenbotham, 93–94

    murder of white children by an enslaved Black woman, 58–59

    for rape by Black men, 58

deaths

    fire resulting from an argument, 123–124, 129–130

    Philadelphia's history of police violence, 18

    women's deaths resulting from abortions, 142–145, 147–148, 152–153

    See also hangings; infanticide; murder

democracy, contemporary feminism and, 163

Dickerson, Hope, 150–151

Dillon, Eva, 112, 128–130

disorderly houses, 24–25

domestic service

    concealing the birth of a baby, 133–137

    the dangers of walking Philadelphia streets, 112–113

    Mary Wright and the murder of Sarah Haggenbotham, 89–105

    poisoning of white people by a Black servant, 71–72

post-emancipation migration of Black women, 64–67

sources of weapons, 4

domestic violence. *See* partner abuse and violence

drugs

    baby farm practices, 149–150

    celebrity crimes, 160–161

    John Haggenbotham's addictions, 97–98, 105

Du Bois, W. E. B., 133 (quote)

    honor of Black people, 26–27

    Philadelphia's history, 19

    on political clubs, 80–81

    stigma associated with unwed motherhood, 141

dueling furies violence, 129–130

duels, 30–31

Durham, John, 103–104

Eastern State Penitentiary, 45, 70, 118–119, 128, 143, 154

Elliott, Josiah, 24

Eloquent Rage: A Black Feminist Discovers Her Superpower (Cooper), 14

Fabrizio, Domenico, 25

family

    the consequences of unwanted pregnancies, 138–140

    sharing the experience of Black womanhood, 167–168

    treatment of enslaved Black women, 55–56

    unwed mothers and, 134–135

    wife-beating laws, 40

Index

femininity, Black
  Black women embracing, 6–7
  Black women navigating the legal system, 68–69, 159
  cultural history of white perceptions of, 19–20
  schism over Black women's vengeance against abusers, 44–45
feminism, defining, 7–8
Ferner, Clara, 97–100, 103, 104(fig.)
Fifteenth Amendment rights, 40–41
fire resulting from an argument, 123–124, 129–130
Fisher, Lillie, 75–82, 84–85, 105–106
food insecurity, 14
Forten, James, 35
fortuity, 85
Franklin, Benjamin, 116
Franklin, Josephine, 119
fury
  as basis of Black vengeance feminism, 9
  collective fury of Black women, 120–122
  defining and characterizing vengeance feminism, 12
  dueling furies violence, 129–130
  infanticide as expression of, 137–138

Gardner, Henry, 90
George v. State, 56
Geyer, Frank, 103
Gibbs, Mary, 117
Graham, George S., 100
Graves, James, 146
Green, William, 125, 126(fig.), 128

Gross, June Maria, 168
guilt, assumption of, 82
  the murder of Sarah Haggenbotham, 93
  wife-beating laws, 38–39
guns
  Annie Cutler's murder of her lover, 33–34
  Black people's prohibition of possessing, 82–84
  Black women's use of firearms for self-defense, 83–84
  conflicting testimony in the murder of Samuel Jackson, 29–30
  corset as defense against gunfire, 84–85
  murder as a response to domestic abuse, 45–46
  murder by a State Liquor League operative, 124–126
  shooting the other woman in a triangle, 49–52
Guy-Sheftall, Beverly, 7–8

Haggenbotham, John, 104(fig.)
  acquittal, 102–103
  alleged attack on his mother, 89–91
  conflicting versions of the murder of his mother, 91–92
  drug use and debt, 97–99
  erratic behavior after the murder, 93
  Mary Wright's relationship with, 87–88
  Mary Wright's trial and acquittal, 103–105, 107
  Mary Wright's version of the murder, 95–97
  sudden marriage, 99–100

Haggenbotham, May, 91–92, 103, 105

Haggenbotham, Sarah
alleged attack by a brick and subsequent murder, 89–94
family and home, 87–88
Mary and John's trials for the murder of, 99–105
Mary and John's versions of the murder, 91–92, 95–99
threatening to fire Mary Wright, 88–89

Haggenbotham, William
defense and support of John Haggenbotham, 100–101
Mary Wright's domestic service, 87–88
on trial outcome of John Haggenbotham, 102–103
on trial outcome of Mary Wright, 105

Hall, Isaac "Lady Washington," 153–154

hangings
calls for hanging immoral women, 43–44
enslaved Black women fighting back, 60
the murder of Sarah Haggenbotham, 93–94

Harper, Frances Ellen Watkins, 135

Harris, Maria, 143–144

Haynes, Ravena, 144

Hitchens, Ida, 153

Hogan, Tenie, 24–25

Holtzclaw, Daniel, 62

homicide. See murder

homophobia
incarceration for, 154
the role of Black feminism in challenging, 8, 13

honor, 33
acts of violence against abusers challenging honor, 46–48
the consequences of unwanted pregnancies, 138–140
the consequences of women killing wife beaters, 41–44
the dangers of walking Philadelphia streets, 112–113
lack of respect prompting women's vengeance, 29–32
vengeance as defense of, 26–27, 30–32, 48

Hood, Carlisha, 163–164

hooks, bell, 13

Hooper, Jennie, 128–129

Howard, Ida, 30, 46–48

Hubbard, Anna May, 83–84

Hubbard, Clifford, 83–84

Hunter, Jane Edna, 138–140

Hunton, Addie, 69–70

immigrants: the origins of baby farms, 152

incarceration
assault against detained Black women, 63–64
of Black badger thieves, 118–120
Black women surviving domestic violence and ensuing justice, 77–78
doctors performing abortions, 142–144
for fornication, 153–154

Index

Ida Payton's sentence for attempted
    murder, 30
Philadelphia's history, 17–18
prison population demographic, 67
self-defense on a Philadelphia train,
    111–112
targeting and threatening Black
    women prisoners, 65–66
vilification of Black women
    prisoners, 70
wife-beating laws, 38
Incidents in the Life of a Slave Girl
    (Jacobs), 35–36
inequity
    arrest and trial for the murder of
        Sarah Haggenbotham, 99–102
    prison population demographic, 67
    social and legal punishment of
        Black women, 72–73
infanticide, 20
    baby farms, 149–152
    economic, political and
        philosophical motives for,
        145–148
    exploitation and stigmatization of
        Black women's reproduction,
        138–142
    forcing a false confession of, 66
    illegal and botched abortions,
        141–146
    Maria Waters's background,
        pregnancy, and childbirth,
        133–137
    prosecution of women for, 146–147
    as reproductive retribution,
        137–138
    women's acquittals for, 146–149
    See also abortion

infidelity: shooting the other woman,
    49–52. *See also* adultery
inquest on the murder of Sarah
    Haggenbotham, 100
Instagram Live video, 160
interpersonal risk assessment, 102
interracial relations
    Black badger thieves targeting
        white men, 116–118
    Black women navigating domestic
        and public spaces, 84
    white men patronizing Black
        prostitutes, 27

Jackson, Mary, 64–67
Jackson, Rachel, 144
Jackson, Samuel, 27–31
Jacobs, Harriet, 35–36
jail. *See* incarceration
Jenkins, Emma, 143–144
Jenkins, Sarah, 144
Johnson, Mary, 154–157
Johnson, Mary/Maggie, 3–6, 17
Jones, Eliza, 119
juries
    acquittals of women having
        abortions, 148
    impaneling of Black jurors, 58
    white jurors' views of Black women,
        68–69
    See also acquittals; legal system
justice system
    enslaved Black women's status,
        54–58
    failure to protect Black women,
        51–54, 61–63, 163–164
    failure to protect enslaved Black
        women, 60

justice system *(continued)*
  murder by a State Liquor League
    operative, 127–128
  police and court bias against Black
    women, 163–164
  See also incarceration; legal system;
    sentencing

Kai, Maiysha, 160–161
Kelly, Joseph P., 38–39
Kelly, R., 160
Knight, William, 32–34

law enforcement. *See* justice system;
    legal system; police forces; police
    violence
lawlessness, 1–2
  Black women arming
    themselves, 83
  Black women leveraging
    dispossession, 159
  defining, 11–12
  as a life-saving mechanism, 164–166
  police corruption and political
    connections, 81–82
  state failure to protect Black
    women, 53–63, 67
  vengeance feminism addressing the
    inequities of, 72–73
legal system
  acquittals for infanticide, 146–149
  Black women surviving domestic
    violence and ensuing justice,
    77–78
  Black women's self-advocacy,
    85–86
  codification of violent
    discrimination, 162–163

failure to protect Black women,
    63–64
feminist violence as response to the
    failures of, 6–8
history of Black people's unequal
    treatment, 56–58
the logic of Black vengeance
    feminism, 10
mainstream Black feminism
    using, 8–9
Mary Johnson's self-defense
    claims, 4–5
the origins and purpose of
    vengeance feminism, 21
perception of Philadelphia's Black
    migrants, 65–67
police scapegoating in the murder
    of Sarah Haggenbotham,
    99–105
retribution for a failed abortion,
    156–157
status of "mulatto" children, 55
unexpected outcomes, 1–2
valuing white people over Black
    women, 70–73
white jurors' views of Black women,
    68–69
wife-beating laws, 37–42
  See also justice system
lewd behavior of white men,
    55–56, 114
Lewis, Jacob, 28–29
liberation of Black women, 120–122
liquor licenses, the cost of, 123–124
Lisbon Street, Philadelphia, 19, 23–30
Lombard Street, Philadelphia, 51,
    75–77
Lorde, Audre, 13

Love, Frank, 24
luck in the legal system, 85–86
Lukens, Nancy, 113

marriage
    John Haggenbotham's hasty
        marriage, 99
    reproductive retribution, 146–147
    seduction of women and girls,
        138–140
    vengeance for betrayal, 32–34
    See also premarital sex
Mason, Julia, 118–119
mental health: the collapse of John
    Haggenbotham, 97
migration: Black women escaping
    enslavers, 63–65
Miner, Edward, 28–29
Minnie's Sacrifice (Harper), 135
Minor, Bessie, 125
Minster Street, Philadelphia, 51
miscarriage, criminalization of a Black
    woman's, 165
misogynoir
    Black women's vengeance
        highlighting sexist double
        standards, 44–45
    history of Black feminist
        violence, 11
    legal codification of racism and
        sexism, 162–163
    the power of vengeance feminism
        against, 159–160
    shaping Black feminism, 8,
        165–166
    women's fight for the right to
        respect, 30–31
    See also sexism

misogyny, 8, 11, 130
mobility of Black women
    Black badger thieves, 112, 130–131
    Pastime Park amusements, 110
Moore, Samuel, 91
morality
    Black badger thieves targeting
        white men, 115–120
    Black women's exclusion from male
        protection, 26
    characterizing Black women, 63
    the consequences of unwed
        motherhood, 138–140
    drunkenness in Pastime Park, 110
    enslavement and the maligning of
        Black women, 53–54
    the feminist perspective of badger
        thieves, 122–123
    the legal system and inequities
        towards Black women, 72–73
    Mary Wright's fraternization with
        her employer, 87–88
    questioning the morality of women
        in public streets, 113
    sodomy and buggery, 153–154
    victimizing women who kill their
        abusers, 43–44
    white judges' and jurors'
        perceptions of female Black
        prisoners, 68–70
    whites' perceptions of Black people,
        26–27
    women raging at misogynoir,
        11–12
    women's insistence on civility and
        respect, 25–26
    See also honor
Morgan, Adolphus, 144

Mother Bethel Church, Philadelphia, 18–19
mulattoes, 54–55, 61
Munchower, Levy, 119
murder
  accusations against Mary Wright, 87–105
  avenging dishonor, 30–35, 41–45
  baby farms, 149–152
  between Black women, 129–130
  domestic dispute escalating to, 27–30
  Mary Crawford avenging abuse and loss of respect, 45–46
  police and court bias against Black women, 163–164
  of Sarah Haggenbotham, 89–94
  the stabbing of a violent domestic partner, 75–80
  by a State Liquor League operative, 123–128
  of white children by an enslaved Black woman, 58–60
  wife beating leading to, 37–40
  See also infanticide
Murdock, Helen, 85
Murphy, Fanny, 39

Negro Courts, 57
news media
  "Baby Murder Syndicate," 152
  Black women attacking white women, 85
  drug use and debt of John Haggenbotham, 98–99
  failed abortion, 155–156
  the murder of Sarah Haggenbotham, 96–97, 100–105
Philadelphia's history, 19
  police and court bias against Black women, 163–164x
  rape of enslaved Black women, 55
  supporting women who killed their abusers, 43–44
  vice and mayhem in Pastime Park, 110
  victim blaming for Mary Johnson, 5–6
  wife-beating laws, 37–38
  women's deaths through illegal abortions, 142–144
Nickoles, Miles, 142–143
nonviolence
  mainstream Black feminism, 8–9
  support for Black women killing their abusers, 42–43

Palmer, Edward, 24
Palmer, Sarah, 119
partner abuse and violence
  Black women's use of firearms for self-defense, 82–84
  Cardi B's victimization, 160–161
  charges against abusers, 5
  consequences of resistance, 167–168
  of enslaved Black women, 55–56
  support for Black women killing wife beaters, 41–44
  the use of guns in self-defense, 82–84
  wife-beating laws, 37–42, 47–48
  See also physical abuse
Pastime Park, Philadelphia, 109–112

patriarchy, the role of Black feminism in challenging, 8

Paul, Frank, 133 (quote), 150

Payton, Ida, 25–31

Pennington, Amanda, 155–156

Pennsylvania Hospital, Philadelphia, 76–77

pennyroyal: abortifacient and toxic qualities, 142

Philadelphia and Reading Railroad, 109–112, 130

Philadelphia County Prison, 46, 85, 111, 118, 143, 146–147, 151

Philadelphia Evening Bulletin, 5–6, 43

Philadelphia Inquirer, 30, 75(quote), 104(fig.)

   badger thieves, 109(quote)

   Mary Wright, 87(fig.), 92(fig.)

   murder by a State Liquor League operative, 126(fig.)

   the murder of Sarah Haggenbotham, 100–101, 103, 104(fig.)

   stabbing deaths of abusive men, 79, 85

   wife-beating laws, 37–38

Philadelphia Radical Club, 40–45

Philadelphia Tribune, 19, 144

physical abuse

   Black women's choices in resistance, 167–168

   enslaved Black women fighting back, 59–60

   police and court bias, 163–164

   See also partner abuse and violence; rape; sexual assault and harassment

poisoning of a white family by a Black servant, 71–72

police violence

   attempting to prevent attempted murder, 28–29

   gang rape and serial rape of Black women, 62–63

   Philadelphia's history, 18

   response to gunfire in Mary Crawford shooting, 45–46

   targeting and threatening Black women prisoners, 65–66

policing

   bias against Black women, 163–164

   Black women's distrust of law enforcement, 51–52

   criminalization of Philadelphia's Black migrants, 65–66

   drunken violence in Pastime Park, 110–111

   men accosting Black women in the streets, 113

   murder by a State Liquor League operative, 125–128

   post–Civil War growth of Philadelphia's police force, 64–66

   raids on political clubs, 81

   retribution for a failed abortion, 156–157

political actors, Black women as, 7–8

political clubs, 80–82

poverty

   Black women's unequal status, 161

   the feminist perspective of badger thieves, 122–123

   the role of Black feminism in challenging, 8

Index

power
  Black women leveraging
    powerlessness, 105–106
  blaming white men's moral
    turpitude on Black women,
    61–62
  the costs of fury, 131
  of vengeance feminism, 159–160
pregnancy. *See* abortion; infanticide;
    premarital sex; reproductive
    retribution
premarital sex
  as act of gender rebellion,
    153–154
  the consequences of unwanted
    pregnancies, 138–140
  loss of respectability leading to
    violence, 32–34
  pregnancy and infanticide resulting
    from, 134
  women's shifting attitudes, 11–12
  See also abortion; infanticide
prison. *See* incarceration
property
  Black women as, 53–58,
    60–61
  women's dispute over, 129–130
prostitution, 24–25
  Better Days's disorderly house,
    128–129
  Black badger thieves,
    114–120
  characterizing enslaved Black
    women, 61–62
  the consequences of unwed
    motherhood, 139–140
  white and Black men's
    patronage, 27

public space, Black women and
  assault on public transportation,
    113–114, 130–131
  questioning the morality of women
    in public streets, 113
  stigmatizing unwed mothers,
    140–141
  treatment of enslaved women,
    55–56
  using a variety of tactics to
    navigate, 84
  See also badger thieves
public transportation, assaulting Black
    women on, 109–114, 130
Purvis, Harriet Forten, 34–35
Purvis, Robert, 23 (quote)
  background and character,
    34–35
  the fight for women's rights,
    47–48
  wife-beating laws and women's
    rights, 36–37, 40–43

racism
  African Americans inhabiting
    public spaces, 140
  assumptions of Black women's
    guilt, 81–82
  Black women weaponizing,
    11–12, 20
  the feminist perspective of badger
    thieves, 122–123
  legal codification of, 162–163
  motivating Black women's
    vengeance, 6–7
  the murder of Sarah
    Haggenbotham, 95–96
  productivity of rage, 13–14

Index

Purvis's activism against, 35, 42
role of Black feminism in
 challenging, 8
stigma associated with unwed
 motherhood, 141–142
violence intersecting class and, 47
white rhetoric about Black
 mothers, 18
See also misogynoir
Rafter, Nicole Hahn, 67
railroad, assault of Black women on,
 109–112, 130
rape
 of enslaved Black women, 54–62
 the legal system and inequities
  towards Black women, 72–73
 police assaulting Black women
  prisoners, 66–67, 70
 resistance of enslaved Black women,
  59–60
 stigma associated with unwed
  motherhood, 141
 white people's hypocrisy over Black
  women and, 69–70
 of white women by Black men,
  62–63
rape laws, 58
religious organizations and orders
 Philadelphia's history, 18–19
 supporting women who killed their
  abusers, 43, 107
reparative work: characterizing Black
 vengeance feminism, 14–15
reproduction
 characterizing Black vengeance
  feminism, 14–15
 criminalization of a Black woman's
  miscarriage, 165

women's shifting attitudes, 11–12
See also abortion; children;
 infanticide; premarital sex;
 sexuality and sexual activity
reproductive justice, 156–157
reproductive retribution
 the absence of retributive justice for
  women, 154–157
 baby farms, 149–152
 illegal and botched abortions,
  141–142
 infanticide as, 137–138
 social, economic, and familial
  factors in, 138–140
 women's deaths resulting from
  abortions, 142–145, 147–148
research methodology,
 documentation, 16–17
resistance
 Black women taking control of,
  167–168
 by enslaved Black women, 58–60
 as tactic of vengeance, 6–7
 tactics of violence, 11–12
respect
 Black women respecting their
  womanhood, 25–26, 30
 forms of resistance, 6
 lack of respect prompting women's
  vengeance, 29–32
 racist double standards applied to
  Black women, 69–70, 122
respectability
 women raging at misogynoir,
  11–12
 women's insistence on civility and
  respect, 25–26
See also honor; morality

retribution
  Black feminist theory, 13
  characterizing Black vengeance
    feminism, 15
  enslaved women's violence in
    achieving, 59–60
  motivating Black badger thieves,
    122–123
  supporting Annie Cutler's right
    to, 43
  See also reproductive retribution
Rhoads, Emma A., 23 (quote), 41–43
Richardsin, Bertha, 86
Riley, Mamie, 116
Robb, Thomas, 116
robbery
  Black badger thieves, 25, 114–120
  Cardi B tactics, 160
  setting the stage for Sarah
    Haggenbotham's murder, 90
Robinson, Joseph, 125, 127
Rolling Stones, 64

Sable Venuses: characterizations of
    Black womanhood, 60–61
safety of Black women
  Black women arming
    themselves, 83
  the state's failure to provide, 51–54,
    60–63, 163–164
  vengeance feminist aims, 15
scapegoating: the murder of Sarah
    Haggenbotham, 99–102
school curriculum: reforming
    heteronormative white
    supremacist ideals, 165
Scott, Ezekiel, 154–157
Scott, Sarah, 70

self-advocacy of Black women, 85–86
self-defense, 75(quote)
  assault on the train, 111–112
  Black people possessing firearms,
    82–83
  Black women's self-advocacy, 85–86
  criminalization of Black women's,
    53–54
  murder by a State Liquor League
    operative, 125–126
  police and court bias against Black
    women, 163–164
  significance for Black vengeance
    feminism, 4–6, 10–11
  the stabbing of William Campbell,
    78–79
  striking back with weapons, 28
  tactical deftness of Black women,
    84–85
sentencing
  baby farm deaths, 151
  Black badger thieves who target
    white men, 116–117
  Black women appealing, 85–86
  Black women attacking white
    women, 85
  police officer's rape of Black
    women, 62
  police perception of Philadelphia's
    Black migrants, 66
  for sodomy and buggery, 153–154
  women shooting wife beaters, 46
sexism
  motivating Black women's
    vengeance, 6–7, 13
  schism over the Annie Cutler case,
    44–45
  See also misogynoir

sexual assault and harassment
assaulting Black women on public
transportation, 113–114
the consequences of unwed
motherhood, 140
the spectrum of sexual violence,
160–161
See also rape
sexuality and sexual activity
Black badger thieves,
114–118
charges of fornication, 153
charges of sodomy and buggery,
153–154
the consequences of unwed
motherhood, 138–140
gender-based double standard for,
144–147
the lack of retributive justice for
women, 154–157
Philadelphia's drugs, dens, and
dives, 97–98
reproductive retribution,
138–140
white people characterizing Black
womanhood, 60–63, 113–114,
141, 148
See also abortion; premarital sex;
prostitution; rape
Shuck, Joseph, 111
*Signs Journal of Women in Culture and
Society*, 13
Simpson, Rose, 125
slavery, 19–20
barring Black people from
possessing firearms, 83
Black women's history as property,
53–54

Cooper's history of enslavement
and liberation, 121–122
legal and judicial treatment of Black
people, 57–58
murder of white children by an
enslaved Black woman, 58–60
persistent characterizations of
Black womanhood, 63–64
Philadelphia's history of, 17–18
post-emancipation migration of
Black women, 63–65
Purvis's activism against, 35–36
the rape of enslaved Black women,
54–62
white women's views of enslaved
Black women, 61–62
Smith, Mamie, 119
sodomy and buggery charges, 153–154
"Some Girls" (Rolling Stones), 64
Somers Point, New Jersey, 87–105
speakeasies, 123–128
stabbings, 75(quote)
assault of a Black woman on the
Philadelphia train, 111–112
Black women's recourse for
harassment and assault, 66–67
Lillie Fisher avenging her dignity
and honor, 75–79, 82
Lisbon Street disorderly houses,
24–25
State Liquor League, 125–127
stereotypes
characterizations of Black
womanhood, 60–61, 63
effects of women committing
infanticide, 148–149
police perception of Philadelphia's
Black migrants, 65–66

stereotypes *(continued)*
  questioning the morality of women
    in public streets, 113
  whites' perceptions of Black people,
    26–27
  women's weaponization of, 20
Stewart, Charles, 128–129
Stewart, Harriet "Better Days,"
    109(quote), 112, 123–130
streetcars: assault of Black women, 114
Stuart, Emma, 117
suffrage, 35–36, 40–41, 44, 47
support systems
  Mary Wright's trial for the murder
    of Sarah Haggenbotham,
    102–103, 105
  the stabbing of William
    Campbell, 79
  for women who kill their abusers,
    43–44
Sydnor, Edward, 3–6, 17

tactics
  abortion and infanticide as Black
    women's defense, 137–138
  Black women leveraging
    powerlessness, 105–106
  Black women's response to state
    failure to protect them,
    163–164
  Cardi B's Instagram Live
    video, 160
  collective strength of
    resistance, 11
  fortuity supplementing, 85–86
  scapegoating Mary Wright
    for the murder of Sarah
    Haggenbotham, 94–95, 102

surviving violence and the legal
    system, 77–78, 84–86
variety in Black women's
    self-defense tactics, 84–85
women living boldly, 6–7
Taylor, Nikki M., 13, 58
Teale, Isaac, 61
temperance organizations,
    123–126
Terrell, Mary Church, 26–27
Thompson, Henrietta,
    145–147
Times Philadelphia, 24, 39, 75(quote),
    104, 110–111, 155
transphobia, the role of Black
    feminism in challenging, 8
trials, 29–30
Turner, Charles, 150–151
Turner, William, 24

Ulrich, Martin, 109–110
Underground Railroad, 35
unwed mothers, 20–21, 134,
    139–141, 148
  See also abortion; infanticide;
    premarital sex
"The Uses of Anger" (Lorde), 13

vengeance feminism
  Cooper's philosophical outlook,
    120–122
  defining and characterizing, 12
  dueling furies violence and,
    129–130
  infanticide as expression of,
    137–138
  as a short-term strategy,
    164–165

victim blaming, 1–2
  biases in the court and police, 164
  blaming white men's corruption on
    Black women, 61–62
  women who kill their abusers,
    43–44
vigilantism, 10–11
violence
  bias crimes, 162–163
  the costs of fury, 131
  defining and characterizing
    vengeance feminism, 12, 15
  dueling furies, 129–130
  murder by a State Liquor League
    operative, 123–128
  See also partner abuse and violence
virtue, white people's hypocrisy over,
  68–70
A Voice from the South (Cooper),
  120–122

Wallace, Michele, 13
Walnut Street Prison, Philadelphia, 18
Ward, Sarah, 49–52, 49(quote),
  52–53
Washington, Robert, 150–151
Waters, Maria, 134–137, 141–142
Watts, Brittany, 165
weapons
  the attacks on Sarah
    Haggenbotham, 89–90, 92–93
  attempted murder with a blackjack,
    27–28
  dueling, 31
  men's violence against men,
    24–25
  motives and tactics of Black
    vengeance feminism, 11–12

  opportunistic use of domestic
    tools, 4
  poisoning of a white family by a
    Black servant, 71–72
  for protection and vengeance, 5
  See also guns; stabbings
Wells, Ida B., 83–84
whipping post, reinstating, 37–39,
  41–42, 47, 116
White, Lizzie, 111–112, 130
White, Mamie, 25
white masculinity: the feminist
  perspective of badger thieves,
  122–123
white men and women
  American feminist origins,
    9–10, 13
  badger thieves' expressions of
    power, 130–131
  Black badger thieves targeting
    white men, 115–120
  Black mobility, 110–111
  characterizing Black
    womanhood, 60–63, 113–114,
    141, 148
  the feminist perspective of badger
    thieves, 122–123
  fighting duels, 30–31
  history of mistrust of Blacks and
    Blackness, 54–56
  hypocrisy over virtue, 68–70
  law enforcement bias against Black
    people, 64–68
  the legal system prioritizing
    white life over Black life,
    70–72
  murder by enslaved Black women,
    58–59

white men and women *(continued)*
  punishing Black women's attacks
    on white women, 85–86, 94,
    105–107
  Purvis's family and background,
    34–35
  white men assaulting Black women
    on public transportation,
    111–112, 114
  See also Haggenbotham, Sarah;
    slavery
white supremacy
  Black badger thieves and white
    men, 120
  school curriculum addressing, 165
  systemic persistence, 162–163
  white men having sex with Black
    women, 116
wife beating. *See* partner abuse and
    violence
wife-beating laws, 37–42, 47–48

Williams, Sarah, 85
women's rights
  origins of American feminism, 8
  transcending suffrage, 47–48
women's suffrage, 40–41, 47–48
Words of Fire (Guy-Sheftall), 7–8
Wright, Mary, 87(fig.), 92(fig.)
  account of the murder, 92–93
  accusations of John
    Haggenbotham, 94–95,
    99–102
  acquittal, 105
  acquittal of John Haggenbotham,
    102–105
  alleged attack on and murder of
    Sarah Haggenbotham, 89–92
  domestic service situation, 86–88
  leveraging powerlessness, 105–107
  social life and amusements, 88–89

Zintl, Joseph (police officer), 51–52

Credit: Ryan S. Miller

KALI NICOLE GROSS IS the National Endowment for the Humanities Professor of African American Studies at Emory University. She is coauthor of *A Black Women's History of the United States* (with Daina Ramey Berry) and author of *Hannah Mary Tabbs and the Disembodied Torso: A Tale of Race, Sex, and Violence in America*. She lives in Atlanta, Georgia.